YEAR OF THE
CAT

How the Carolina Panthers
Clawed Their Way to the Brink of the
SUPER BOWL

**SCOTT FOWLER AND
CHARLES CHANDLER**

Simon & Schuster

SIMON & SCHUSTER
Rockefeller Center
1230 Avenue of the Americas
New York, NY 10020

SIMON & SCHUSTER and colophon are registered trademarks
of Simon & Schuster Inc.

Designed by Bonni Leon-Berman

Manufactured in the United States of America

1   3   5   7   9   10   8   6   4   2

Library of Congress Cataloging-in-Publication Data
Fowler, Scott.
Year of the cat : how the Carolina Panthers clawed their way to the brink of
the Super Bowl / Scott Fowler and Charles Chandler.
p.   cm.
Includes index.
1. Carolina Panthers (Football team)—History.   I. Chandler, Charles (Charles
Elliott)   II. Title.
GV956.C27F69   1997
796.332'64'0975676—dc21   97-23936
CIP

ISBN 978-1-4165-7798-0   ISBN 1-4165-7798-X

Photo Credits:
1, 2, 3, 4, 6, 7, 9, 10, 11, 12, 13, 15, 16, 18,
20, 21, 22, 25, 27, 30: Bob Leverone
5, 8, 14, 17, 19, 23, 24, 26, 28, 29: Photos
by Christopher A. Record

To Mom, Dad, Mary, and Heidi.
And to Elise and our new life together.
—Scott Fowler

To Kim, my wife and my world.
And, always, to Mom, Dad, Jim, and Tim.
—Charles Chandler

CONTENTS

INTRODUCTION

WHEN YOU'RE IN THE MIDDLE OF A GOOD DREAM, YOU rarely realize how hard it is to recapture later. You simply go along with it—smiling in your sleep, watching events unfold, delighting in the next unexpected turn.

The 1996 Carolina Panthers season felt like that to us. It was a dream that lasted for nearly six months. When it was finally over, we were supposed to shake ourselves and wake up. We hit the snooze button instead.

We wanted to write this book to take a closer look at the most remarkable sports season either of us had ever covered in a combined 25 years in the sportswriting business. We reported on the Panthers, play by play and practice by practice, for *The Charlotte Observer* throughout the 1996 season and as it stretched into 1997. We developed relationships with the players, visited their homes, and wrote about their struggles and their triumphs. We interviewed Carolina coach Dom Capers so often that we found ourselves accidentally mimicking his speech patterns from time to time, talking to each other in deep voices about the "sense of urgency" our next newspaper deadline had. But we never got to take three steps back during the frantic year to enjoy the gorgeous view. We were too busy studying each tree to understand the forest.

For this book we tried to recreate that dream of a season, but in richer detail than before. We did that through more than a hundred postseason interviews with the Panthers and the people who cared most deeply about them. We talked for hours with everyone from quarterback Kerry Collins to team owner Jerry Richardson, from controversial center Curtis Whitley to Panthers mascot Sir Purr, from exuberant linebacker Lamar Lathon to TV analyst John Madden. All of those interviews were on the record. Many of them were surprising. We found that the dozens of players we talked to shared an innate understanding of how special the season had been and wanted its full story to be told once and for all.

Even if you are a diehard fan who followed the Panthers in 1996 as closely as you would follow your own two-year-old—worriedly trailing after every step—you will find many anecdotes in this book that you never knew before. You'll also discover some startling revelations. If you are a casual sports enthusiast, we invite you to hop aboard the Panthers bandwagon right now, before there's no more room. If you hurry, you won't even have to buy a permanent-seat license to get a seat.

This book is not a sustained cheer for the Panthers. No sports team is perfect; the Panthers certainly were not. This is a "warts-and-all" documentary of the 1996 season, complete with some of the team's personal failures along with many of their successes. Years like this don't come along very often. Teams like this don't, either. Even in the middle of the dream, we were vaguely aware of that. After it ended, we realized it more acutely. It was the year when the Panthers, in only their second season, crept up on the entire National Football League and attacked. Of course, the Panthers could win the Super Bowl this season and trump what they did the season before, but no matter what happens in their third season and in the seasons to come, the magic won't be as enchanting as it was in 1996.

Now the Panthers don't belong to just the Carolinas. In 1996 they grew up, changing from a regional to a national team before our eyes. Their 1997 schedule includes four prime-time games, two on Sunday night, two on Monday night, and their team memorabilia have locked in a place among the top 10 NFL teams in American sales.

Last year, that wasn't the case. Before Lamar Lathon screamed into TV cameras after one of the Panthers' biggest wins last season, "Do you know where Charlotte, North Carolina, is now, BABY?!" not everyone who was watching did know. But fans around the country learned. The Panthers have gotten very big, very fast.

For the most part, Carolina's first season in Ericsson Stadium was as innocent as a first kiss. At times, it was just as awkward. Always, it was as memorable.

We invite you back into the dream for a while.

Scott Fowler and Charles Chandler

PROLOGUE

I Found My Heart in San Francisco

ERIC DAVIS WAS FURIOUS.

The Carolina Panthers cornerback had just made the most gorgeous, most important play in franchise history—but he was still hopping mad.

It was late afternoon on December 8, 1996. Davis's fourth-quarter interception of 49ers quarterback Steve Young had silenced the crowd at 3Com Park in San Francisco and preserved the Panthers' improbable 30–24 win. It marked the second time in as many tries that the Panthers had upset the 49ers that season.

Davis usually cherished this sort of moment. He sometimes talked about the awesome power he felt when 60,000 screaming fans suddenly stopped yelling because of something good he had done on the field—a feeling that came only when he made a spectacular play on the road in a National Football League game. While Davis steamed, his teammates danced on the sidelines, bursting with raw emotion—as happy as kids running through a water sprinkler on a hot August day.

The Panthers' volatile team meeting of a month before—the one whose details made up one of the team's two deepest secrets—had served its purpose. Carolina hadn't lost a game since and had even overcome the suspension of their starting center, Curtis Whitley, a player whose problems were far worse than any of his teammates ever imagined. Now, just a few weeks later, the Panthers players were screaming loudly enough to be heard 30 rows up from the field. Their joyous noise was eerie—the only sounds amid the silence. The rest of the stadium was so quiet you could hear a pin drop. To add insult to injury, the usually reserved Carolina safety Brett Maxie started yelling at the crowd. Maxie is normally as mild-mannered as Clark Kent, but he had gotten sick of some of the 49ers fans in the front row who had heckled the Panthers all afternoon. In a voice as deep and soulful as singer Barry White's, Maxie started whooping at the fans.

"Go ahead, go on home!" Maxie boomed. "Beat the traffic!"

Davis heard this and the rest of the revelry, and even though he had started the sideline celebration with his interception of former teammate Young, he wanted no part of it.

Before joining the Panthers in the 1996 off-season as a free agent, Davis had been a proud veteran of the 49ers teams that dominated the NFL in the early 1990s. He was a large part of their success, and with that success came a certain sense of professionalism. So while Carolina's offense rolled to a couple of first downs to clinch the game, Davis started yelling at the excessiveness. He strode angrily to several of his teammates on the sideline and barked at them one by one. "Act like you've been here before!" he shouted.

Normally, his teammates would have listened to him closely. But this time they yelled back to him "Thank you!" for the interception, patted him on the helmet, and ignored him.

The Panthers had not been here before. In fact, they hadn't been anywhere near here before.

Davis didn't immediately appreciate the implications of his interception, though most of the other Panthers did. That's why, on the sideline, near the 40-yard line, linebackers Lamar Lathon and Kevin Greene laughed to themselves as they filled up a large cooler with ice and water. They had painstakingly poured in one cupful at a time, since there were no full coolers left. They wanted one brimming with ice water so they could go out and create some mischief.

Lathon, Greene, and quarterback Kerry Collins—who had all used the game as a national coming-out party—knew the Panthers deserved this celebration more than anyone else. They had made an experienced team self-destruct like an instructional tape on *Mission Impossible.* Carolina's game-sealing first down had come when San Francisco linebacker Ken Norton, Jr., son of the former heavyweight champ and usually one of the league's smartest and best players, head-butted Panther Frank Garcia. That penalty gave Carolina an automatic first down with 1:08 left in the game and assured that San Francisco would not get the ball back. It was the 49ers' seventh penalty for unsportsmanlike conduct or personal fouls in the game, part of a San Francisco team record of 15 penalties for 121 yards.

"We came unglued," San Francisco coach George Seifert said later. "We got too caught up in the in-your-face football. They appeared to be the team with all the tradition and poise, not us."

The Panthers' win gave them a season sweep in the series with San Francisco. Both teams had 10–4 records after this game, but Carolina jumped into first place in the NFC West because of a 2–0 season record over the 49ers. And even though Carolina still wouldn't be discovered by many casual NFL fans until five weeks later, when they would beat the Dallas Cowboys in a playoff game with an even larger scope than this one, it was this 49ers game that made that one possible. This win was the one that gave Carolina a first-round bye in the playoffs, and with that came the mystical confidence from knowing you were part of something much better, much larger, and much purer than yourself.

"We knew in San Francisco that we were writing a storybook," Panthers receiver Willie Green said. And he was right. This was the win that shouted to the world that the Panthers had arrived. A franchise built on an empire of cheeseburgers, permanent-seat licenses, and unlikely dreams had been flipped like a seared piece of beef at just the right time. The Panthers—who had been expected to contribute massive cash to the NFL coffers and then be quiet about it at least until the year 2000—had become the National Football League's feel-good story of the year.

CAROLINA WAS AN NFL TODDLER—A BABE AMONG wolves. But here they were, in only their second year of existence, striking a death blow to the 49ers. This was unheard of in the NFL. No expansion team had done so well so quickly. The 49ers were mortally wounded. The balance of power officially shifted with this victory.

San Francisco, the dominant team in the NFC West since Ronald Reagan's first term, would finish the season as a wild-card playoff team, thanks to the Panthers' season sweep of the series. They would soon be eliminated from the playoffs, and the organization's impatient brass would pull a power play that would basically force head coach George Seifert to resign. Seifert would join three other NFC West coaches as victims who had lost their coaching jobs partly because of the Panthers' meteoric rise in 1996. New Orleans's Jim Mora, Atlanta's June Jones, and St. Louis's Rich Brooks also bit the dust after Carolina shocked the NFC West with a 7–1 division mark. After only his second season as a head coach, Carolina coach Dom Capers would emerge as the dean of the NFC West.

No one knew any of that yet on December 8, 1996. But everyone knew that the Panthers had proved—in the shadow of the Golden Gate Bridge, against one of the most feared teams in football—that they could beat the 49ers or just about any other team, anywhere or anytime. This win gave Carolina a 3–1 record vs. San Francisco and catapulted the Panthers franchise into the realm of the NFL's elite.

Carolina's sideline dancing at the end of the 49ers game was only the latest, and the cleanest, in a series of emotional eruptions that day. The 49ers had talked so much trash before the game, you would have thought they were teaching a course in how to fire up your opponent. Steve Young, the 49ers' magnificent but aging quarterback, would later call his teammates "overzealous" in their desire to recapture the NFC West throne. In reality, they were far worse than that.

During pregame warmups, San Francisco fullback William Floyd yelled at several Panthers players, "All y'all ain't nothing but punks!"

Floyd tried to be a one-man pregame wrecking crew. When the Panthers offense was introduced one by one and gathered together on the field, the players briefly stopped for a huddle. "Win on three!" one Carolina player yelled. "One, two, three—WIN!"

That huddle kept the Panthers on the field just long enough for the 49ers to come storming out near them. Floyd was first. "Get off our field!" Floyd screamed, throwing in every expletive he could think of for emphasis. Soon after that, he started spitting in the direction of Panthers players, screaming, "That's what I think of y'all!"

"William Floyd's out there spitting at us," Panthers tight end Wesley Walls told some of his teammates. Walls was angry and excited at the same time. He pointed Floyd out, in case any of the nearby Panthers were missing it. "Look! He's spitting at us!"

Linebacker Lamar Lathon was already watching. "When I saw that, I was very confident," Lathon said afterward. "You could feel it. We were going to kick their ass. They were afraid of us."

During the pregame, Eric Davis again tried to advise his current teammates not to get too worked up about Floyd. "This is a business trip!" he told them. "Just win! Then tell them to look at the score-board. All those horrible things they're calling us—well, they'll be lower than us, because we'll beat them!"

Earlier in the week, Floyd had dismantled the 49ers' campaign to make sure that the Panthers would not be able to play the "no re-spect" card in this one. After Seifert and Young had gone out of their way to praise the Panthers, Floyd told San Francisco reporters he was sick of Carolina getting "too much respect." That comment had stoked the Panthers' fires. Floyd had not even played in Carolina's first win over San Francisco. But here he was "talking junk," in the players' vernacular. When quarterback Collins heard Floyd's words, he smiled and thought, "I can't ask for anything more. Please, keep talking. Please." Collins later explained, "To hear that from a player, that's perfect. That's when I knew they weren't sure."

After the first Carolina–San Francisco game of 1996, when several 49ers couldn't play because of injuries, San Francisco offensive line coach Bobb McKittrick labeled the Panthers' 23–7 win an "aberra-tion." Carolina coach Dom Capers made sure that all his players heard those inflammatory words. He read them to the team the Saturday before the game at a 9 A.M. meeting at the team hotel in San Francisco.

"We respect them," Capers told his team, his voice edgy. "Obviously, they don't respect us."

Although Capers has a reputation as a steady, intelligent coach, he knows how to push a player's emotional buttons when he needs to. Those Panthers who love to feed off emotion—like Lamar Lathon, linebacker Carlton Bailey, and center Frank Garcia—were red-hot by game time. But even before the game, tempers had flared.

NFL players routinely warm up together, one team on one side of the 50-yard line and one on the other. Usually they treat each other like cats and dogs, ignoring one another and trying to steer clear of paths that would lead into the other's territory. On this day, though, there were numerous confrontations. Besides the Floyd incident, there was another flare-up before kickoff, involving San Francisco cornerback and special-teamer Curtis Buckley and Carolina's Frank Garcia. "This is our house!" Buckley screamed in Garcia's face. "This is our house!" Buckley did it enough times to irritate Garcia, whose fuse is short anyway. Garcia finally shoved Buckley away like a fly, and Buckley, furious, ran back toward Garcia, forgetting that the Panther outweighed him by a hundred pounds. The two had to be separated.

"You kind of got the overall feeling that their attitude coming into this game was that we didn't even deserve to be on the same field with them," Collins said.

At least that's what the oddsmakers thought. Carolina was a 10-point underdog to a team they had pounded just a few months before.

Linebacker Kevin Greene was incredulous. Not only did he want to prove everyone wrong, he also wanted to really stick it to a team he despised more than any other. "I've known the 49ers for years and I've just grown to hate them," Greene said. He didn't think the 49ers played fair, believing that their offensive linemen routinely "cut-blocked" defenders and didn't worry about the injury risk involved. "I wanted to beat them bad," he admitted after the game.

• • •

JUST AS THE NOTES FROM POP SINGER HUEY LEWIS'S rendition of "The Star-Spangled Banner" were fading, Carolina showed that the oddsmakers might have underestimated the Panthers once again. On their first possession, Collins took the Panthers on an impressive 73-yard touchdown march. Near the goal line, he was so composed it looked as if he were playing a backyard game of catch. Collins winked at tight end Wesley Walls in the huddle before he threw him a five-yard touchdown pass. Walls said, "Right then I thought, 'Oh man, this guy is on. He's got confidence. He's going to make the plays today.'"

From that point on, though, it was a well-played, vicious battle. Fights broke out all over the field. At one point, during one of the game's many scuffles, Fox-TV analyst Jerry Glanville joked on the air that the 49ers and Panthers were now arguing about whether or not they should send each other Christmas cards. But the shocking thing was that the 49ers offenders weren't just young players or special-teamers like Buckley. Linebacker Gary Plummer, 36, got ejected for bumping an official while arguing a call. On one play, San Francisco defensive end Chris Doleman flung Collins down so late that he may as well have stayed around for the Panthers' next huddle. The 49ers looked like the other team across San Francisco Bay, the heavily penalized Oakland Raiders.

San Francisco Chronicle columnist Scott Ostler would rip the team the next day, writing that the 49ers had decided to forgo their usual classy act in favor of a turn as MTV's Beavis and Butthead. Ostler wrote, "The 49ers not only lost a big game, they turned into junior-high kids, acting tough, talking trash, standing on the street corner, and flipping off passersby."

And the Panthers? Well, they looked like division champions, shredding San Francisco's normally stingy defense for 27 points in the first half and then protecting the lead well enough late into the game to win on Davis's interception.

Bill McPherson, San Francisco's assistant head coach, was sent down from the coaching booth high in the stadium to try and restore order on the 49ers sideline. At halftime, the 49ers talked about not committing dumb penalties the rest of the game, but none of it worked. Frustrated by a second-year team, San Francisco just kept talking and getting yellow-flagged until Norton's head-butt effectively ended any chance to save face at the end of the game.

Ironically, the 49ers organization was slated for a fiftieth-anniversary "golden gala" the next night in San Francisco. The title of the banquet: "Winning with Class." The 49ers hadn't shown either of those elements on this day. "They don't let many teams get in their heads like we did," Brett Maxie said.

"Forty-Niner style of football," San Francisco lineman Jesse Sapolu told reporters after the game, "is that you don't talk much. You stop doing all that macho crap!"

But even the Panthers couldn't resist some of that "macho crap" during their sideline celebration at the end of the game. As the clock wound down, several players gathered in groups of four and five, hugged each other fiercely, and responded to Curtis Buckley's "This is our house" tirade of hours before.

"Whose house?" they screamed.

"Our house!"

"Whose house?"

"Our house!"

While the other players cheered, Lathon and Greene kept dumping water into the cooler. They were determined to douse coach Capers. "We wanted to hit him with some water to let him know we were leading the division," Greene said. "It was a big win. We wanted to wash him!"

Capers had taught the Panthers to out–San Francisco San Francisco. His team was the one that had played with poise and pride in this game, as they had done for the entire year.

But Capers wasn't celebrating. Even though he hadn't been here before either—this was only his thirtieth game ever as a head coach—he stayed in character, grimly focused until the end. Always observant, the coach spotted Lathon and Greene's sly water refill of the cooler shortly before the final gun. He resolved to stay away from them.

As the game ended, Capers darted toward midfield for a quick handshake with Seifert and a few of the 49ers players. Then he kept moving fast, running away from Greene and Lathon more success-fully than most NFL quarterbacks. But Lathon and Greene stayed in pursuit, the ice water hoisted between them. The water started get-ting heavy. "This guy can run a lot better than we thought he could," Greene huffed to Lathon.

Finally, Capers got held up by player traffic, and Lathon and Greene flung the water at him in an icy spray. It was only a glancing blow. Capers received a partial bath, enough to soak his shirt. He stopped running and shivered for a second. Then he walked toward Lathon and Greene. "Great game, men," he said quietly. "Thank you."

THANK YOU. THAT WAS A COMMON REFRAIN THROUGH-out the Carolina Panthers' spectacular 1996–97 season.

Fans thanked Panthers owner Jerry Richardson for putting up mil-lions of his own money to bring an NFL team to the Carolinas. Richardson thanked Panthers fans for financing the $187 million Er-icsson Stadium by buying permanent-seat licenses. Panthers players thanked Capers not only for his innovations but also for treating them with fairness and consistency. And Capers thanked his players for giving him everything they had, game after game. It was a grateful franchise, and now a successful one, too.

No one had a bigger part in Carolina's instant success than Ca-pers—a man so precise that he used to edge his family's lawn in a small town in Ohio with a fork to make sure it looked perfect.

While Capers was one of the season's finest heroes, others played very large roles in the success as well. One of the brightest stars was Kerry Collins. Even though at 24 the quarterback looked more like a singer in an MTV video than an NFL quarterback, Collins was the man who ran Carolina's improving offense. Part of the new crop of Generation X NFL quarterbacks that includes New England's Drew Bledsoe, Jacksonville's Mark Brunell, and Green Bay's Brett Favre, Collins is the foundation for the Panthers' future. He is a 6′ 5″, 240-pound quarterback with an odd delivery and a fondness for play-action passes, Pearl Jam, and partying. He once sang the Beastie Boys' rap tune "You've Got to Fight for Your Right to Party" at a Charlotte nightspot. During a recent visit to New Orleans, he was as much a staple on Bourbon Street as jambalaya and jazz. But Collins's maturity on the field translated into fewer interceptions and more points for the Panthers. And after his second season, he had the strong-armed potential to become one of the best at his position.

The Panthers defense was led by swaggering linebackers Kevin Greene and Lamar Lathon, dubbed "Salt & Pepper" by Greene. Greene was a 34-year-old sackmeister with a wild streak, and Lathon was by far the defense's most controversial and most valuable player.

Ultimately, though, it was the foresight of team owner Jerry Richardson and general manager Bill Polian that brought them all together. Richardson, the only current NFL owner actually to have played in the league, was once a wide receiver for the Baltimore Colts and even caught a touchdown pass from Johnny Unitas in the 1959 NFL championship game. He invested the $4,864 in playoff money he received that season and opened his first Hardee's restaurant in 1961 in Spartanburg, South Carolina. Richardson grew up in Spring Hope, North Carolina, but attended Spartanburg's Wofford College, so he knew both Carolinas well. He amassed his fortune by selling cheap hamburgers and expanding his restaurant business into a huge operation that also ran Denny's and Quincy's franchises.

But Richardson wasn't happy just being rich. He always burned with a vision of giving something back to the Carolinas. In 1987 he announced that he wanted to enter the race for an NFL expansion team. In 1993, after a boatload of lobbying and an outpouring of support by fans in the Carolinas, he finally got one.

Richardson immediately said he wanted to win a Super Bowl within ten years. People once thought he was being ridiculously bold by saying that. Now, his statement seems somewhat conservative.

Then there was general manager Bill Polian, the former GM of the Buffalo Bills Super Bowl teams who was the architect of this Cinderella squad. Polian's mode of operation was to stay relentlessly pessimistic in public, and then to go out and acquire the players that enabled the Panthers to accomplish the near impossible. In March 1996, when San Francisco coach George Seifert and Miami coach

Jimmy Johnson both claimed that Carolina could make the playoffs in their second year of existence, the Panthers general manager sounded like he thought they should both be committed. He called the playoffs "absolutely impossible" for the Panthers. Anyone suggesting otherwise, Polian said, must be "smoking something." But Seifert and Johnson were dead-on.

While Polian outwardly poor-mouthed the Panthers' lack of players, he privately glued a phone to his ear and tried to convince free agents that Charlotte was at the center of something remarkable. Polian negotiated for cornerback Eric Davis, tight end Wesley Walls, special-teams specialist Michael Bates, and linebacker Kevin Greene to come southeast to Carolina as free agents in the 1996 off-season. All four came. All four made the Pro Bowl.

Eric Davis, the cornerback who made the key interception in the second San Francisco game, was a locker-room leader and the closest thing the team had to a philosopher. "You've got to be larger than the moment," he would tell players who started getting overwhelmed. "Don't let the moment be larger than you." And as the Panthers won game after game in 1996, Davis kept challenging his teammates to improve. "You haven't done anything yet," he'd say. Each week he'd set the bar higher and higher. Each week the Panthers would clear it.

THE FACT THAT THE PANTHERS WERE ABLE TO MELD so many disparate personalities into one team with a common goal was a tribute to Dom Capers. Wide receiver Willie "Touchdown Machine" Green was a talkative Muslim who lost his starting job early in the season to a rookie and then came back to reclaim it with a wonderful late-season run. Cornerback Tyrone Poole was so quiet you could forget he was standing beside you. Long snapper Mark Rodenhauser dabbled in computer graphics and T-shirt design. Running back Anthony Johnson was a devout Christian who drove a 1990 Toyota Celica and lived in a three-bedroom apartment with his wife and four children. Tight end Wesley Walls was a southern-fried pass catcher who grew up in Mississippi near Elvis Presley's birthplace and had the softest hands on the team.

On the field, Capers's right-hand man was linebacker Sam Mills, a

37-year-old NFL veteran and former high school photography teacher. Mills kept his dignity intact and survived innumerable jokes about his lack of height (he is 5′ 9″) while trying to make one last run at the NFL championship that had always eluded him. Mills was the leader of an aging, ornery defense with six starters over 30, nicknamed the "grumpy old men."

The Panthers' character and heart captured the imagination of Carolina sports fans in Year 2. In Year 1, the team had played their home games in Clemson, South Carolina, 140 miles away from their real home in Charlotte. They had to because Ericsson Stadium had not yet been completed. Only one game out of eight at Clemson sold out. Home games were blacked out on TV in most of the Carolinas, and for road games the Panthers' TV ratings were mediocre at best.

But when the Panthers came home to Charlotte in 1996, the honeymoon began in earnest and ran for six months nonstop.

Television ratings soared to levels never before seen in the Carolinas. Every game was a fast sellout in 72,685-seat Ericsson Stadium. A group of 8,500 single-game tickets sold for the Dallas-Carolina playoff game in Charlotte almost caused riots in a number of ticket venues and sold out in four minutes.

But not everyone in Charlotte immediately turned into a Panthers fan. A school bus full of kids passed the Panthers' practice field early in the season and the kids gleefully shouted, "Cowboys! Cowboys!" The Panthers still had much to prove. But by playoff time, the team had endeared itself to everyone.

The Panthers' magical season even reached all the way to the White House. President Bill Clinton postponed a January cabinet meeting so that Erskine Bowles, a Charlotte investment banker and Clinton's chief of staff, could watch the Panthers in the playoffs.

It was a dream season for the Panthers and their fans.

It was the year Carolina went from being a whimsical curiosity to a snarling NFL contender.

It was 1996—the year of the cat.

CHAPTER ONE

Dom Capers and the Art of Obsession

DEEP UNDER THE SEATS AT ERICSSON STADIUM—FAR, far away from the places where fans go on Sundays—is a black leather sleeper sofa. There is no chance of someone stumbling upon it by mistake. You need security clearance and a computerized photo access card to get there. The sofa stays folded out as a queen-sized bed most of the time. Its owner always spreads a hunter-green comforter over the top and neatly tucks it into the corners.

The walls surrounding the sofa are gray cinder blocks. The desk next to the bed is always immaculate. A black phone sits on the desk. Nothing else. In the one tiny closet, all the shirts are nicely pressed and face the same way. As you look across the wall, nothing breaks up the monotony of the cinder blocks except for a mounted color TV. Its screen is always turned toward the wall. The spartan setting looks like the college dorm room of a neat freak or the cell of a prisoner. Actually, it serves as the second home of Carolina's head coach, Dom Capers.

· · ·

EVERY TUESDAY AND WEDNESDAY NIGHT DURING THE 1996 football season, Capers slept on that sofa. Sometimes he stayed there on Monday nights too. Ericsson Stadium became his home away from home on those nights so he could save himself the 30-minute commute to his 5,000-square-foot house—the one with the beautiful view, and the full-sized panther statue on nearby Lake Norman.

His house was much nicer, but "the cell" was more convenient. That's how Capers laughingly referred to his second home. "I've got a radio down here, a shower, a john, a fold-out bed, and a desk," Capers once said of the cell. "I've got everything I need. I could move right into a minimum-security prison and not miss a beat."

Capers would undoubtedly do well in a prison environment. He is a smart, simple man who needs little to survive, does well in a stark setting, and has great respect for others' personal space. You'd have to make him the warden, though, because it would be extremely difficult to think of a situation where Dom Capers would commit a crime. You won't find a straighter arrow than Capers, unless you start visiting monasteries. Even then it would be difficult. "Dom is the perfect coach for the Bible Belt," Panthers cornerback Toi Cook has said.

The Panthers coach is also a model of controlled obsessiveness. Before each team meeting in 1996, he wrote down every word he would say. He had his speech typed up and he highlighted each sentence with either blue or yellow marker, depending on its importance. He used blue for the main topics and yellow for the subtopics. After the speech, he took the pages, punched holes in the sheets, and carefully inserted them into a large black binder. Capers had a binder for every season. He kept a record of every speech. Every team meeting. Every practice session.

He kept a personal journal, too, in which he recorded the length of every jog he took and documented almost everything he ate. He studied opponents' game film so incessantly that Panthers players often shook their heads in admiration during team meetings, as Capers pointed out, say, the four primary weaknesses in another club's third-string tight end. All of that took a great deal of time. It was no wonder that his wife, Karen, picked out all of his casual clothes at home and Panthers equipment man Jackie Miles selected all the ones for work. Capers, 46, routinely put in a 110-hour work week, an intense schedule that made others start to worry about his future candidacy for coaching burnout. On the odd occasion when he did go home to sleep, he usually left home at 5:30 A.M. the next day and didn't get back until 11 P.M.—"unless I have to work late," as he explained it.

"Get a life," his few friends outside the coaching profession said.

"I've got one," he told them. "Just the one I want. I couldn't imagine doing anything else."

Because of his leave-in-darkness, return-in-darkness schedule, Capers sometimes forgot what the outside of his own house looked like. In this he was similar to former Green Bay coach Vince Lombardi, who once drove past his own home, parked his car in another family's garage, and walked into a neighbor's kitchen before figuring out he was in the wrong place.

In November 1996, during the heart of the Panthers' playoff run, Capers saw his home in Lake Norman for four hours while the sun was up. "That was kind of weird," he admitted. "But it just goes to show you how much you actually don't need a house."

Football was life for Capers—all else was incidental. The only TV show he watched was ESPN's *NFL PrimeTime* highlight show every Sunday night. He usually fell asleep in his chair after that, exhausted from the week's work. He missed voting in the 1996 presidential election because it would have interfered with his work on developing the game plan for the New York Giants. When Capers's assistants delayed a meeting so they could watch the announcement of the O. J. Simpson verdict, Capers sat alone in the meeting room, oblivious. "Did everyone quit?" he wondered aloud. Capers ho-hummed when he was told the "not guilty" verdict—O.J. had dropped off Capers's radar screen as soon as he retired from football.

Capers had no children. His second marriage survived the 1996 season in part because his wife, Karen, kept herself busy working as a flight attendant for United Airlines and planned her schedule around her husband's. She took her overnight trips early in the week during football season, because she knew that if she was in Charlotte, she'd probably have to go visit her husband at the cell if she wanted to see him.

Karen Grupp Capers had worked as a flight attendant for 23 years. The two met on a United Airlines Chicago–Pittsburgh flight in 1992 after Dom's first marriage dissolved—partly because of his gruesome schedule. Capers sat in coach class in those days. (A career assistant then with the Pittsburgh Steelers, he didn't get to go first class until 1995, after the Panthers offered him his first head-coaching job.) As he boarded the plane, Capers noticed the cute, blonde flight attendant near the door. He had most of his things packed in a carry-on. Since this was Capers, the bag was gently packed and not over-stuffed, but still, it was heavy. Karen Grupp had had hundreds of bags shoved at her just like this one over the years as grown men shouldered past her and muttered, "Put this up for me." She thought another boor was coming, but Capers quietly surprised her.

"I remember that he hung up his own garment bag, and I thought that was nice," Karen Capers said. "A lot of people give us these two-hundred-pound bags and say, 'Here, hang it!'" Not him.

DESPITE THE OBVIOUS QUESTIONS ABOUT WHETHER or not anyone could sustain Capers's work pace in 1996, it appeared that the Panthers could not have made a better choice for head coach. This was ironic, because really, he was their second choice. Former Washington Redskins coach Joe Gibbs turned down the job before Capers ever got a sniff at it. Interestingly, it was Gibbs whom Capers seemed to resemble most on the sideline. Gibbs also slept on an office couch during the Redskins' best years in the 1980s. His first Washington team started 0–5, just like Capers's first Panthers team in 1995. And Gibbs too was clueless when it came to current events: He didn't know who Oliver North was during the middle of what was then the biggest scandal in the country. Gibbs, now a TV analyst for NBC and a successful NASCAR car owner, has said publicly several times that he couldn't have done as good a job as Capers did with the Panthers. He has also jokingly warned Capers not to win so much so fast, or expectations will rise faster than talent. Capers good-naturedly ignored the warning.

One of the ways Capers tries to maintain his level of success is through intense physical conditioning. He has no real hobbies except for physical fitness—five-mile runs and years of gym work have given him a weightlifter's chest and an impressive 6-foot, 200-pound physique. He needed his size to help him win respect from some of the players. Most of them understood that the Panthers were an anomaly—the owner had played in the NFL but the head coach hadn't. On many teams, it's the other way around. Even though he never played professionally, Capers understood what it meant to stay in good shape, which gave him something in common with the men he coached. "When I first met him, it was February 1996, and he had on this big sweater," remembered tight end Wesley Walls. "He was all thick, like he'd been working out. He really seemed to care about the way he looked."

Capers did care, although he liked to pretend that he didn't. He ate and drank carefully—his favorite drink was diet Coke, his favorite food, pasta.

Back at Meadowbrook High in Ohio, Capers had always worn crisply pressed dress pants to school. Thirty years later, his clothes were still unwrinkled. And close observers of the coach's appearance noted that he seemed to have a lot more hair on his head during the 1996 season than during 1995. So had Capers joined the hair club for men?

"No, no," he said, blushing slightly. In reality, Capers had noticed some newspaper stories where writers had referred to his thinning hair.

"I just cut it differently," he said. "It used to be a lot longer [on one side] and I combed a lot more of it over my head."

Capers still favored wearing a cap most of the time, but with the new part, he looked younger. And he always looked strong—"like he wanted to put on the pads and come out there with us," as Walls said.

That first encounter with Capers really made Walls feel concerned. "I was a little nervous," the tight end recalled. "He looked like he'd work my tail off."

And he did.

In the summer of 1996, Capers ran what Walls would later call a "military-style" training camp. Players were fined for missing breakfast or for being one minute late to meetings. That sort of stringent discipline carried on throughout the regular season: Capers suspended key reserve Shawn King before the Dallas playoff game because of King's chronic tardiness.

Although regarded as a player's coach in many ways, Capers is also very demanding.

"When I played for San Francisco, we held a plane one time for forty minutes because Ricky Watters [a star 49ers running back at the time] was late," Panthers cornerback Toi Cook said. "When Kerry Collins was a few minutes late for the plane this year before one game, we just left him."

A good day for Capers was one where everything ran on time. Capers expected that, but he also expected a little more. His players were all supposed to work extra hard, just as their coach did. It was part of the way the Panthers evaluated their players. Who finished the regular job? Who did a little more?

When choosing a player, Capers said, "You've got to be able to ask the tough questions. How does this guy handle criticism when all of a sudden things start coming down on him? Is he a guy that will be accountable? If he's supposed to lift weights at seven-thirty in the morning, is he going to be there? Is he going to be willing to spend some extra time to look at tape after practice? Or can he not wait to get out of here because he's going to do just the bare essentials? Will he do more than what you ask him to do?"

Capers prepared his whole life to become a head coach, so it was no surprise, when he got the job in early 1995, that he had a plan extending far beyond wanting players with a good work ethic. The plan had been honed to a fine point for the past two years. Capers would recite parts of it to you even when he wasn't asked to. An answer to a question about a particular player would suddenly veer back to Capers's philosophy, which was never far from the front of his mind. It went like this:

"When you set a higher standard, you're going to have to pay a steeper price," Capers preached. "It's human nature that we all want to do what we want to do when we want to do it. It's human nature sometimes to look for the quick fix, the easiest way. But if you want to do anything out of the ordinary, it's going to take some sacrifice."

DON'T EVER HIRE SOMEONE TO JUMP OUT OF A CAKE for Dom Capers. Don't ever throw him a birthday party without telling him. He likes his life as organized and prepackaged as the products in your local grocer's frozen-food section. He already has a timetable set up for every day of the Panthers' upcoming 1997 season, hour by hour. If you wanted to know where he will be at 2:14 P.M. on November 13, 1997, Capers could tell you exactly.

"I don't like surprises," Capers said. "We would take a player with lesser talent who would be consistent in his effort as opposed to an extremely talented guy who would be up and down, because then your team will reflect that. We don't want to be a team that's up and down like a yo-yo."

Capers's favorite three words are "belief," "trust," and "consistency." His favorite expression is "sense of urgency," and he certainly always seems to have one. People around the Panthers on a daily basis joke about what Capers must be like to live with: "Karen, we must eat with a sense of urgency tonight, because I urgently need to go buy some more highlighter pens." Panthers offensive lineman Matt Elliott said, "You would almost go as far as saying he's anal retentive. But maybe 'meticulous' is a better word."

Capers owns a 27-foot boat that he keeps on Lake Norman and docks outside his home. In the spring of 1996, during some of his rare downtime, he sometimes took the boat out to the middle of the lake. There he would sit on the deck and work on whittling down his correspondence, sometimes with a light-rock station playing in the background. Capers tried to answer every letter he received, although that got harder as the Panthers got more popular.

Perhaps because of the boat, Capers's favorite analogy in 1996—the one that made players groan because they heard it so often—involved sailing. "There are thirty teams in training camp," Capers told the Panthers when they gathered in Spartanburg, South Carolina, for preseason workouts in July 1996. "They all have the same goals. It's like climbing into a big boat. We have a map of where we want to go. We want to sail across this big body of water. And when we get in that boat, everybody's got to get that oar in the water and they've got to do their part. There aren't any passengers, because if there were, it's going to be too heavy.

"As you start out, everybody knows where they want to go," Capers continued. "But the next thing you know, once you get in that water, some of them start getting off course. And the key is, once you get off course, how do you find a way to get back on?"

Capers used this analogy so often during the season that players could recite it with him if they wanted to. Only once in 1996 was there a crack in the boat story. Capers was adding some color to his description of the boat, making the players visualize it hitting some big waves. But instead of saying that the boat was smashing against waves, he accidentally said it hit an iceberg instead. Fullback Howard Griffith looked back at one of his teammates and said, "Oh, man, we hit an iceberg? We can't sail through that! The man has just sunk us!"

Most of the time, though, Capers's analogy ran right on course, as it did that first day of training camp. "Some teams have the ability to get through stormy weather," he said. "Some teams don't. And some guys get thrown off that boat along the way." In other words, if you don't do your part, you get fired. That happened to Barry Foster, the former Pittsburgh Steelers star running back who was Carolina's best-known player for a short time in the summer of 1995.

Capers thought Foster wasn't trying hard enough to come back from a mild knee injury. Soon, Foster was history. Capers always based much of his weekly game plan on running the ball on offense and stopping it on defense, and he quickly decided Foster was too unreliable to carry the mail for the Panthers.

"I have a great disdain for excuses," Capers said. "To me, this is a bottom-line business. It comes back to accountability and guys being able to look in the mirror and say, 'Are we or are we not getting the job done?' To me, that's the common thread in the ships that get off course. If I come into a press conference and start making excuses, then the assistant coaches see that. Then they do it. Then the team does it and it just runs rampant. If you've got the offense pointing fingers at the defense or the defense pointing fingers at the offense—you show me that and I'm going to show you a loser."

CAPERS'S PHILOSOPHY FOR THE 1996 SEASON MIGHT have sounded a little hokey, a little too 1950s-ish, but it worked, precisely because he believed it was true. He went out of his way throughout the season to take the lion's share of blame when something went wrong, and he avoided embarrassing players in public the way superstitious people avoid black cats.

"What I admire most about him is the way he respects everybody on the field," running back Anthony Johnson said of Capers. "Whether they're a practice squad player or a limelight guy, he treats everyone with the same amount of respect. That just doesn't happen in this league. It's unheard of, really."

"I've played for eight NFL head coaches in ten years," Panthers quarterback Steve Beuerlein said, "and I've never seen one who won't scream at a guy in front of everyone else occasionally. I've also never seen one who—if you look only at him on the sidelines—you have no idea if you're fifty points behind or fifty ahead."

Capers's normal expression is one of concentrated neutrality. He is the Switzerland of NFL coaches—and one of the most popular head men among NFL officials because he only complains when he is nearly certain he is right.

But he's not always robotic. Although it is often hidden, Capers occasionally displays a nice, self-deprecating sense of humor. He loves to tell the story of how Karen was supposed to pick him up at the security gate one sunny afternoon at Ericsson Stadium but got held up at a hair appointment. After the security guard left, Capers slipped inside the booth and waved to everyone who was leaving. Player after player and employee after employee did a double take as they looked for the familiar security guard and instead saw Capers outside the black gate, waving back at them.

"What are you doing here?" they asked him.

"I'm taking on some extra responsibilities!" he would shout. Some people believed him, too.

Capers also gets angry sometimes. The surest way to see that happen is for a player to blame someone else for his own mistake. The second-surest way is to give him a piece of equipment that doesn't work.

Capers sets a huge amount of stock in the 9 A.M. Saturday team meeting he holds the day before each game, when he reads aloud any press clippings he can find that he thinks may motivate the team. He also chooses six to eight plays from the opponents' offense, defense, and special teams as teaching tools—final pointers to think about in the 28 hours before the game usually kicks off.

On Saturday, December 14, however, the film projector set up by the Panthers' videotape crew didn't work. Capers turned red. He fooled with the projector for a while. The players hid their smiles. Finally Capers sputtered, "Okay, break the meeting—we'll reschedule this!" No one had ever seen him so angry.

"I guess I had a hard time hiding my emotion that day," Capers said. "That kind of hit right to the bone with me because I don't feel that we can ask our guys to do anything that we don't do. I think we set the tempo as a coaching staff. I talk all the time about attention to detail, the little things make a difference whether you win or lose. . . . I was extremely frustrated. I don't want our players to ever have to come into a meeting and wait on us to fiddle with film."

Veteran wide receiver Dwight Stone, who had played under Capers at both Pittsburgh and Carolina, was concerned enough to approach him about it in the hotel later that day. "Coach, when the tribe sees the chief get ruffled, they start to get concerned," Stone said. "I just wanted to see if everything is okay. We still love you. It wasn't your fault it happened like that."

Capers was more embarrassed than angry by that point. "The reason I blew up is, I sit here all week long and tell you all how organized and focused you have to be to make things happen," he said. "For me to say that to you and then come here on Saturday and have the film not working, that makes the players look and say, 'Hmmph. The coach doesn't have his work done, why should I have mine done?'"

Capers got the meeting rescheduled, of course—for one hour

later—and from then on the Panthers' video people triple-checked the projector before each Saturday morning meeting.

Capers's love of narrating videotape to his players was legendary. When he was defensive coordinator at Pittsburgh, Steelers linebacker Greg Lloyd once said Capers had the "most monotonous voice in the world."

ON ONLY A HANDFUL OF OCCASIONS HAS CAPERS NOT been anxious to watch more film on an NFL player. One of them was his first date with Karen.

The two had talked enough on that 1992 flight that Capers had gotten Karen's number. She lived in Chicago. He lived in Pittsburgh—but she could fly free as a United employee. So he called her up and asked her out to dinner in Pittsburgh a few weeks later.

They were still cute telling the story together four years after it happened. Capers loosens up around Karen faster than around anyone else in the world. Karen was scheduled to arrive at the Pittsburgh airport at 5 P.M. Dom planned to leave the office just after 4:30 to pick her up and head off to dinner.

"About four-thirty, [Pittsburgh Steelers head coach] Bill Cowher walks in and wants to talk defense," Capers recalled. "Well, I can't say, 'Bill, I've got this date, okay? We can't talk defense. Let's let this go.' So, it gets to be five-thirty. It gets to be six o'clock."

Meanwhile, Karen had no clue what was happening. The last flight back to Chicago on United had already left. She stood there, nervous, wondering what had happened to the assistant coach she had met on the plane. "I had talked to him enough to know that he wasn't the kind of person who would stand you up, though," Karen said.

Finally, Capers made up an excuse to duck outside for a minute. In a mild panic, he asked his secretary to call the airport, page Karen, and tell her to meet him near the USAir room for frequent travelers. At 7 P.M., two hours late, Capers finally got to the airport. He found Karen. If he had been able to, he would have fined himself.

"Here it's the first time we've ever gone out, and I'm two hours late," Capers said. "I figure, 'Hey, if she sticks around, she knows exactly what she's getting into.'" They were married in June 1994 and still reserve every Friday night as "date night."

ERNEST DOMINIC CAPERS GREW UP IN TINY BUFFALO, Ohio, a no-stoplight town of eight hundred people about a 6½-hour drive north of Charlotte on Interstate 77. His younger brother, Julius, and his mother, Jeanette, still live there. They remain close to Dom and drive down to games as often as they can. Capers calls his mom once a week, and by the fall of '96, he had sent her enough Panthers regalia to outfit her from head to toe on Sundays for Panthers games.

Capers was a good high school athlete and a decent one at Division III Mount Union College in Alliance, Ohio, but he had no chance to make the pros in either football or baseball, his two main sports. He began his football coaching career immediately after graduating from Mount Union in 1972 and leapfrogged from one assistant's job to another after that, working under well-known college coaches like Don James and Johnny Majors.

In 1992 Cowher gave Capers his big break, naming him defensive coordinator of the Steelers. By that time, Capers had been an assistant for six collegiate teams and two pro teams—not an uncommon résumé for someone determined to find a head coaching spot. His longest stint came under Jim Mora, who hired Capers as an assistant in the United States Football League for the Philadelphia-Baltimore Stars and then brought him along to the New Orleans Saints in 1986. Capers was the defensive secondary coach in New Orleans for six seasons, working with future Panthers Sam Mills, Brett Maxie, and Toi Cook.

He started his personal log in 1982, after his father, Eugene, gave him a large leather-bound notebook for Christmas in 1981. Shortly after that, his father died of a heart attack at age 57.

"My father was a very, very important figure in my life," Capers said. "He gave me a start. He was my mentor. He's never far away. I think about him all the time. . . . One of the things he told me when I was real young, I'll never forget it. I've used it in most of the decisions I've made professionally: If you surround yourself with good people and you learn from those people and you work as hard as you can, good things happen."

The elder Capers was a highway project engineer and a part-time carpenter. Dom was the oldest of the Caperses' three children— Julius is four years younger, and his sister, Nina, is ten years younger. Capers's mother, Jeanette, wasn't sure she would ever be able to have a family until Dom came along. She had two miscarriages before carrying Dom to term, and took up to 38 hormone pills per day to prevent a third miscarriage.

Eugene and Jeanette Capers gave their first-born son the name Ernest after a great-grandfather who had lived in Italy. Capers never went by that name and doesn't appreciate anyone's calling him that now, even in jest. The family's surname was originally Caprera, but Dom's grandfather, Giovanni Caprera, changed it when he journeyed from Italy to Ohio to work in the coal mines.

Dom was a well-mannered, athletic kid, and a big fan of the Cleveland Browns. His good behavior fueled a friendly sibling rivalry. "As a kid, I did everything, and I got caught," Julius Capers said, laughing. "He never did anything. I always got compared to perfection."

Dom Capers developed small, neat handwriting as a kid and never varied from it. An autograph from Capers is actually not a signature at all, but tiny printed letters that almost look typewritten. Pittsburgh's coach Bill Cowher once marveled, "Dom writes so small. It's amazing how he can economize one piece of paper."

Capers took the Panthers head job, edging out the other top candidate, Rich Kotite (after Gibbs turned down the job), shortly after his last Pittsburgh team got upset by San Diego in the AFC championship game. Capers had never been to a Super Bowl as a coach, and he sure didn't want to go to the 1995 game as a league invitee after getting so close to it. But the NFL wanted to introduce the Carolina and Jacksonville head coaches at a press conference two days before the game, so Capers had to fly down to Miami and grit his teeth through two days' worth of sympathy—partly for the Pittsburgh loss, and partly for taking the head job of an expansion team that seemed destined to flounder at the bottom of the NFC West. "I'll never forget going to the Super Bowl," Capers said. "It was the last place I wanted to be. The Chargers had beaten us and I didn't want to go down. But I had to. So I sat there [during the game] and just watched the 49ers go up and down the field.

"I was thinking, 'We don't have our staff completed. We've got about ten to twelve players under contract. We have no identity. And we have to play the 49ers not twice, but three times [including once in the exhibition season] next year.' That was a little bit of an over-whelming feeling."

When Capers got overwhelmed during the '96 season, he compensated by breaking a job down into small tasks. It made him feel better to do a small thing well, rather than a big thing ordinarily. And he obsessed endlessly about the small things—about the football equivalent of whether there was a speck of dust in the corner or a spiderweb underneath the deck. "To me, if you want to be special, if you want to be there at the end, you've got to condition yourself to do a lot of the little things that most people won't do," Capers said. "They'll talk about it. They'll talk a good game. But they aren't willing to pay the price it takes to be special. A lot of teams end up being ordinary because of that."

Want a special yard? Edge it with a fork. Want a special team? Respect everyone, but don't let any of them get away with anything.

Capers has always been a statistics nut, too. When the Panthers started off 0–5 in 1995, Capers tried to build them up by letting them know they were among the NFL's best in kickoff return yardage allowed. He loved all sorts of stats about field position and turnovers. He gladly noted after the season that Carolina was now 19–5 in the regular season when its turnover ratio was zero or on the plus side and 1–9 when it was minus-one or worse.

The Panthers players would good-naturedly tease him about this tendency, too. It became a running joke to some. "The Panthers are five and one this year when eating chicken for the pregame meal, but only three and two when they eat pizza," the players would kid.

By the end of the 1996 season, the players didn't notice the wear and tear the brutal workweeks had taken on their coach, but his family did. "He doesn't get much sleep," Julius Capers said of his brother.

"He really is running himself ragged. I see this season wearing on him. It always does at the end of the season. He starts losing some weight. But he still handles anything they throw at him. And he won't let up. He never will."

Capers did make some concessions to age. He keeps a heater in his large daytime office upstairs from the cell in case his feet get cold while he works. He doesn't pull all-nighters. He tries to eat right. But he has worked hard all his life for the job he now has, and if it eventually kills him maybe he couldn't think of a better way to go out, than on the football field with a big smile on his face.

CHAPTER TWO

Laying the Foundation

IT IS RARE WHEN A COACH FINDS NO DEFEAT IN A loss, but the Carolina Panthers' 1995 season was such a source of pride for Dom Capers that despite a 20–17 loss to the Washington Redskins in RFK Stadium on a frosty-cold Christmas Eve, he brimmed with pride. It was the final game of the Panthers' smashingly successful debut season. The most games any previous NFL expansion team had won in its first year was three. The Panthers' 7–9 record had set a mark that might never be surpassed by a first-year team, and they had done it after starting the season a dreadful 0–5. There were some startling accomplishments along the way: a four-game winning streak, seven wins in the final 11 games, and a 13–7 victory over the defending Super Bowl champion San Francisco 49ers. No previous expansion team had ever beaten a reigning champion. These positive elements established a solid foundation on which to build the team's future, so Capers wanted to make sure he sent his players into the off-season with a message of affirmation.

"I don't want today's game to detract from anything about the rest of the season," he told his players after the Washington game. "When we started out nobody really knew anything about us. One of our goals was to gain an identity and to gain some respect around the NFL. I'm proud to say that we did."

Even as he spoke, though, Capers knew that major changes would be on the way. To take the next step toward owner Jerry Richardson's Super Bowl dream, the Panthers would need to improve their talent and their depth via free agent signings and draft picks.

The winds of change were already blowing in RFK's open-air press box in the minutes before the Redskins game. Panthers president Mike McCormack was watching the Green Bay–Pittsburgh game on television when Packers tight end Mark Chmura made a catch and sprinted downfield ahead of Pittsburgh's defenders. "That's what we need, right there," McCormack said.

He meant a new tight end. At the time, it seemed like he might also mean Chmura, who was due to become an unrestricted free agent in February. Panthers general manager Bill Polian, Capers, and McCormack began meeting in January to outline the team's needs heading into the 1996 season. They decided it was essential to add a game-breaking running back, a tight end with speed, and bigger, faster wide receivers. The offensive line had to get bigger and more athletic. A pass-rushing boost was sorely needed on defense, and the kickoff and punt return teams needed upgrading, too.

"We are far, far from being a complete football team," Polian said at the time. "There's no question we will be infusing new talent onto this team."

To create roster openings, tough decisions had to be made. In the months ahead, Polian would have to release three players who had originally helped him build the Buffalo Bills into a Super Bowl team: quarterback Frank Reich, Carolina's first starting quarterback; tight end Pete Metzelaars, who caught the Panthers' first-ever touchdown pass; and wide receiver Don Beebe. Two other players who wouldn't be back for '96 were the colorful cornerback Tim McKyer and the immensely popular Derrick Moore, an effervescent running back who had led the team in rushing with 740 yards.

The success of Carolina's first season already had their fans talking about making the playoffs in Year 2, but Polian, true to his nature, tried to downplay the team's potential by adamantly warning against unrealistic expectations. "It's conceivable that we could be a better team next year and have the same record, or maybe even a little worse," Polian said. "When you talk about challenging the 49ers for the division, we're a long, long way from that."

Only Polian knows whether he actually believed that statement or not, but in the key off-season months, February through May, he would set out in search of the missing pieces that could someday complete a championship puzzle.

THOUGH HE WAS ONE OF THE PANTHERS' LARGER-than-life characters, Polian had never played or coached a down in the NFL. Yet everyone called him a good "football man" anyway. A red-headed, tempestuous risktaker, he was a master team builder, the constructor of the Buffalo teams that reached four Super Bowls in four consecutive years. The Panthers were his latest project. Polian's specialties included luring free-agent players (like Lamar Lathon in 1995) and plucking talented collegiate players (like quarterback Kerry Collins) out of the NFL draft. "It's a lot like trading stock on the stock market," Polian once said of the draft. "There's lots of sound and fury around you. Phones are ringing. Decisions have to be made instanta-neously."

His temper and his knack for scouting were equally legendary. Po-lian, who was 53 when the season began, is a New Yorker through and through. When he first joined the Panthers, owner Jerry Richard-son sometimes slipped him notes during group meetings with a four-letter word written on them: C-A-L-M.

Richardson's and Polian's personalities couldn't be further apart, but to put a successful team on the field, Richardson knew that he would have to put up with Polian's temper to reap the benefits of his football knowledge. Their styles were very different, but that was one of the reasons the two were so effective together.

"Bill has tried really hard to get along with what I call the Carolinas culture and way of doing business," Richardson said. "We're not a confrontational culture. New York City is confrontational. When I go to New York City, it happens even before you get out of the car. You're riding into the city and people are blowing their horns and going bananas over crazy stuff—like the light doesn't change in time or something. It's just a different way of life. Our culture is more calm and not quite as in-your-face."

Polian's star-searching method during the 1996 off-season wasn't as regimented as Capers's routine, but it came pretty close. Polian usually got to his Ericsson Stadium office around 8:45 A.M. The first thing he did each day was double-check what the Panthers' salary-cap status was. Negotiating contracts to fit under the cap was one of his most important duties. Shortly after that, he'd hook up his telephone headpiece and go to work. Polian often spent five hours on the phone a day, and he didn't like to linger very long over any one of the conversations. The average call length was perhaps five to six minutes, which meant it wasn't infrequent for Polian to make or receive a hundred calls a day. He drank diet Coke and chewed gum during much of this time. (The gum replaced the Salem Menthol cigarettes he used to smoke.) He ate lunch at his desk and rewarded himself at the end of most days with a jog, either outside or on the treadmill. "My best problem-solving time—which is what this job boils down to—usually comes when I'm running or when I have quiet time to think," Polian said. "That's probably between seven and ten P.M."

Polian usually tried to get home by 10 P.M., but it wasn't uncommon for him to stay up until 1 A.M. trying to work a deal—particularly if he was negotiating with players or agents on the West Coast.

The bane of Polian's existence is sports agents. In his opinion, they are the ones who hold players out for more money, care only about their commissions, and in general, make a GM's life extremely difficult.

When in Buffalo constructing the Bills' Super Bowl teams, Polian once challenged an agent to get down into a three-point offensive line stance and come at him. The agent wisely declined. Polian's favorite line to use with a wayward agent was "I'm going to come through this telephone and tear your tonsils out!"

When Polian heard late in the 1996 season that a movie called *Jerry Maguire* was about to come out with Tom Cruise portraying a sympathetic sports agent, he muttered, "The apocalypse is upon us."

But Polian dealt with the agents because they brought him the players, and that's how he made his living. "My greatest strength is that I'm a good judge of talent," Polian said. "I have a good feel for where people fit within the framework of a team."

Everyone knew this, and it became even more apparent as the Panthers became successful faster than anyone thought possible. During the '96 season, Polian's name got mentioned for a general manager job every time one opened up—or even when there wasn't an opening. But Polian was hot even before his excellent 1996 off-season. In March he was named *The Sporting News* Executive of the Year in a vote by his peers for his work during Carolina's 7–9 season of 1995.

The players respected him too. "He's got that edge to him," Collins said of Polian. "That's why I think he's so good. People say a lot about his temper, but the man is good."

Well regarded throughout the league, Polian had even worked a year in the NFL office for commissioner Paul Tagliabue after he lost his job in Buffalo because of a front-office dispute.

"Bill has a unique combination of energy and intelligence, along with a unique mix of sports background and management skills," Tagliabue said shortly after the Panthers hired Polian. "He did a tremendous job for us."

And did he ever have a temper. Bob Ferguson, who used to negotiate contracts with Polian in Buffalo and now works for the Arizona Cardinals, once said of his former colleague, "I don't think anyone in the world can scream as loudly into a telephone as Bill."

In the press box, Polian, a devout Catholic, would sometimes greet a bad Panthers play by sputtering, "Jesus, Mary, and Joseph!"

Sports agent Ralph Cindrich, who has negotiated many contracts with Polian, once said, "When you go in talking to Bill Polian, you'd better know your business, and you'd better know your client. Otherwise, you're breakfast."

Polian learned his trade the hard way, on muddy, far-off practice fields in Canada and at small colleges around the United States. He scouted and coached football players in anonymity for much of his professional life—often taking just enough time for a fast lunch of doughnuts, diet soda, and cigarettes before rushing off to watch some other prospect.

Polian's son Chris, the second oldest of Bill and Eileen Polian's four children, works in the Panthers' scouting department. But Bill Polian didn't know anyone in the NFL well enough to get an early break. He grew up in the Bronx and attended New York University in the 1960s. There he played strong safety and captained the football team. He graduated from NYU in 1966, but wasn't talented enough to play football at a higher level, so he tried coaching. Over the next nine years, Polian assisted at three small colleges as a football and baseball coach. He also did some pro football scouting on the side and sold some advertising for *Farm Journal* magazine to help generate extra income. His break came in 1975, at age 32, when his college coach, Bob Windish, then personnel director of the Montreal Alouettes of the Canadian Football League, asked Polian to join him. The head coach of that team was Marv Levy.

Polian scouted for Montreal, the Kansas City Chiefs, the CFL's Winnipeg Blue Bombers, and the USFL's Chicago Blitz from 1975 to 1983. Gradually he developed a reputation for having a fine eye for talent. After getting hired by Buffalo in 1984 and working his way through the organization, he became the Bills' point man in signing quarterback Jim Kelly, drafting defensive end Bruce Smith, and hiring Levy as head coach.

Polian's reputation for preparation was exemplary. He once acquired a videotape of a knee surgery done on a running back he was interested in drafting and showed it to several doctors, trying to get an idea of how likely it was that the player could recover. The doctors said the operation had been done correctly, and that's how Polian decided to take Oklahoma State running back Thurman Thomas. Eventually, Polian was forced to resign in Buffalo after constantly butting heads with Jeffrey Littman, a tax expert who lived in Detroit and helped manage the wealth of Buffalo owner Ralph Wilson. Wilson kept Littman. Polian had to go.

The Panthers scooped him up, warts and all, and gave him the freedom to build a team. He was different than everyone else in the

Panthers' front office—a scoop of Rocky Road in a carton full of vanilla. But he was also wonderful at his job.

"We never want to squelch his passion and personality," Richardson said. "That would be counterproductive."

It also would have made life around the Panthers far less interesting.

POLIAN KEPT HIS 1996 FREE AGENCY SHOPPING PLANS top secret. He didn't want any other team to know that he believed New Orleans tight end Wesley Walls, not Green Bay's Mark Chmura, would be a perfect fit for the Carolina offense. Or that Oakland's Greg Skrepenak was the big right tackle he wanted, not Pittsburgh's Leon Searcy. Or that San Francisco's Eric Davis was the cornerback he coveted, not Arizona's Aeneas Williams. But when Friday, February 16 arrived—the first day of the NFL signing period for unrestricted free agents—Polian was ready to start speed-dialing the agents of the players he wanted to sign. He knew he would have to move quickly, because the best players usually get gone fast.

Polian was armed with plenty of spending money because the Panthers were approximately $16 million under the league's $38.773 million salary cap figure for the '96 season. Most teams had less than half that. Polian had enough room under the cap to shop for new free agents, re-sign a few of the Carolina players whose contracts had expired, and pay for the draft picks he'd make in April.

By February 21, just five days into the signing period, Polian had managed to sign Walls, Skrepenak, and Davis. In Walls, Carolina finally had a speedy tight end who could "stretch the field" and replace the aging Pete Metzelaars. Davis, a first-team All-Pro for San Francisco in 1995, would take Tim McKyer's place at cornerback—a signing that was doubly impressive because the Panthers were taking him away from the rival 49ers. And Skrepenak, a 6' 6", 340-pound lineman who had been with the Raiders for four years, was immediately penciled in as a starter on an offensive line that needed his size and experience.

Polian's next major target was Cornelius Bennett, the outside linebacker he had drafted when he was general manager of the Buffalo

Bills. The Panthers had decided to pursue the 31-year-old Bennett to play the outside linebacker position opposite Lamar Lathon. The Panthers had come tantalizingly close to signing Bennett but had been outbid in the end by the Atlanta Falcons, who emerged as a surprise player in the negotiations on the eve of the bidding deadline set by Bennett's agent, Eugene Parker.

The next outside linebacker on Carolina's free agent list was Pittsburgh's Kevin Greene. Greene, who had been cast off by the Steelers, watched the Bennett sweepstakes closely. He knew his best chance for employment in 1996 was with the Panthers since Capers was one of the few coaches who still used the 3-4 defense tailor-made for his pass-rushing talents.

But Bennett's decision didn't hasten a Carolina move to sign Greene. The Panthers instead turned their attention to the college draft in April, where they thought they might find an outside linebacker to complement Lathon on the other side. They didn't, so they pursued Greene.

On May 3, Carolina signed Greene, who was part Hollywood and part Dick Butkus. He instantly became the first nationally recognized superstar to play for the Panthers. He had zoomed into prominence the previous three years in Pittsburgh, partly because of his Fabio-length blond hair and partly because of his reckless abandon on the football field. Now he was a Panther, and the hair was almost gone. Only a few thin blond slivers remained, hanging down the middle of his back. In a gesture symbolic oʻ his divorce from the Steelers, Greene had instructed his wife, Tara, to give him a haircut. She snipped for hours, giving him a normal-length cut, except for the narrow string of perhaps a dozen or so long hairs that remained as a reminder of what had once been.

"I had grown my hair out for three years with Pittsburgh as an attitude statement because I believed in what the Steelers were trying to accomplish," Greene said. "I wanted to show that I was doing everything I could to get that team to the Super Bowl, that I was going the distance."

Greene had thought he would retire a Steeler, but Pittsburgh's decision not to re-sign him and to allow him to go to another team had hurt him deeply and forever changed his feelings about Steelers coach Bill Cowher.

"I'm an athlete who plays with a passion and a love for the game and I try to establish relationships," Greene said. "I put my heart on the line for the coach who plays me. I thought I had established a wonderful relationship with Coach Cowher that would last beyond football. I really cared for him. But I was disillusioned."

Exit Bill Cowher. Enter Dom Capers.

And enter a few talented rookies and some key backup players, too.

THE PANTHERS HAVE HAD TWO INCREDIBLY LUCKY breaks in their brief history. The first: Capers was available to be hired after Joe Gibbs turned down the job. The second: drafting star Michigan running back Tshimanga Biakabutuka with the eighth overall pick in the 1996 draft.

Biakabutuka, a back with blazing speed and shifty moves, was coming off a 1,818-yard season at Michigan. He was also the player the Panthers wanted more than anyone else—the breakaway franchise back Polian thought the offense needed as a complement to Collins's passing. But Polian was so skeptical about the Panthers' chances of getting Biakabutuka with a pick as low as No. 8 that he later admitted he had considered it "a mortal lock" that some other team would get Biakabutuka first. As it so often happens in the NFL draft, however, the early stages of the first round were full of surprises and Biakabutuka was still available when the Panthers' turn came around. Polian was so thrilled he later called it the happiest moment of his entire off-season. "Of all the different scenarios we planned, we knew that one would be the hardest," he said.

The selection of Biakabutuka was the first sign that the Panthers were going to use the draft to try to add firepower to their offense. In the second round, they chose Michigan State wide receiver Muhsin Muhammad, whose strength and ability to run after catching the ball had drawn comparisons to Dallas star Michael Irvin. In the third round, they added New Mexico running back/kick returner Winslow Oliver, a speedy 5′ 7″ dynamo who was likened to New England Patriots mighty mite Dave Meggett.

The selections drew rave reviews from the national media, including this glowing reaction from ESPN announcer Chris Berman during the cable network's live coverage of the draft: "I think what we're watching is like Dallas in the early sixties under [Tom] Landry and the Dolphins in the early seventies under [Don] Shula. You get the feeling here is a team that will be in the playoffs for the next decade."

And the Panthers didn't stop there. Right before the draft they also picked up free agents Steve Beuerlein and Michael Bates: Beuerlein to be the much-needed backup to Kerry Collins and Bates to play on special teams. The team was primed for the start of the 1996 season, but first, a few matters concerning some of the players needed to be sorted out before the start of training camp.

TRAINING CAMP IN THE NFL IS LIKE A HYBRID OF A military boot camp and a summer boys' camp. Sometimes it's grueling. Sometimes it's fun. Either way, it's a sure sign that vacation days are over. For five weeks, a team's players and coaches spend every day and every night together. They eat, drink, and sleep football, frantically preparing for the season ahead.

Jobs and careers are at stake. So is the fate of the upcoming season. No coach wants to have a bad camp. No player does, either.

Because the Panthers' training camp facility is in the Deep South—75 miles southwest of Charlotte at Wofford College in Spartanburg, South Carolina—the summer heat and humidity become just as much of a challenge as two-a-day practices and roster cutdowns.

All 30 NFL teams are optimistic when training camp opens, and the Panthers were no different. Offensive tackle Blake Brockermeyer marveled at how much more talent and speed the team had, compared to the first season, but he wasn't as enthused as outside linebacker Lamar Lathon, who was already famous on the team for his brash predictions. Lathon told Brockermeyer that he planned to buy the fastest, newest Ferrari on the market *after* the Panthers won the Super Bowl in January. *You must be crazy,* Brockermeyer thought.

One of the early highlights of training camp came on opening day, when team owner Jerry Richardson addressed the team. He had begun this tradition the previous year. Richardson was very popular with the players, and many were anxious to see him for the first time since he had undergone successful surgery for prostate cancer less than two months before.

"You could tell he was still pretty shaken," said Kerry Collins. "But he was strong, too. He reiterated what it means to be in this organization and what's expected of you. It really got us all fired up."

Richardson said that he was proud of the team and that he expected all of the Panthers to be winners on the field and in the community.

He also told the players about the large panther statues that would be unveiled at Ericsson Stadium the following week. He said the statues, which would be positioned outside the stadium's main entrances, would look strong, powerful, and graceful. "If you ever wonder what it is we expect of you on that playing field, just walk around and look at those panthers," Richardson said. "That will tell you everything you want to know."

The players could hardly wait to see them.

TRAINING CAMP WOULDN'T SEEM COMPLETE WITHOUT a player holding out because of a contract dispute or without a significant player getting injured. Both are major nuisances to a coach's attempt to build a cohesive team quickly.

Dom Capers faced both.

The Panthers' top two draft picks, Biakabutuka and Muhsin Muhammad, missed the beginning of camp because their agents hadn't yet reached contract agreements with Polian. Muhammad's deal got done fast enough so he was hardly a holdout at all, but the Biakabutuka negotiations were as tough as gristle. Muhammad only missed the first four days of camp, but judging from the heated confrontations between agent Carl Poston and Bill Polian, Biakabutuka looked as if he would miss many more. The most sensational of the confrontations came in the early days of training camp, when Poston labeled Polian a "dinosaur" for not considering what the agent believed to be a modern-era contract structure.

Polian's public outbursts on the matter came in spurts and almost always included a claim that he had made a final, take-it-or-leave-it offer to Poston. Polian would later classify his tussle with Poston as a "garden variety" holdout, but it looked plenty exotic to the rest of the NFL.

Each day Polian would give daily updates on the negotiations to Capers, who was frustrated that the team's first-round pick was missing so many training-camp practices. The longer the holdout dragged on, the more it looked as if Biakabutuka might not make it to Spartanburg at all, especially after he threatened to sit out the entire season unless a satisfactory contract settlement was reached.

While Biakabutuka sat out, the other players fought for a spot on the 53-man roster.

One of the camp's pleasant surprises was Matt Campbell, a promising prospect at offensive tackle. Campbell was a converted tight end who had been one of the team's original ten signees in December 1994. As the Panthers coaches were experimenting with possible combinations on the offensive line during training camp, they found that Campbell had a natural ability to play tackle. He was extremely athletic and his quick feet were ideal for pass protecting. There were times during practices when he looked better than Brockermeyer, who had been a first-round draft pick in 1995. The coaches also liked his work ethic. He was a blue-collar player. He worked hard, did his job, and never complained. Campbell was unquestionably the surprise player of training camp and he quickly became a favorite of Capers's. Eventually he made it into the starting lineup in a series of position changes that included moving Greg Skrepenak from tackle to guard. While Campbell later found out that his status on the team was secure, plenty of other players worried daily about whether or not they would make it through the next cut.

One was wide receiver–special-teamer Michael Bates, the free-agent signee who would later go on to be one of the stars of the season. Bates had spent his first three seasons with the Seattle Seahawks and Cleveland Browns and wasn't prepared for the intense environment at Camp Capers, where players were expected to do everything at full speed all the time. "I had never experienced anything like that in the NFL," said Bates. "It was a lot rougher and stricter than anyplace I'd been before. On those other teams, it was easy to wait until the regular season to play hard. But not here."

More than once, wide receivers coach Richard Williamson ripped Bates for not running full-out during a pass pattern, especially on practice plays where Bates could tell the quarterback had overthrown a pass. Special-teams coach Brad Seely, who believed Bates could be a major contributor if he made the team, warned Bates that he was close to getting released. "It wasn't that I was late to meetings or was missing my curfew," Bates said. "It was just my output on the practice field. I guess you could say they thought I was too nonchalant."

That changed, and so did Bates's fortunes.

It took much longer for running back Anthony Johnson's value to the Panthers to crystallize. He seemed so much like a bit player during training camp that he asked Capers to be released so that he could go to another team that needed a running back more than Carolina.

"Dom's response was that he was kind of taken aback," Johnson said. "He said in no way would he release me. He said he had a plan for me." But not even Capers knew how well his plan would turn out.

THE DRUDGERY OF CAMP SUBSIDED ON THE SPARKling Saturday afternoon of July 27, when the Panthers got to move practice from Spartanburg to Charlotte for their first workout at Ericsson Stadium. Officially, it was known as PSL Appreciation Day, an event open only to the fans who had dished out hundreds or thousands of dollars each to purchase the permanent-seat licenses (PSLs) that had helped fund the $187 million facility.

Though the Biakabutuka holdout was still going on, Capers considered it one of the best practices of the preseason. Clearly, the players were excited to be in their new home. The fans were, too. Cornerback Eric Davis called it "the nicest stadium I've ever seen."

"We want to start to establish a certain type of attitude so that every time we come into this stadium it's going to be a special place for us," Capers said. "If it's a special place for us, we'll make it a special place for our fans."

The panther statues Richardson had told the players about on the opening day of training camp were everything he'd promised. There were six of them—two guarding each of the three main entrances into the stadium. They weighed 2,800 pounds each and were 22 feet long, all coal-black except for their green eyes. They were known collectively as "the Indomitable Spirit." Sculptor Todd Andrews had written in his proposal, "You'll be able to look into the panther's throat with the realization that you could fit inside." The animals looked exactly as he had envisioned them, and already the sculptures were the favorite picture spot at the stadium for every fan with a camera.

The Panthers players also took their turns gazing at the statues before and after that first practice. "When you saw those panthers, you almost felt like you were one of them," said linebacker Sam Mills. "You'd stand under them and it seemed almost like that thing was going to come to life and pounce on you. You'd see the muscles bulging out and the mouth open. There was such a toughness to them. We knew immediately that's the way our team had to be. We had to be able to pounce on people."

One week later, the Panthers did just that to the Chicago Bears, winning 30–12 in the opening exhibition of the preseason, the first game ever played at Ericsson Stadium. "First and foremost, our goal this year is to not lose at home," Lamar Lathon said in the locker room after the game. "We're off to a good start."

The next week, the Panthers were off to Greeley, Colorado, for three days of practices with the Denver Broncos before the two teams' scheduled exhibition game in Mile High Stadium.

Lathon didn't make the trip. He stayed in Charlotte to have minor arthroscopic surgery on his left knee to remove loose cartilage fragments. The procedure was done at Lathon's insistence and not entirely with the team's full blessing. "I made the decision that in order for me to have a great season I needed to have that surgery," Lathon said. "I know they got pissed off, but I didn't give a damn. They said they were going to work with it and give me therapy [instead of the surgery]. But I didn't want to spend the season in the training room. I *hate* the training room. The big thing was, the knee was swelling up on me. My body never swells. It never has. So I promised them I'd be back quickly, but I had to have that surgery."

One of the things Capers liked about practicing against the Broncos was that it gave the Panthers a chance to work against—and hit—somebody besides their own teammates. Perhaps it was the change of scenery, but the players didn't dread practices nearly as much as they had in Spartanburg. Plus, there was the Smiling Moose, a bar located less than a mile from the Broncos' practice facility and the University of Northern Colorado dormitories that housed the two teams. Players from both teams made frequent Moose visits during their free time at night.

Kerry Collins enjoyed the stay in Greeley so much he said it felt like a "field trip." It was in Greeley that Collins got to know Broncos quarterback John Elway, a 14-year veteran whom Collins had grown up admiring.

One of Collins's favorite stories of the entire season was how he was almost injured riding in a golf cart driven by Elway. Elway used the cart to maneuver quickly around the Northern Colorado campus during training camp. One night he was in a hurry after returning from a Mexican restaurant with Collins and three other Panthers—Walls, Beuerlein, and center Curtis Whitley. The four Carolina players were close to being late for a team meeting, so Elway loaded them all onto his cart and sped to get them all there on time. Collins was standing on the back of the cart with nothing to hold on to. When Elway zipped around a curve, Collins lost his balance.

"Whoa!" Collins said. "John, you've got to slow down, man."

"All right," Elway said with a chuckle.

But Elway hit the next curve at full speed, and Collins went flying off the back of the golf cart, screaming as his body rolled over and over on the asphalt parking lot. Elway slammed on the brakes and ran back to Collins. He was horrified. He thought he'd just debilitated another team's quarterback—one of the NFL's brightest young stars. He could already envision the newspaper headlines the next morning: ELWAY WRECKS COLLINS, CAROLINA SEASON.

"Are you okay?" Elway asked frantically.

"Yeah," Collins said, laughing. He wasn't hurt except for a couple of nasty scrapes on his hands.

You wouldn't know it, the way Collins played several days later. His three-interception performance in the exhibition game against Denver led to a 40–28 Panthers loss.

COLLINS'S SPILL WAS ONLY ONE OF THE TALES THE Panthers would carry with them as reminders of training camp.

Fullback Howard Griffith's favorite times were the nights he and Collins and others watched the Olympics in Steve Beuerlein's dorm room at Wofford. "We'd all sit around and be judges," Griffith said. "We'd come up with who we thought should and shouldn't be winning."

Beuerlein usually had a batch of his wife's delicious homemade cookies for snacks, so his room always attracted a crowd. Griffith especially liked kidding Beuerlein during the diving competition. Beuerlein formerly had been a diver and had actually competed against gold medalist Greg Louganis.

"We let Beuerlein have the final say on the diving judging," Griffith said.

Sam Mills's favorite memory was of the dramatic skit put on by the rookies, a training camp tradition on all NFL teams. What made this one special was that Winslow Oliver, who at 5' 7" is two inches shorter than the 5' 9" Mills, playacted Mills by walking on his knees.

Long snapper Mark Rodenhauser passed the time by creating a World Wide Web page, where he tried to keep Internet users informed with behind-the-scenes events involving the team and himself, including frequent updates on his wife's pregnancy.

Even the media got in on the preseason shenanigans. Collins, Beuerlein, and wide receiver Willie Green helped several newspaper reporters who covered the team regularly pass off a fake scoop to David Newton, a reporter who covered the team for *The State* of Columbia, South Carolina. The other reporters had been telling Newton throughout training camp that he was missing out on a huge story: the Panthers practicing the shotgun offense—something Capers had made it clear he had no intention of doing. In an attempt to get Newton to bite, the reporters tape-recorded authentic-sounding quotes by Collins, Beuerlein, and Green about the installation of the shotgun in that day's practice. When Newton heard the tapes at approximately ten P.M.—close to his deadline—he rushed to his portable computer and began writing a story about the Panthers' sudden decision to experiment with the shotgun. He was seconds away from transmitting it via modem to his editors when the other reporters in the press room informed him he'd been had.

"Really?" Newton said, pausing for a few seconds. "Well, I knew it all along."

Yeah, right.

The next day, Collins got a good laugh when he was told how much he had helped make the stunt work.

"Anytime you guys need me for anything like that, just let me know," he said.

NOT EVERYTHING WAS FUN AND GAMES THROUGHout camp though, and one of the more serious events occurred when the Reverend Billy Graham, the world-renowned evangelist, dedicated Ericsson Stadium on August 17, before the kickoff to an exhibition game against the Buffalo Bills. It was one of owner Jerry Richardson's proudest moments. Of course, he would have enjoyed it even more had the Panthers won the game; instead, they had their worst performance of the preseason, losing 24–0.

The good news was that first-round draft pick Tshimanga Biakabutuka finally signed his contract the day before the game. Biakabutuka's bitter holdout lasted 27 days and caused him to miss 31 practices, including all of training camp in Spartanburg. In the end he got a seven-year, $12.653 million contract.

Biakabutuka was thrust into practice quickly, but carefully, the next week and made an appearance in the Panthers' final exhibition game against the New York Giants. He gained 32 yards on seven rushing attempts in an impressive 34–7 Carolina win. The victory was exactly the kind of sendoff Capers wanted heading into the regular season. About the only bad news was that Matt Campbell, who had won the starting left tackle job, had suffered a broken left fibula and would be lost until midseason.

Otherwise, Capers felt the Panthers had bounced back strongly from their two straight losses to the Broncos and the Bills and were close to being ready to open the regular season at Ericsson Stadium against Atlanta in nine days.

"Everything we've done for the last five weeks we've done with one thing in mind—to get ourselves as ready as we can be for the regular season," Capers said. "From this point on, everything we do is for real."

CHAPTER THREE

Opening Day

THERE IS NOTHING ELSE QUITE LIKE OPENING DAY. It is the day when anything seems possible, when the air is full of sunlight and mystery and hope blossoms on every tree.

That's how it felt for the Carolina Panthers when September 1, 1996, finally came around. They would break in Ericsson Stadium for real now, hosting Atlanta in the regular-season opener.

The Falcons, a playoff team a season ago, entered the game with high hopes of their own and as a three-point favorite. Coach June Jones's run-and-shoot offense was one of the NFL's most unorthodox, predicated on spreading the field with four receivers and throwing on most downs. Quarterback Jeff George, a temperamental player with a balding head and a rifle arm, would direct the Falcons in the "I-85 rivalry" against a Panthers team that was searching for an identity.

"Everybody was trying to find out what kind of football team we had," quarterback Kerry Collins said.

No one knew for sure. Panthers general manager Bill Polian thought the club he had built might be a playoff team, but only if running back Tshimanga Biakabutuka came through in a big way.

Coach Dom Capers had been asked hundreds of times already for a prediction on the season's outcome. Characteristically, he refused to give one, but he thought quietly that the team might be able to make a quantum leap. He believed he had noticed the beginnings of serious team chemistry early in training camp. Most members of the media—and the fans, for that matter—figured the Panthers would win somewhere between six and nine games. Atlanta would be an ideal test.

The day dawned bright and glorious with the temperature for the 1 P.M. start at 76 degrees. The first thing the Panthers players noticed on their way over to the stadium from their hotel was almost simple enough to be overlooked: The commute took no time at all. The Panthers spent the night before all home games in the Westin hotel in uptown Charlotte. The commute to the stadium took about eight minutes, compared to the 2½ to three hours each way it had taken to get to their temporary "home" stadium in Clemson, South Carolina, the year before.

Owner Jerry Richardson's heart swelled as he saw his $187 million dream fill with people. The weather was perfect and Panthers T-shirts and caps were the fashion of the day. Richardson couldn't have asked for a better beginning. Now, if only the Panthers could win.

Charlotte had been a small-time sports town until 1988, when the NBA's Charlotte Hornets came to town. Before that, people had played softball and watched high school football, pro wrestling, and boxing. College basketball had an avid following, but the state's glamour teams—North Carolina and Duke—were 150 miles away. Auto racing was huge—Charlotte Motor Speedway had opened in 1960 and was one of the nation's preeminent race tracks. In fact, stadium scoreboard operators planned to include updates on the Southern 500 in Darlington, South Carolina, during the Carolina-Atlanta game.

But pro football? It was an unknown entity here. For years, Charlotte had been Washington Redskins territory. How many of those fans would willingly change over to the black and blue of Carolina?

From the looks of the traffic on opening day, an awful lot. Fans tailgated outside the stadium. The sizzling scent of hamburgers on the grill permeated the air. A lot of dressed-down yuppies quaffed microbrewed beers. Eventually, everyone filtered into the stadium—69,522 people in all, including NFL commissioner Paul Tagliabue. For only the second time ever, a Panthers home game had sold out. (The only other sellout had been at Clemson when the Panthers hosted the

49ers.) That meant the fans who couldn't get tickets still got to see the game on TV.

The players, used to playing in front of 20,000 empty seats at Clemson in 1995, couldn't believe the sheer number of people. "The atmosphere was wild," cornerback Tyrone Poole said. "The fans were into it. It felt like our own personal Super Bowl."

Linebacker Sam Mills said, "You really wanted to do a good job of opening up that stadium. You felt a lot of pressure because it seemed like the only way you were supposed to open that stadium, with those big panthers out front, was with a win."

CAPERS ALWAYS TALKED TO HIS TEAM FIVE MINUTES before game time. He never gave a "Win one for the Gipper" speech, but he often harked back to his basic system of belief and trust. Usually, the players paid fairly close attention to their head man, but on this day, there was just too much going on. This was what the Panthers had been pointing toward since the previous Christmas Eve— the last time they had played a game that counted.

"The guys were so cranked up in the locker room before Dom talked, I don't even know if they heard a word he said," assistant coach Brad Seely said.

Darius Rucker, lead singer of the pop group Hootie & the Blowfish, blasted out the national anthem and the season was on. Darius and the boys were already big Carolina fans and attended Panthers games throughout 1996 whenever their concert schedule allowed it.

Carolina won the toss and chose to receive the opening kickoff. The first drive was a jewel. Collins and Biakabutuka, the two No. 1 picks of their respective drafts, started off dominating the game. On a nine-play drive, Biakabutuka carried four times for 23 yards. His 27-day, 31-practice training camp holdout didn't seem to have affected him much. Biakabutuka had already impressed his teammates with his can-do attitude, and this drive bolstered that reputation even more.

"He came into the huddle, and he wasn't some little lost boy looking around in awe," Panthers wide receiver Mark Carrier said. "He wanted the ball."

Collins threw four passes on the drive and completed all four. The final one went 12 yards to Carrier for a quick touchdown. Only five minutes into the game, Carolina led, 7–0.

"That was one of our best drives ever," Collins said.

It was also strikingly similar to Carolina's first drive ever as a franchise. The year before, playing at Atlanta, the Panthers had reeled off a touchdown drive on their first possession, too—with Frank Reich throwing to Pete Metzelaars for the score. Now the offense was much younger and—the Panthers hoped—much better.

Atlanta got the ball on the kickoff and got ready for the expected array of blitzing. The Falcons had used much of their preseason preparing for the Panthers zone blitz, a series of "safe" blitzes where rushing extra men would not force Carolina into man-to-man coverage and the possibility of getting burned on a deep play. Capers had brought the defensive scheme with him from his days in Pittsburgh and had used it successfully in Carolina's last game against the Falcons. This defense had given the Falcons so much trouble the year before that they had spent tons of time preparing for it.

Carolina didn't use it at all.

The Panthers spent almost the entire game using only the standard number of four pass rushers. The move baffled the Falcons.

Atlanta did manage a field goal late in the first quarter to cut the lead to 7–3, and then Collins—whose mission this season was to cut down on turnovers—lost a fumble at the Carolina 19 after being blindsided by Atlanta defensive tackle Travis Hall.

On third-and-six from the Panthers 15, George saw something he thought he could exploit in the Carolina defense. He audibled for a screen pass—a play he was sure would pick up at least the necessary yardage for the first down, maybe more.

Then, for the first time, Carolina's home crowd came into play. Urged on by defenders Lamar Lathon and Carlton Bailey, the crowd roared "Dee-FENSE! Dee-FENSE!" as George attempted to call the signals. "Half the guys heard it, half the guys didn't," George would later say of the audible. "That's the advantage of the twelfth man."

The play flopped and on fourth down, Morten Andersen uncharacteristically missed a 23-yard field goal. The Falcons had come up empty.

Carolina added a field goal early in the second quarter after a flea-flicker play resulted in a 30-yard pass from Collins to Mark Carrier. John Kasay's 32-yard field goal sailed through the middle of the goalposts, and it was 10–3, Carolina, with 13:21 left in the second quarter.

Atlanta sped downfield, however, and got to the Carolina 14. Then came one of the best plays of the game—and what cornerback Eric Davis would later say was his favorite play of the entire season.

On third-and-one from the Panthers 14, the Falcons tried to punch the ball up the middle with Craig "Ironhead" Heyward, their 250-pound bowling ball of a back. Panthers linebacker Sam Mills—officially listed at 232 pounds, but a player who, Kevin Greene would say, "weighed 210 pounds soaking wet"—knew Heyward would get the ball. He guessed the hole Heyward would run toward and ran there himself.

"I knew he was going to get the ball and I could possibly have a shot at him," Mills said. "I knew it would be interesting."

BOOM! The collision was thunderous. The hole Heyward tried to run through was "just big enough for a guy to go through with no moves," Mills would later say. Mills, using his low center of gravity to his advantage, plowed into Heyward. For a millisecond, it was unclear which way Heyward would fall. And then, like an oak tree, he tumbled backward into the Atlanta backfield. The run lost a yard.

"Sam absolutely *dropped* that guy," Davis said. "Everyone around the league knows about the power Ironhead carries. It was awesome to see."

It was a play that helped define Carolina's season.

Because of the stop, Atlanta had to settle for a field goal and it was 10–6, Panthers, midway through the second quarter.

With 3:27 left in the first half Kasay kicked another field goal for Carolina to increase the lead to 13–6, and after an Atlanta punt, Collins found his rhythm again. He pushed the Panthers downfield on a ten-play, 65-yard march.

With 26 seconds left now, tight end Wesley Walls burst off the line of scrimmage at the one-yard line and found himself wide open. Collins hit him—a TD combination that would become more and more familiar as the season wore on—and Walls caught it. As soon as the tight end held on to the ball long enough to ensure that Carolina had taken a 20–6 lead just before halftime, he immediately dropped to the ground and began firing an imaginary gun into the air.

"We were playing the Falcons, see?" Walls would explain later. "So I was shooting the birds out of the air. That TD really broke their backs, so I was using my pump-action shotgun and bringing them down."

That was classic Walls. He always had something to say, and often it was very funny. The Panthers had spent all that money ($4 million over three years) to acquire a tight end who could get deep and catch everything thrown at him. They didn't realize they had gotten a Southern storyteller thrown in as well.

WHEN YOU VISIT WALLS'S 4,300-SQUARE-FOOT HOUSE in South Charlotte, you had better plan on staying awhile. If he likes you—and he likes most everyone—he can tell you a tale about almost anything. "I'm still just an ole redneck from Pontotoc, Mississippi," Walls would say, and then launch into some story—maybe the one about how he lost his front tooth in a college bar-room brawl.

That much is true—Walls got it knocked out while playing at Mississippi when a guy "sucker-punched" him. He then preceded to beat the daylights out of the guy after that. He got a fake front tooth made, which he wears almost all the time, but for games—and for sleeping—he takes it out. "I'm afraid I'll swallow the thang," he said.

Walls's accent is strong, but no stronger than his hands or his mind. He graduated with a 3.31 grade-point average from Ole Miss. He played both ways for a while as a Rebel, catching passes and also running after quarterbacks as a 6′ 5″, 250-pound outside linebacker. He met his wife, Christy, at a friend's wedding and caught her as gracefully as he did most everything else. She was an incoming freshman at Mississippi; he was a junior. Within four months they were engaged. Walls wanted to keep her away from the frat boys at Mississippi. Plus, "I saw a dadgum good thang," he said.

But Walls wasn't ready to set a marriage date, so for the rest of his time at Mississippi and for his first year as a backup tight end in San

Francisco, he and Christy saw each other whenever they could. One day Walls was taking her back to the San Francisco airport—trying to rush her there and then get back home for a 49ers function—and the traffic was terrible. There was only one way out of it. "Just stay," Walls told Christy. "We'll get married next weekend." They did, flying to Lake Tahoe and squeezing in a one-day honeymoon between football games.

Marriages were always getting bumped around by football in the Walls family. When Walls was a high school junior in Pontotoc, he was stuck in some "dadgum single-T thang" offense. Walls was the quarterback, but the team stank and the family worried that Wesley's talents weren't being properly showcased. Wesley wanted to transfer schools and his father—a burly man who worked a graveyard shift as a maintenance man—agreed with him. Mississippi had a law that said no transfers could be made for athletic reasons, so the Walls family legally moved Wesley's household. Charlie and Betty Walls split up for a year, and Charlie went to live with Wesley on the other side of town, so he could go to Pontotoc High School. (Ironically, Kerry Collins's life would run a somewhat parallel course a few years later in Pennsylvania).

The Wallses quickly got back together after Wesley finished his stellar senior year and got a scholarship. "It was the biggest, greatest thing they ever did for me," Walls said.

Walls could always catch the ball, and he was tough, too, but he had bad luck early in his NFL career—getting buried by then Pro Bowler Brent Jones on the 49ers' depth chart. In five seasons, Walls caught a measly 11 passes.

He caught hundreds more on a practice field from Joe Montana, though. Montana needed someone to help his comeback. Walls got drafted, since he wasn't doing much of anything else. Montana couldn't throw the ball five yards when they started—"couldn't lob it through a windowpane," Walls said. But Montana got better and eventually resurrected his career, leaving Walls far behind. Walls still gets angry when reminded that Montana hardly gave him any credit for the comeback and didn't even invite him to his retirement party.

Walls left San Francisco in 1993 and went to New Orleans, where he would catch 95 passes over the next two seasons but still start only part time. He burned up the Panthers in the 1995 season, so they hired him as a free agent in 1996. For the first time in his life, Walls, 30, was a full-time starter. Best of all, he would be the go-to man near the goal line. Collins already loved him just from training camp, and one of Walls's favorite sayings was "Love Thy Quarterback." "If there's any one position on this team that has really improved the most and come alive from last year, it's tight end," Collins said.

THAT SEEMED APPARENT AS THE FANS GAWKED IN delight, watching Walls shoot imaginary birds out of the Carolina blue sky. The Panthers went into the locker room with a 20–6 lead and a firm grasp on their first-ever real win at Ericsson Stadium.

The second half of the game belonged to the Panthers defense. Outside linebackers Lamar Lathon and Kevin Greene started using George as a pinball, bouncing him back and forth to each other. Lathon sacked George three times, and Greene got him twice more and punctuated both sacks with strutting dances—dedicated, he said, to the wrestler Ric Flair, in the stands. (Greene and Flair had wrestled against each other over the summer as part of a staged tag-team match, and Greene harbored dreams of being the next Flair or Hulk Hogan after football ended.)

Kasay kicked three field goals for the Panthers in the second half, and the Panthers defense didn't allow a single point to Atlanta. Safety Pat Terrell was struck by how quickly the defense gelled, particularly the three star linebackers.

"There are eleven different personalities out there, but they were working together like a symphony when the ball was snapped," Terrell said. "Sam Mills was the general—intense, focused, making the defensive calls. Lamar—you just had to try and keep his voice down. He was always either talking about what he just did or what he was about to do. Then there was Kevin—he was the one that really made being out there a lot of fun. He grunted. He hollered. He squealed. He brought a lot of energy to the huddle. He always kept saying, 'You wouldn't want to be anywhere else but right here, right now. Remember that.' And we did."

Jeff George was particularly impressed with Greene, especially after getting knocked on his back a couple of times by the 34-year-old linebacker. "The crowd loves him," George said. "And he definitely backs it up. You have to take your hat off to him."

Carolina kept rushing four men and having success with it. For the first time in 25 games, Atlanta scored fewer than 10 points. Atlanta coach June Jones called the Panthers defense "vanilla" because it was so plain. Falcons running back Jamal Anderson called it "elementary." But it worked.

The final score was posted everywhere on the huge scoreboards as the clock wound down: CAROLINA 29, ATLANTA 6.

"They had a great scheme and pretty well kicked our butts," George said glumly.

Biakabutuka surprised his teammates by playing reasonably well despite his 27-day, 31-practice holdout. He ran 26 times for 69 yards. After the game, though, he said he was "physically exhausted" and he still felt as if he was in "training camp shape." The Panthers' other rookie runner, Winslow Oliver, had actually looked more dynamic, returning three punts for a fine average of 21.0 yards.

Kasay, after missing half his attempts in preseason, had gone a perfect five-for-five on field goals and scored 17 of the Panthers' 29 points. He had been helped by new punter Rohn Stark, who had joined the team in the last week of preseason and taken over as Kasay's holder.

Capers had finally gone with Stark, even though he had claimed to love preseason punter Kevin Feighery only 24 hours before he fired him. This was as close as Capers would get to misleading reporters all season, and reporters pressed him on the issue before the Atlanta game. "We cut Feighery even though I love Kevin Feighery, all right?" Capers said.

How did Capers explain his statement the day before cutting Feighery then?

Quoting an old Stephen Stills song, Capers said, "You love the one you're with."

That meant the Panthers would have to love quarterback Collins as well—but that wasn't hard to do on opening day. Collins had thrown for 198 yards—186 of them in the first half. Most important, for only the fourth time in his 14 starts Collins had not thrown an interception. He had fired 19 pickoffs the year before, when he often tried to force the ball into a receiver like a New York cabbie forces his way into traffic. He finished a dismal twenty-ninth in the NFL pass ratings, ahead of only Tampa Bay's Trent Dilfer. But this game was different. Collins looked like he knew what he was doing almost all of the time.

"That's one of the best games Kerry has ever played," said Carrier, who had paced the Panthers with six catches for 78 yards. "He did it on the field, but he did it on the sidelines and in the huddle, too. Kerry has taken control of the offense from a leadership standpoint, and we really needed that."

Despite Collins's performance, it was Greene and Lathon who were the talk of the day. Five sacks from a two-person combination? That doesn't happen more than three or four times a season in the NFL, and the two had done it in their first game together. Lathon had talked about how they would call themselves "Salt & Pepper" throughout the season. They had come up with the nickname in the preseason, a play on the fact that Greene is white and Lathon is black.

"We're going to put some spice on their ass this season!" Lathon said. "We go together pretty well, don't you think?"

But did they?

CHAPTER FOUR

The Salt & Pepper Shakeup

LAMAR LATHON THOUGHT HE HAD PLAYED THE GAME of his life.

Too bad the media hadn't noticed.

In the locker room after the win over the Falcons, reporters and cameramen swarmed around Kevin Greene, not Lathon. Though Lathon had three sacks to Greene's two, it was Greene who was the center of the media's attention. His postsack dances had energized the sellout crowd and his aggressive play had inspired his teammates. Greene's debut game as a Panther had been a success.

"It's a blessing to play this game," Greene said. "We're out there getting paid good money and getting cheered by fans. What else would you want to do for a living?"

Lathon, whose locker is less than ten yards from Greene's, went unnoticed by most of the reporters. He couldn't believe it. The more he thought about it, and the longer he watched the crowd hovering around Greene, the more jealous he became.

Even though Salt & Pepper had just shaken up the Falcons with a combined five sacks, they were far from being bookend buddies. In fact, their relationship was plenty shaky. It would remain that way for weeks.

"How in the hell can they give him all this bliss when I kicked ass from the first play to the last play?" Lathon thought to himself. "I'm running all over the field making tackles. I'm running guys down. I'm knocking the shit out of people. How can he get all this attention? It's not right."

Lathon had spent much of the preseason in a funk about Greene's signing. The Panthers had given Lathon a huge contract before the 1995 season and he felt that made him the team's designated franchise player on defense. He didn't want Greene, a flamboyant new addition, challenging that distinction. Lathon had tried to build at least a working relationship for the regular season with Greene, but now, suddenly, everything he'd feared about Greene's joining the team seemed to be coming true.

Greene was stealing his show.

"I knew right then and there I was going to have to deal with that crap all year," Lathon said. "I was ticked off. I was dejected. I knew if I allowed it to screw up my head, I wouldn't be effective the whole year. I didn't want to be miserable."

But he was.

Later that night, Lathon's rage peaked when he saw ESPN's *NFL PrimeTime* show. After the Carolina-Atlanta highlights were shown, the score was posted on the screen along with some of the key statistics. One of them said "Kevin Greene, two sacks." The graphic said nothing about Lathon having three.

"What the hell is going on?" Lathon screamed at his television set. His anger at Greene was intense. "At that point," he would say later, "I was really hating his ass."

Lathon picked up the phone and called his agent, Marvin Demoff, who gave him some simple advice: "Get used to it."

"Marvin told me Kevin's a rah-rah guy who has to have the attention and that if he doesn't get it, it's going to kill him," Lathon said.

Greene definitely enjoyed the attention he got after the game, but he also stressed that all of his actions on the field—from the wrestling struts to his crowd interaction—were natural and unscripted. "I play by pure love and passion of the game," Greene said. "When I'm having fun, it's evident. I cannot just have fun and be ho-hum about it."

And the fans loved watching him.

"I'm sure a lot of people see that Kevin is a little kid out there running around and playing football because of all the silly crap he's doing out there on the field," Greene said. "They see he's not just a big-money, high-priced player who's uppity, snobby or whatever. They see this guy is a hard worker, who comes to play, makes plays, has fun, and sometimes freaks out and starts dancing around.

"That day, I knew Ric Flair was in the stands. I was just pinned by him a few months earlier in the wrestling ring, so what I did on the field was to say, 'Hey, Ric Flair, this is my town, not your town.'"

Still, it was killing Lathon that Greene was getting so much attention. It got even worse the day after the game, when the front sports page of *The Charlotte Observer* featured a gigantic picture of Greene pumping his fist into the air. The newspaper's columnist at the game, Tom Sorensen, wrote extensively about Greene and didn't even mention Lathon's name.

Lathon decided he wasn't going to speak to the media at all for the rest of the season. There was no way he could stand by this decision for very long, but he did retreat into a temporary shell. On Wednesday, in the media's first open–locker room interview period since the Atlanta game, Lathon declined all interviews. The only explanation he gave was a huffy remark he made as he walked briskly through the room: "A guy has to get fifty sacks around here to get any attention."

Lathon never meant to say it, but what it did was let everyone know why he wasn't talking.

"After that, all the reports were that Lamar and Kevin weren't getting along," Lathon said. "Well, it wasn't him. It was me."

It had been from the beginning.

ONE OF THE MOST IMPORTANT DAYS OF THE PANthers' 1996 off-season was the day they signed Greene to a two-year, $2 million contract. It thrilled Capers to have Greene again. Greene had starred for Capers when Capers was the Pittsburgh Steelers defensive coordinator. Back in 1994, Greene had led the NFL in sacks with 14 and had made the All-Pro team. Capers believed an outside linebacking tandem of Greene and Lathon had the potential to be as good as the Greene–Greg Lloyd combination he had in Pittsburgh. Capers also knew Greene was a mature veteran who would work hard and study for games as thoroughly as Sam Mills. He knew Greene would set an example for the team's younger players, including Lathon.

"The two years I was with Kevin in Pittsburgh, there was never a doubt in my mind about his preparedness for a game, his intensity, and the fact that he'd be playing as hard the last play of the game as he was the first play," Capers said. "He's a proven producer."

Capers also knew there would be competition between Greene and Lathon—not for playing time, because they would both start, but for status and statistics. Capers often joked that most all of the NFL's top pass rushers "bowed to the sack God," so he knew how much importance Greene and Lathon would place on who led the team in sacks. He was right about that.

Greene joined the team brimming with personal motivation. He felt the Steelers had betrayed him by not re-signing him, and he wanted to prove that he could still play at a top level. He also wanted to use his two years with the Panthers to try and pass former New York Giants star Lawrence Taylor as the No. 1 all-time sack leader among linebackers. Taylor finished his career with 132½ sacks. Greene entered the '96 season with 108. He would need 25 in two years to break Taylor's record. "I have something to prove and that's that I'm the best linebacker playing this game," Greene said at the news conference where his signing was announced. "I have the opportunity to do that here over the next two years. That's my goal. And, of course, I'm here to help this team get to the big one."

By that, of course, he meant the Super Bowl.

LATHON WAS IN HIS HOMETOWN OF HOUSTON WHEN he learned the Panthers were going to sign Greene. The news immediately made him uneasy. He felt threatened because he knew he'd had a disappointing season in 1995, nothing like what the team expected when they originally signed him to a five-year, $13 million contract.

Lathon also liked playing with Darion Conner, the Panthers' other starting outside linebacker—partly because they were friends and partly because Conner posed no threat to Lathon's status as the team's defensive "franchise" player. Conner, unlike Greene, was a quiet player who didn't draw—or attempt to garner—much attention from the press. Lathon liked being treated and perceived as "the man."

"When I first heard about Kevin, I was kind of scared, to be perfectly honest," Lathon said. "After having a crappy season, I'm thinking, 'Okay, they're bringing in Kevin. What if they keep Darion? They've also got Duane Bickett.' In the back of my mind, I'm thinking, 'What are their plans for me?' "

Lathon was a nervous wreck. He had put immense pressure on himself to have a big season in '95 and he'd failed, partly because he'd played most of the season hurt, with a variety of injuries that were worse than anyone involved with the team knew. A bone chip in his shoulder had become reattached to his shoulder joint. He had bone spurs in both ankles, and late in the season he developed back spasms. "I wanted to go out and have a press conference and just tell someone, 'My body is messed up,' " Lathon said. "But talking about it, to me, would have made me weak."

His goal that year had been to lead the NFL in sacks, but he finished with eight—a mediocre number for a player of his talent and salary. He was nine off the league lead. "As the weeks went by, all I could think about was the 'bust list' of all the guys who are not worth the money," Lathon said.

Ten days after the '95 season ended, Lathon underwent three surgeries at once—to remove the bone spurs in his ankles and to reconstruct his shoulder (which was much more damaged than his doctors thought). By the time the Panthers signed Greene in May, Lathon's physical recovery was well under way. But his psyche was still fragile. He was stubborn about his rehabilitation, choosing to use a personal trainer in Houston rather than recuperate under the team's supervision in Charlotte.

"They were mad as hell about that," Lathon said. "But it was second nature to me. I've been hurt before. I know my body better than anyone." In June, Lathon reluctantly reported to the team's minicamp at Winthrop University in Rock Hill, South Carolina. The workouts would be the Panthers' last together before training camp opened at Wofford in mid-July. Some of the biggest news of minicamp came when Lathon unexpectedly didn't show up for practice one day. Then he missed a second straight day. The official reason the team gave was "a death in the family." One of Lathon's cousins had died, but Lathon was more concerned about his status with the team.

"I was depressed," Lathon said. "I was still feeling the remnants of the previous year. I was still feeling the pressure. I would think, 'Am I going to finish my contract out? Will they cut me? Do I need to retire?' I had all kinds of crazy thoughts. I also had a lot of personal issues to deal with. There were money pressures, debt—just a lot of things that were stressing me out."

After Lathon missed minicamp practice for a second straight day, general manager Bill Polian decided to visit Lathon at home. It was a convenient stopover, since they live in the same Lake Norman development, but it was a gesture that would mean a great deal to Lathon.

"Having Bill come over to my house was a real motivational factor for me," Lathon said. "To me, every general manager should be like him. He really cares about the players, and he takes it a step further. When something happens, he's right there at your front door and wants to get the problem nipped in the bud. It's not just with me, it's with a lot of the players."

Polian asked Lathon what was wrong and what could be done to make it better.

"I told him I felt like I needed to talk to someone professionally, that I needed to have an outlet," Lathon said. Polian and the Panthers arranged for Lathon to see a therapist at Carolinas Medical Center, the Charlotte hospital that services the team. "The doctors were probably a little more panicky about it than I was," Lathon said. "They would ask me questions like 'Are you suicidal?' I would say, 'Oh, no, I just need an outlet.'"

He was given a prescription of Librium, an anti-anxiety drug, which he took for about two weeks. Eventually, he decided he no longer needed the drug or the therapy. He felt he was ready for football again. He knew training camp would be opening soon, and about the only thing that made him anxious about that was the fact that Kevin Greene was one of his new teammates.

LATHON SHOWED UP AT TRAINING CAMP IN SPARTAN-burg in July determined to have a season worthy of his salary—good enough to get selected to his first Pro Bowl, to help lead the Panthers to the playoffs for the first time, and to outshine Greene and every other linebacker on the team.

"I know these guys aren't better than me," he told himself. "They can't outplay me. There's no way. If I'm healthy, I know what I can do, and I feel healthy again."

Lathon worked harder in this training camp than he'd ever worked in his pro career. When night practices ended, he'd go to the weight room. He was doubly motivated by seeing Greene in there, too.

"I'm the money guy on the team," Lathon told himself. "I'm the man they're building the defense around. Kevin? So what? I'm Lamar. He's going to have to play catch-up to me."

But there was no question that Greene's mere presence irritated Lathon, especially the way Greene would get excited on the practice field. Greene had always been energetic, but Lathon wasn't used to it. Greene would shout "Sackerooski!" whenever a defensive player rushed the quarterback, and he always seemed to be chattering something, including his favorite phrase: "Physical, baby, physical!"

"I didn't care for all of Kevin's fanfare," Lathon said. "It was so annoying when reporters kept asking me about him. So many times, I wanted to say, 'I don't give a damn!' I really wanted to say it, man, but instead, I tried to tune it out."

But tuning out Greene was almost impossible. The outside linebacker was playing on every station in Lathon's mind. "I really felt he was what every sport wanted—a white superhero," Lathon said. "To me, he was the Larry Bird of football. He really is a hell of an athlete, but he's great in *this* scheme—the three-four defense. I could play in *any* scheme. So I disliked him for being who he was—Kevin Greene, the blond-haired, blue-eyed Great White Hope."

Luckily for the Panthers, Greene didn't have similar feelings about Lathon. Instead, he spent much of training camp—and the regular season—trying to build and maintain a relationship with Lathon. "I was well aware that Lamar had me at a distance when I first came to the team, but so did Greg Lloyd when I went to Pittsburgh," said Greene, who spent his first eight NFL seasons with the Los Angeles Rams before joining the Steelers in 1993. "Greg actually was a little on the ballistic side back then. But I showed him I was a guy who was committed and would play his butt off and make big plays.

"Here, Lamar was the big-money linebacker, the player of the future. I know I probably have a reputation for being a wild-and-crazy-maniac type of guy. Plus, I love to get sacks. But I tried to immediately establish a relationship with him because this team did not need two of its star players head-butting.

"It took a lot of give and take. But the bottom line was that Lamar did not need to be jealous at all. I'm sitting here in the last two or three years of my career. I'm just trying to play the thing out and go out on top. He's still young and he's making more than two and a half times what I'm making."

It probably would have come as a surprise to Lathon that Greene's frustrations in the preseason were also media-related. Reporters kept reminding Greene, in interviews and in newspaper stories, that he didn't have a sack in any of the four exhibition games. Greene also wasn't amused when a reporter told him a sports magazine had rated the top 30 outside linebackers in the NFL. Lloyd, his former Pittsburgh teammate, was ranked No. 1. Greene was No. 26. Greene would use that rating to help motivate himself during the season. "I felt like the media treated me with skepticism when I got here," Greene said. "I was coming off two Pro Bowl years. The bottom line was that sacks in the preseason mean nothing. And, as far as those rankings, well, all that was crap, too."

GREENE'S AND LATHON'S BACKGROUNDS COULD HARDLY have been more different. Greene grew up in a military family that moved all around the world. He had a strong father figure in his dad, Therman Greene, a U.S. Army colonel.

Lathon was raised by his mother, Alma, in the small town of Wharton, Texas, near Houston. He had no male authority figure because his father left the family when he and his sister were toddlers.

Greene still keeps time the military way. Seven in the morning to Lathon is 0700 hours to Greene.

Greene's family lived in 12 places—some outside the United States—while he was growing up because of his father's military assignments. One of his earliest football experiences came when he played on an Army youth team in Mannheim, Germany that was coached by his dad. After graduating from high school, Greene attended the Military Police Academy at Fort McClellan, Alabama, and the Airborne School at Fort Benning, Georgia, and was in the Army ROTC during his college playing days at Auburn. He became a captain in the U.S. Army Reserves and has been on the inactive list since 1990. His specialty: tanks.

Greene admitted he got in the "attack mode" at times on the football field, but he bristled when asked to make an analogy linking his sporting career to his military background.

"I want to make something clear," he said. "There is no correlation between fighting a war and playing a game. Those guys out there being trained and dodging bullets, they know every sense of the word 'reality.' That's the ultimate form of reality, when you have a chance to lose your life any second.

"Too many people want to say a football game is like fighting a war or waging a battle. Getting paid hundreds of thousands of dollars to play a game is nothing like getting paid pennies to defend your country, or somebody else's democracy."

Greene's father was a logistics officer in the Vietnam War. His brother, Keith, was a Blackhawk helicopter pilot who was decorated with a Bronze Star in the Gulf War. Although Greene makes a clear distinction between playing sports and waging war, there is no question but that his military background helped structure the way he approached his football career. It taught him discipline, commitment, and accountability.

When he left the Auburn football team in 1980 after failing as a walk-on punter and 190-pound halfback, he realized that quitting wasn't acceptable. Determined to succeed in football, he spent more than a year in the weight room before returning as a 235-pound linebacker—his position of destiny. "It was more a matter of getting my mind and my heart right than getting my body right," Greene said. "Your body will let you down in certain situations, so a man has to play with his heart. The heart pushes the body."

Those who have spent time around Greene, including Capers, say his heart is enormous. Most of the quarterbacks Greene has chased over the years would agree. It is while pursuing an opposing passer at full throttle that Greene comes fully alive. He is at his best then, hunting down prey with determination and ferocity. "What I do is slick my ears back, slick the hair back and foam at the mouth," Greene said. "I'm one of those guys who just keeps coming. It may sound sick, but I really enjoy coming after those little fragile guys standing in the pocket, all helpless. You have a chance of crunching the number one quarterback and seeing what the number two quarterback looks like. Nothing on purpose, I assure you, but you do try to hit people as hard as you can."

Greene admits he loves playing football so much that he has a hard time imagining what he'll do after retirement. "I guess I'll end up in a park somewhere late at night and clip somebody when they're drinking water out of a fountain," he joked. "I'll just come out of the woods with face paint on or something, or maybe I'll go low-crawling through the bushes with a helmet on."

That's Kevin Greene. Wild. Intense. One heck of a football player.

NONE OF LATHON'S PANTHERS TEAMMATES KNEW HE was still known among friends and family back home in Houston by his childhood nickname, Titty.

"My grandmother used to call me Titty Baby when I was real little because I breastfed all the time," Lathon said with a chuckle. "Every time I would cry, that's what I'd want. When I got older, they dropped the 'Baby' part and just called me 'Titty.'"

If the Panthers had given him a nickname, "Mr. Moody" would have been a good one. Catch Lathon on a good day and he's full of laughter and jokes. Catch him on a bad day and he will be off by himself, brooding.

"He's all over the map in terms of emotions," said nose tackle Greg Kragen.

"Lamar can be a fun guy, but he can be abrasive, too," said defensive end Gerald Williams. "If you don't know how to take it, he can rub you the wrong way."

"I'm an extreme personality," Lathon admits. "I'm hot or cold, and there's no in between. Some days I'm radical, joking, doing all the male stuff in meetings and making Coach Capers laugh. That's the joking Lamar. The other side is quiet—not mean, just quiet. People who know me know not to mess with me when I'm feeling that way. Basically, I think I'm the type of guy every team needs. I'm a guy who doesn't take any bull."

For most of his life, Lathon has been trying to learn how to control his emotions. He got kicked off his high school team for cursing out his teammates. He was booted out of school for fighting. When he played for the Houston Oilers, he was infamous for getting into fights during practice. Some of that emotion has carried over to the Panthers, and at times he's had trouble controlling his temper when coaches have corrected him.

"Sometimes Lamar overreacts when someone is trying to teach him something," said backup linebacker Duane Bickett. "Instead of thinking they're trying to help him, he thinks they're insulting him, and he has a tendency to get a bit combative about it."

But there's a compassionate side to Lathon, too. He has lost count of how many cars he has bought for family members and friends. Two years ago, he purchased a full-fare plane ticket for a woman who was crying at Houston Intercontinental Airport because she was desperate to get home to Greensboro, North Carolina, in a hurry. "He's lovable, kind-hearted, and he'll give you the shirt off his back," said his mother, Alma.

Lathon bought his mother a home after the Oilers picked him in the first round of the 1990 NFL draft, moving her from suburban Wharton to an upscale Houston neighborhood. He bought her a new

Mercedes for Christmas in 1995. He has tried to help his sister, Gloria Ann, defeat her crack addiction, but so far that has been the most disappointing failure of his life. Lathon has paid for Gloria Ann's stays in rehabilitation centers, but she has relapsed each time. While he was preparing for the 1996 season, his sister was serving a jail term in Texas.

"This is sad to say, but when she's in prison, I am so much happier," Lathon said. "I don't have to think about her being on the street. When she goes to jail, I know she's safe. Some people tell me to let her hit rock bottom, to let it go. But she's my only blood sister, and family is all I have. If she falls again, I'll be there to lift her up. Besides, who knows what rock bottom is? It could be death."

Lathon felt like he bottomed out in the summer of 1994, when he was charged with choking a topless dancer at a Houston night club called Michaels International. The Panthers investigated the incident before signing him to his big contract in the spring of '95. Lathon denied choking the woman, Regina Williams, but he admitted that they argued.

"I went to the club with some of my friends and saw this girl that I'd known from another club," Lathon said. "I had always talked to her and had always been nice. She had never danced for me, though. She was a very beautiful black woman. She had it all. My whole thing with her had always been 'What are you doing in a club? This is not you.' She told me her story about how she ended up in a club and we became friends.

"The night this incident happened, I could not understand why she was being belligerent to me. Her whole thing was 'You football players come in here and you don't want no sister. You want the white girls.' That wasn't the case at all, but one thing led to another and we started arguing and we shot each other the bird. I told her the whole thing was ignorant and she told me to get the hell out of her face. She slapped my hands and slapped me. I never strangled her, but I pushed her off of me." The story was reported in Houston newspapers and on television stations. It was an embarrassment to Lathon, a local hero who was still with the Oilers and had previously played college football at the University of Houston.

"My name was like mud there for a while," Lathon said. He eventually pleaded no contest to a misdemeanor assault charge, which was later removed from his record. The woman, Regina Williams, filed a civil suit against him and was hoping for a six-figure settlement. She was awarded only $12,000.

The embarrassment of his confrontation with Williams was among the many factors that caused Lathon to begin reevaluating himself. By the time his second season with the Panthers was approaching, he had already undergone therapy and counseling. He soon found that his soul-searching was becoming even more intense.

"There are a lot of things I've still got to resolve," he said. "I'm struggling with God. I feel like I know God, but then again I don't. My conscience bothers me—about everything. Having sex before marriage bothers me, but there's the temptation to do it, and *that* bothers me.

"I think about it when I don't make plays in a game. I say, 'Man, Lamar, if you start living better, this might change.' At some point in time, I have to make a decision—either live right or be totally in left field. That's why I'm trying to bridge the gap. I'm trying to pull myself in."

LATHON KNEW HIS ATTITUDE TOWARD GREENE DIDN'T bring out the best in him, and so did Greene. When Lathon's animosity became more and more apparent in training camp, Greene decided to tell Lathon the story of a man named Isaac Russell. Russell, who is black, had been Greene's best friend for the previous 17 years.

"I wanted Lamar to know about Isaac because it shows there are no racial boundaries in my relationships," Greene said. "Isaac's a great friend, someone I tell openly that I love." Greene didn't necessarily believe there was anything racial about Lathon's feelings toward him, but he figured it could only help the situation if Lathon knew him better. He explained that Russell was his business partner, and that they owned a Gold's Gym together in Anniston, Alabama.

Their relationship dated back to 1980, when Greene was playing football at Auburn. They met in a military gymnasium in Anniston. Their friendship grew over the next several years and Greene became close to Russell's family—his wife, Valerie, and their daughter, Sheree, and son, Carlson.

"It was such a wonderful household," Greene said. "I always said I wanted to meet a woman who would love me like Valerie loved Isaac and I wanted to have children just like they had."

In 1983, tragedy struck the Russells. Valerie was killed when the car she was driving got hit by a train.

"When she died, Isaac was crushed," Greene said. "He began to lean on me, and I leaned on him the rest of my time at Auburn. I've continued to do so for all twelve of my years in the NFL. He's been my workout partner, and my best friend, ever since."

Greene telephones Russell, who has never remarried, before every game he plays. He even invited Russell to the Panthers training camp to meet Lathon.

Lathon admits that this story softened his feelings about Greene and that he actually began to like Greene the day the Panthers held their first practice in Ericsson Stadium on July 27, one week before the team's exhibition opener against the Chicago Bears. The two were sitting on the grass in Ericsson, talking.

"You know what, Lamar?" Greene started. "I have been through a lot of camps, but this has been a good camp. I have never had a relationship with another outside linebacker like I have with you. It's just a pleasure playing with you. I look across the field at you and I've got my brother on the other side. I like that."

Lathon was surprised. He didn't think they had a good relationship at all, but he found himself tugged emotionally by what Greene said. "I figured wherever he'd been, whether it was the Rams or Pittsburgh, that maybe people didn't like him," Lathon said later. "For some strange reason, I kind of felt like maybe he had felt alone. I actually felt a little sorry for him. It was weird, but I actually started liking him a little bit right there.

"The truth is that Kevin has pressure on him to be better than the average guy. That's why he works harder than anybody else and he watches more film than anybody else. That's what gives him the edge. If he didn't do those things, he wouldn't be Kevin Greene.

"I started to realize he had come to a point in his career where he could go either way. It could either be a good situation for him or a bad situation. My heart went out to him when I heard him say, 'This is a great stadium and I've got my brother right here with me. We're going to show 'em, aren't we, Lamar?'"

THE POSITIVE SENTIMENTS LATHON HAD BEGUN TO feel about Greene disappeared in the locker room after the season-opening win over Atlanta and in the days that followed, however. Lathon was especially steamed by what he perceived as Greene's attempt to keep him from being presented a game ball by his teammates for his play in the Atlanta game. The team routinely hands out game balls for offense, defense, and special teams after each game. The voting is done by the players, so the award is considered a major distinction.

"Everybody was ready to vote me the defensive player of the game because I'd led the team in sacks and I'd had a lot of tackles [six]," Lathon said. "But Kevin stood up and told Coach Capers he thought the whole team deserved a game ball, so that's what happened. I told Kevin later he knew he wasn't going to get a game ball, so he tried to screw me out of it. It ticked me off. I was mad. That was supposed to be one of my game balls. Do you have any idea how hard it is to get a game ball in this league?"

Greene insisted he wasn't trying to keep Lathon from winning the vote, that he merely wanted the team to share the award. But there was no convincing Lathon of that.

After only one game, the Salt & Pepper combination looked great on the field, but their relationship still had a long way to go.

CHAPTER FIVE

Winning Ways, Wounded Knees

KERRY COLLINS'S SEASON ENDED ON SEPTEMBER 8, 1996.

At least, that's what he thought as he lay crumpled on the hard green turf of New Orleans's Superdome.

The game was deep in the fourth quarter. Carolina trailed the Saints, 20–19, and Collins was leading a potential game-winning drive. He faded back for a quick five-yard pass to Muhsin Muhammad. To his left, New Orleans linebacker Winfred Tubbs started an all-out blitz. Tiny Carolina scatback Winslow Oliver got a piece of Tubbs as he stormed by, knocking him a little off balance but failing to halt his forward progress. Collins threw the short completion, but Tubbs, spinning uncontrollably after Oliver's hit, fell—a 6′ 4″, 250-pound slab of muscle—and landed a direct hit on Collins's left knee. The impact unnaturally straightened Collins's knee, buckling it in a way no human joint was ever designed to bend. "I felt something go *pop!*" Collins said. "I didn't hear it. I *felt* it."

Collins bashed into the turf. His knee felt as though someone was stabbing it with a knife. Lying on his back, he grabbed his helmet with both hands, feeling equal parts pain and frustration.

"This is the big one," he thought to himself, "A-C-L"—the anterior cruciate ligament in the knee that, if torn, ends your season—and possibly your career. Those three letters, A-C-L, give all football players nightmares at one time or another.

Tubbs hadn't hit Collins on purpose. "Tell Kerry I'm sorry," he said later. "I didn't mean to. I just got blocked into him and lost my balance."

Collins got up gingerly, testing the knee. A squadron of doctors and trainers rushed to the field to help him. On the sideline, backup quarterback Steve Beuerlein started firing 15-yard passes—hurriedly trying to warm up for the most important series of the game. Things didn't look good for the Panthers as Beuerlein jogged in, patted Collins on the back, and took over a team still trailing by one. Already, Carolina had been outplayed for much of this game, and except for one play made by Oliver, they wouldn't have even had a shot at winning.

AT 5′ 7″, WINSLOW OLIVER WAS ONE OF THE SHORTEST players in the NFL. People around the Panthers organization sometimes called him Little Winnie—his baby-faced smile and bubbly personality made him an immediate favorite in the locker room. Carolina had drafted Oliver, a third-round pick out of New Mexico, with the hope that he could generate some speed on punt returns and third downs. So far, so good—Oliver had played well in exhibitions and in the Panthers' first game, against Atlanta.

Like Panthers linebacker Sam Mills, Oliver was a superb athlete who happened to be encased in a small package. He had set a record for running backs at the NFL scouting combine in February by bench-pressing 225 pounds 25 times in a row—nine times more than the first running back picked in the draft, Lawrence Phillips. He could also run 40 yards in 4.47 seconds.

Married with two small children, Oliver and his wife, Julie, had needed government aid after having their second child during his college years at New Mexico. He had grown up in a difficult situation, too. His mother, Sandra Elmore, had to work two jobs to support her children. She worked as an accountant during the day and delivered newspapers at night.

After Oliver left his hometown of Houston to become a star at New Mexico, however, the only aid he needed on the field came from his blockers. He totaled 5,375 all-purpose yards in four years with the Lobos and as a senior ranked second in the nation in kickoff returns with a 31.7-yard average.

He was electric on punt returns, too—which is where the Panthers really wanted to use him. He had almost broken one in the Atlanta game and in the Panthers' final two preseason contests. After the Saints scored a touchdown on their first possession vs. Carolina, they were forced to punt on their second. Oliver jogged out to return it. In the stands, his mother and two dozen other family members watched him closely.

Saints punter Klaus Wilmsmeyer boomed one 52 yards. Oliver gave chase all the way back to his own 16-yard line. He caught the ball, found a hole, and broke to the sideline. Surprised, the Saints overran the play. They hadn't counted on Oliver's speed. In a blink, he was in the clear. "I looked up and saw nothing but sidelines," he said. Only one player was left to beat—Wilmsmeyer. The punter waited for Oliver, trying to guess which way he would go. It didn't matter. Panther Dwight Stone took care of Wilmsmeyer before Oliver got there, leveling him with a huge block that owner Jerry Richardson would still be talking about three hours later. Oliver burst into the end zone, tying the game at 7.

Carolina needed that play badly. The Panthers had been totally outplayed in the first half. The Saints had outgained the Panthers 171–54 in yardage, and Collins had been sacked three times and had completed only four passes. But because of Oliver's return and two John Kasay field goals, the Panthers trailed only 14–13 at halftime. As they headed for the locker room, they realized that New Orleans didn't have much of a home-field advantage at all—there were 22,000 empty seats in the 65,000-seat Superdome, and what fans there were didn't make much noise.

Despite being down, Capers wasn't worried. "I remember at half-time walking from the offense to the defense in the locker room and I liked what I saw. You can always tell by looking in a guy's eyes. I had a feeling of confidence we felt we were going to come back out and win that game. That's what good teams do." Still, the Panthers had to find a way to stop Saints quarterback Jim Everett, who was picking the defense apart. New Orleans had gone 65 yards for a TD on their first drive and 85 on their third. Everett had lost to Carolina the previous season, throwing interceptions on three straight passes, but before the game he had told a New Orleans newspaper that the Panthers' zone-blitz scheme wouldn't fool him this time because New Orleans had "figured out" Capers's game plan.

Everett wasn't as dominant in the second half, though. New Orleans managed only two field goals against Carolina's defense, while Kasay kicked two more. So when Collins limped out of the game unassisted with less than five minutes to go, the Panthers were only down by a point.

Beuerlein, Collins's backup, could throw the ball well and was smart, but Carolina wasn't about to risk anything—not with Kasay's hot foot. So the Panthers kept the ball on the ground six straight times until Kasay could come in and try a 23-yarder. He knocked it home. Kasay was now 10-for-10 for the season.

An unflappable, deeply religious player, Kasay had a good relationship with the media. A journalism major in college at Georgia, he sometimes understood what reporters were driving at better than the reporters knew themselves. And his temperament was exactly opposite that of most kickers.

"He's such an even-keel guy," Panthers special-teams coach Brad Seely said. "I've worked with other kickers, and they find every excuse in the book why they missed a kick. It was the snap. Or the hold. Or they installed the goalposts wrong. John takes the good and the bad exactly the same."

Kasay's field goal put the Panthers up 22–20 with 2:09 to go. New Orleans would get the ball back one last time. On this last series, Everett misread a route from his receiver and made a bad throw. It was on fourth-and-three at his own 31-yard line. Quickly the game was over. Carolina had gotten away with one.

Lathon, who had had two more sacks to maintain his NFL lead, pounded his heart with his fist as the game ended. The Panthers had shown some heart here, he meant, and it was true.

Although New Orleans was supposed to be the Big Easy, this victory was anything but. The Panthers didn't play well but somehow "willed" themselves to win, linebacker Kevin Greene said.

Every point the Panthers scored came from their special teams. The Panthers stressed special-teams play as much as offense and defense, and on this day that philosophy paid off. "That day sold our team on the importance of special teams," Coach Seely said. "Our guys totally bought in to that theory after that."

Capers said the win demonstrated the strong character the Panthers were developing. "Those are the kind of games you have to win to have a real good team and a real good season," he said.

The Saints players were furious at themselves. "I believe they know they got away with one," Everett said. "That was a gift to Carolina."

"We gave the game away," Saints tackle Willie Roaf said.

The Panthers agreed. "That was a pretty pitiful performance by our offense," Panthers offensive tackle Blake Brockermeyer said. "We stole this one. I feel like we should have lost."

No matter what the players thought, though, the record was what counted. And Carolina was 2–0.

DESPITE THE VICTORY, THE PANTHERS WORRIED ABOUT Kerry Collins. Losing Collins for the season would be a disastrous blow. The initial diagnosis was a minor sprain of the medial collateral ligament in his left knee—a diagnosis that made Collins cautiously happy. It wasn't until the team got back to Charlotte, where Collins had a magnetic resonance imaging test, that he found out for sure that his ACL was still intact.

Collins publicly expressed hope that he could play against San Francisco on September 22. The Panthers had a bye that next Sunday, and so had two weeks between games. Privately, Collins already knew he wouldn't play against San Francisco, but the Panthers didn't let that information leak out because they wanted San Francisco to have to prepare for either Beuerlein or Collins.

"It was actually three to four weeks [out of action] from the beginning," Collins admitted. "I think three weeks was being pretty optimistic, but they [the Panthers coaches] wanted to keep other teams in the dark. I don't know how effective that is, but our feeling was we were not going to show them our hand—just say the knee was questionable and go into it that way."

So the Panthers would have to prepare for at least their next two games—against San Francisco and Jacksonville—with Beuerlein. The battle against the 49ers seemed lopsided. It would be a journeyman quarterback against a fearsome 49ers defense that had caused two safeties, sacked the quarterback seven times, and forced two turnovers in their last game, a 34–0 shellacking of St. Louis on September 8.

"It's hard to find a weakness in attacking the San Francisco defense," Dom Capers said. "You look at their first two games and you get a little discouraged."

With Collins out, a victory seemed virtually impossible. Beuerlein was shorter and slower than Collins, and not as strong. He also didn't know the offense as well, since he had only arrived from Jacksonville over the summer. In 1995, he had compiled a 1–5 record as a starter there, until Jaguars coach Tom Coughlin handed the team over to Mark Brunell, who turned out to be a much better choice than Beuerlein.

But Beuerlein was tough. And a quick study. And he had faced situations like this before. "As a competitor, as a quarterback, this is the kind of challenge you live for and dream about," Beuerlein said. "Unfortunately it had to happen at Kerry's expense, but I am excited."

BEUERLEIN, 31, HAD TRAVELED AROUND THE NFL SO much that he seemed to play one of his old teams about every third week. Carolina was his fifth NFL employer in nine NFL seasons. In only one of those, 1993 in Phoenix, had he started more than half his team's games.

The former Notre Dame quarterback always seemed to be on the fringe of a full-time job, starting 46 games over his career. He was the embodiment of mediocrity in those starts, going 22–24—not quite good enough to win a permanent starting job, but not quite bad enough to be considered no more than a steady backup.

Beuerlein could tell you stories about many of the most famous coaches over the past 10 years, because he had played for most of them: Lou Holtz, Mike Shanahan, Jimmy Johnson, Buddy Ryan, Art Shell, Gerry Faust, Coughlin, Capers—they had all barked orders at Beuerlein at one time or another. He had won a Super Bowl ring in Dallas as a backup in 1992, had been labeled a cancer by Buddy Ryan in Arizona in 1994, and felt he had gotten "blackballed" by Oakland owner Al Davis in 1990.

Beuerlein had started the first game ever against Carolina—for Jacksonville in the Hall of Fame game in July 1995. That was the first game either team had ever played. Carolina won 20–14.

A natural athlete, Beuerlein was one of the best golfers on the team. Besides the usual baseball-basketball-football combination in high school that so many NFL players completed, Beuerlein was also a diver for his swim team at Servite High School in Anaheim, California. At Notre Dame, a Fighting Irish team quarterbacked by Beuerlein lost to Miami 58–7. The Hurricanes were coached by Jimmy Johnson. "I hated Jimmy Johnson's guts then," Beuerlein said. "Everyone at Notre Dame did. It was pounded into your head."

It was a surprise, then, when Dallas Cowboys coach Jimmy Johnson rescued Beuerlein years later. He saw Beuerlein languishing in Oakland and traded for him, getting him out from under the thumb of Al Davis, the strange, Big Brother–ish owner of the Raiders. Johnson wanted Beuerlein to back up Troy Aikman, a job similar to the one the Panthers had in mind when they hired him away from Jacksonville to back up Collins.

At Dallas, Beuerlein once quarterbacked four straight wins to earn the Cowboys a playoff berth. That was his shining moment—for a while Cowboys fans even wondered whether Beuerlein might get a chance to start over Aikman full time. The Panthers were hoping he could pull off a similar feat now. Mediocrity just wouldn't do against San Francisco.

THE PANTHERS FANS COULDN'T BE MEDIOCRE, EITHER. Starting offensive tackle Blake Brockermeyer would try and take care of that. Brockermeyer had come from Texas; he grew up in Fort Worth and played college ball in Austin for the Texas Longhorns. In that football-rich state, little boys practically grow up with helmets on, and everyone knows to scream for the defense on third-and-eight when the other team's offense has the ball. Brockermeyer felt like the Panthers fans hadn't quite grasped that concept yet. He saw the big splotches of empty seats after halftime in the most expensive seats at Ericsson Stadium. Many of the fans were used to the longer halftimes of college football, so many of them didn't return to their seats until halfway through the third quarter. The fans were okay—the Panthers were selling out every game, at least—but he wanted to tweak them a little.

Brockermeyer was an interesting character with a slightly obsessive tinge to his personality. He loved dogs, and he and his wife, Kristy, shared their house with two Labrador retrievers, 90-pound True Grit and 110-pound Big Chief. He also loved cigars, so he stocked a couple of hundred good ones in two humidors and read *Cigar Aficionado* on road trips.

Now, Brockermeyer had a mission: fan support. He had become a 6′ 4″, 305-pound cheerleader during the Panthers games, yelling at the fans and waving his helmet at them every time the Carolina defense was on the field. He did that against Atlanta. That made it better, Brockermeyer thought, but still, he wasn't satisfied. So he drew up a list of fan commandments that was published in *The Charlotte Observer* before the San Francisco game.

Among the best:

- When the Panthers offense is on the field, don't do the wave.
- Don't leave the game if it starts raining.
- Boo the officials every time they call a penalty on the Panthers.

"Whenever a close call doesn't go our way, boo, even if the officials made the right call," Brockermeyer explained. "Do it even if you can tell they were actually right after you see the replay. Make the officials think they made the wrong call, so maybe they'll come back and give us a good call later in the game."

THE BUILDUP TO THE SAN FRANCISCO GAME WAS fairly intense for an early-season contest. Much of it centered on Beuerlein, but Eric Davis, who would be playing his first game against his old teammates, was also questioned repeatedly. Everyone wanted to know about the old practice battles he used to have every day against Jerry Rice, the best receiver ever to play the game. While Davis was on a conference call with San Francisco reporters during the week, a surprise questioner sneaked into the room. "Hey, Eric," the man said. "Are you worried about those offensive linemen hitting your skinny little ass?"

The questioner was San Francisco offensive lineman Derrick Deese, who had tiptoed into the session just to see what his former teammate was up to. Davis recognized the voice immediately.

He told the 275-pound Deese, "It's not going to be how hard I hit you, it's going to be how many times."

Davis felt confident like that all week, and the rest of the Panthers weren't scared of San Francisco, either. After all, they had split with them in their first-ever season.

"We had beaten them before and we felt like we could do it again, especially with Eric Davis around," linebacker Sam Mills explained. "Eric is the guy who gives you so much confidence."

At times Mills would listen to Davis talk about all of his former teammates' weaknesses in San Francisco and wonder, "Are we talking about the same team? He makes it sound like they aren't very good at all."

They were very good, of course, but the Panthers didn't have the same wounds that most teams in the NFC West did, having gotten beaten year after year by the 49ers.

"We don't have a history of being scarred by that team," Mills said.

"So when we take the field to play San Francisco, there's no history of them beating us. . . . When this team was being built, we didn't model ourselves after San Francisco. We set our standards to be better." That statement seemed ludicrous before the game—and totally appropriate five minutes into it.

Beuerlein came out blazing. Counting on Beuerlein's football smarts, the Panthers had installed a number of "check-with-me" plays—plays that Beuerlein basically called at the line of scrimmage off a limited number of options.

They worked beautifully. Carolina took the opening drive 80 yards in nine plays, delighting the crowd of 72,224 waving blue "growl towels" on another perfectly sunny day. (The towels, handed out at the ticket gates, were the size of a dish towel and turned the stadium into a sea of blue.) Beuerlein hit Oliver on a screen pass for 25 of those yards. Then he found Walls for a 19-yard touchdown pass that the tight end neatly snagged with one hand. That made it 7–0. Quickly, it became 10–0 on the Panthers' next drive later in the first quarter, after Beuerlein found Willie Green for a 38-yard pass to set up a field goal.

On the Panthers' third drive they scored again. They were shredding a 49ers defense that had pitched a shutout the week before. Beuerlein was on. All told, he completed 15 of his first 16 passes. Walls caught the touchdown pass again—this time a seven-yarder to cap a 69-yard drive.

Walls couldn't believe it. He would later call this his favorite game of the season—partly because of his two TDs, partly because the Panthers were playing better than anyone had imagined.

"I was so nervous about playing those guys," Walls said. "I had a lot of confidence in their ability. I had seen [safeties] Tim McDonald and Merton Hanks in practice for years while I was out there. The way it unfolded—seventeen points in our first three possessions, the fans going nuts—it was magical. It was inspiring."

The defense, meanwhile, was slamming the door on the 49ers offense. Quarterback Steve Young was obviously less mobile than usual because of a nagging groin injury, and he wasn't getting any time to throw. Left outside linebacker Greene—in the rare position of rushing a quarterback's blind side (Young is left-handed)—manhandled 49ers offensive tackle Harris Barton. Once, after pressuring Young into another incompletion and knocking him down, a kneeling Greene put his hands on his hips and simply smiled at the crowd.

"I believe that may have been my best game all year because of how many times I hammered Steve Young," Greene would say after the season ended.

Carolina's 17–0 lead held up through halftime. Beuerlein's only flaw through the entire first half was an underthrown ball that got picked off in the end zone. He completed 17 of 20 passes altogether. Carolina had outgained the 49ers in yardage by a startling 251–66 advantage in the first half, and the second half wasn't much better for the 49ers.

San Francisco managed to get one touchdown in the third quarter on what coach George Seifert would later term a "sandlot" play—Young scrambling around until he found tailback Derek Loville sneaking behind the defense for a 44-yard touchdown. But that was it. The Panthers dominated the game on both sides of the ball. The defense silenced every weapon the 49ers had. San Francisco wide receiver Jerry Rice caught 127 yards' worth of passes but never found the end zone. Brett Maxie had made a big interception in the end zone to stop one 49ers drive. And Carolina's unique formations—the Panthers sometimes used only two defensive linemen, five linebackers, and four defensive backs—flummoxed Young.

"That's when I finally, really believed," Panthers safety Pat Terrell said. "I realized then this is a close team and we've come together really quickly. Honestly, that's when I knew we could go as far as we wanted to."

Kasay made two more field goals to complete the scoring—Carolina won, 23–7. No one had missed Collins and it would have been easy to forget he was gone, had he not helped Brockermeyer lead cheers from time to time on the sideline.

The fans, caught up in the moment, were wonderful from beginning to end. Like teenagers with braces trying to learn how to kiss, they had finally gotten it just right. They sang, "Na-na-na-na, hey, hey, hey, GOODBYE!" as the 49ers trudged off the field at game's end.

"That place was *rockin'!*" Greene yelled. "When we needed the fans on defense, they were there. And when we were on offense, you could hear a pin drop."

San Francisco was stunned.

"I'm struggling for words," coach George Seifert said, "because I don't know what the hell to say. . . . We looked like we were in another world. We've been beating on our chests about what a great defense we have. And we didn't do anything."

An exultant Walls said, "There's something special going on here in Carolina. If this didn't get the word out, we'll just keep beating people until everybody figures it out."

Beuerlein had played so well that the Panthers now had a new problem. Was he actually better than Collins? Neither of Collins's first two games of the season had been as statistically impressive as this one. Beuerlein had finished the game with 290 yards and two touchdowns. Beuerlein dismissed that theory quickly. "This is still Kerry Collins's team," he said; he knew he had at least one more start coming up against Jacksonville before Collins would be ready. "There's no doubt of that. But today was the most fun I've had in years."

Center Curtis Whitley strode proudly around the locker room. Not only had Carolina won, but Whitley's wife, Tracy, had had a baby boy six hours before kickoff. They named him Curtis Jr. Whitley joked, "The last thing the baby told me before I came over here was 'Daddy, beat the 49ers. And tell the boys to bring the noise.'"

They had done that. Unlike Carolina's 13–7 win over San Francisco last season—in which the 49ers outgained the Panthers by 200 yards but kept fumbling the ball near the goal line—this one wasn't lucky in the least. "The year before had been kind of a fluke when we beat 'em," Brockermeyer said. "But this was pretty much an ass kicking."

Team owner Jerry Richardson was floating. The Panthers were 3–0, and his stadium had never sounded so good. "This is not something that just happened," he said. "The culture of this team didn't just show up. The culture of the Carolina Panthers was throughout that entire stadium. It's unique."

But no one was happier than Greene, who had spent his first eight NFL seasons with the Los Angeles Rams trying unsuccessfully to knock the 49ers off their high NFC West throne. "They had been beating my butt since I've been in the league," Greene said. "It felt great to hammer them, and hammer them we did. I said to myself, 'Yeah! Now I'm on a team that doesn't have to freakin' bow down to the San Francisco 49ers!'"

CHAPTER SIX

Jerry's Dream

THE REVEREND BILLY GRAHAM APPEARED STRONG AND vibrant despite his five-year battle with Parkinson's Disease. Still a powerful speaker at 77, he stood on a stage erected on the sidelines of Ericsson Stadium to address the 65,000 believers who had come to hear the first sermon of his four-night crusade. The event had been years in the making—a homecoming crusade for Graham, the world-renowned evangelist born and raised in Charlotte. It was Thursday, September 26, 1996, four days after the Panthers beat the 49ers in the same stadium that was now serving as a spiritual sanctuary.

"I watched a part of the football game on Sunday," Graham said in his opening remarks. "I don't watch football on Sunday usually, but I had to see the Panthers. . . . I couldn't believe it when they said the score was what it was."

This was the second time in six weeks that Graham had been to Ericsson Stadium. He had previously dedicated it "to the glory of God and to the advancement of Charlotte and the Carolinas" prior to an exhibition game against the Buffalo Bills on August 17.

"I'm delighted that the Richardson family allowed me to have a part in the dedication of this great Ericsson Stadium, which is certainly the most beautiful stadium, I believe, in the world," Graham told the crowd on the opening night of his crusade. "I think I've been to—I've preached in—many of the great stadiums of the world. . . . But there's no stadium so beautiful and state-of-the-art as Ericsson Stadium here in Charlotte. God bless you and God bless the Panthers." Many times over the course of the 1996 season, it seemed like He was doing just that.

Graham had been a Dallas Cowboys fan during the era of coach Tom Landry, who is a devout Christian. But he had a new favorite team now.

Jerry Richardson sat in his owner's box watching Graham preach. The owner's heart filled with emotion. Richardson thought about the nine years he had worked to bring an NFL expansion team and a new stadium to Charlotte. Now he was watching an entirely different kind of history being made. "It really hit me like a ton of bricks," Richardson said later. "If we hadn't built this stadium, where would they have held that crusade in Charlotte? Probably nowhere, so it wouldn't have happened.

"When we get asked the question about the economic impact [of the Panthers on the Charlotte area], I've always said it would be positive but that the real issue was the emotional and psychological benefits. How do you put a value on the Billy Graham crusade being in that stadium for four days? I don't think you can. But I know in my mind it's far greater than a winning season. No doubt about it."

Four months earlier, Richardson had feared for his life. He had been diagnosed with prostate cancer and was facing surgery. To be alive—to see the stadium's grand opening, the Panthers' 3–0 start, and the beginning of the Billy Graham crusade—was an answer to his prayers. And his dreams.

THERE'S AN EMPTY SPOT ON THE WALL OF THE LOBBY in Ericsson Stadium where Jerry Richardson plans to put the glass case that will someday house the Panthers' Super Bowl trophies.

That is not a misprint. It says trophies—plural. It's an issue Richardson is possessive about. "Darn right," he said. "I want a *large* case. We're going to win Super Bowls. How many are we going to win? I'm sixty years old and I expect us to win a lot of Super Bowls, I can tell you that."

The Vince Lombardi Trophy, presented annually to the Super Bowl champion, has been at the heart of Jerry Richardson's NFL dream since the day in April 1987 when he decided to try and bring a team to the Carolinas. He was driving in his car when he heard on the radio—to his amazement—that Charlotte, under the direction of George Shinn, had been awarded an NBA franchise. Richardson instantly decided to try for an NFL franchise and got the financial backing of Hugh McColl, Jr., the chairman and CEO of N.C. National Bank (now NationsBank). He hired Max Muhleman, the marketing whiz who had helped George Shinn land the NBA's Charlotte Hornets, and in 1989 he hired NFL Hall of Famer Mike McCormack to serve as an executive consultant. McCormack was essential to the bid-winning formula, for he supplied the credibility within the NFL that Richardson needed. McCormack had played and coached in the league and been a team executive, most recently serving as president of the Seattle Seahawks. Richardson's son Mark, who seemed to have been born with a savvy business sense, was on the front lines with his father from the beginning.

The drive to bring an NFL team to the Charlotte area was a long, uphill battle. Jerry Richardson had to overcome the fact that his was the only bid among the major contenders—St. Louis, Baltimore, Jacksonville, and Memphis were the other finalists—that didn't include a rent-free stadium scheduled to be paid for with public funds. Richardson's plan was to build and own his own stadium, without having to ask taxpayers for help. It was a goal many critics called unattainable.

"I never got discouraged over it," Richardson said, "but the longer I stayed in the process, I realized it was just like fighting a fight with one hand tied behind your back or trying to run a race with somebody on your back."

Ultimately, in order to keep his bid alive, he had to initiate what amounted to a stadium user's fee. He and Muhleman put together the concept of selling permanent-seat licenses (PSLs) to fund the stadium. In order to obtain season tickets to games at the new stadium, fans first had to purchase the rights to those seats in the form of PSLs. The concept contributed more than $100 million toward funding a stadium that would eventually cost $187 million. The permanent rights cost anywhere from $600 to $5,400 per seat. That was a one-time charge, but you still had to buy your season tickets every year. Richardson predicted then that PSLs would be the wave of the future in NFL stadium financing. He was right.

Following a successful PSL campaign, Richardson set out on October 26, 1993 to win the prize he had been seeking for more than six years. That was the day NFL owners finally planned to award two expansion franchises during their meetings in Chicago. There was a problem, however. They couldn't find two cities worthy enough to be granted a franchise at that time, so they decided to add only one and to wait until the fall to choose another.

The one they picked first, ahead of all the others? By a landslide, it was Richardson's bid for Charlotte and the Carolinas. Amazingly, he was unanimously granted a new team, getting an affirmative vote from every one of the league's 28 owners.

Richardson's live television response to the people who had bought the PSLs was an exuberant "Thank you! Thank you! Thank you! Thank you!"

The next day, former NFL commissioner Pete Rozelle, who had been an ally, adviser, and confidante to Richardson throughout his bid for an expansion team, typed a letter of congratulations. "You gave the league no choice," Rozelle wrote. "The combination of the financial package, plus your clearly demonstrated marketing skills and personality, presented an unbeatable bid. . . . It should be a marvelous experience for the Richardsons. . . . I am very happy for you." At a pep rally in front of 50,000 fans on the site where Ericsson Stadium would be built, Richardson promised the Panthers would win a Super Bowl within ten years.

After Carolina went 7–9 in its first season—easily the best record ever by an NFL expansion team—Richardson admitted that he might have been conservative in his Super Bowl prediction. But he wasn't about to amend his vow to a more specific timeline for winning a championship. He subscribed to the ASAP theory. "I don't buy this stuff with dates," he said. "I've never had a five-year plan or a three-year plan. I expected when we got the franchise that we wanted to start that day wanting to win every game we played—*every* game."

Richardson still keeps a note on his desk that he wrote before the

Panthers played their first game in September 1995. It said preparing and planning to win every single game was "the most logical thing for us to do."

As confident as he was, Richardson was not so arrogant that he didn't believe in the power of luck, fate, and divine intervention. In fact, he admitted, "I think fate has had a lot to do with the success we've had."

He felt most fortunate to have been able to put together the triumvirate of the team president, Mike McCormack, the general manager, Bill Polian, and the head coach, Dom Capers. McCormack was available to him in 1989 because Seattle had undergone a change in ownership and didn't retain McCormack. Polian was not attached to a team in January 1994 after leaving the Buffalo Bills. And Capers had not yet been discovered when the Panthers were hunting for a head coach near the end of the '94 season.

Initially the Panthers had hoped to hire as their first coach Joe Gibbs, the former Washington Redskins coach, who had moved to Charlotte to operate the auto-racing team he owned. Carolina courted him and made him a lucrative offer, but he ultimately decided he did not want to return to coaching.

Without another obvious choice available, the Panthers took a chance on Capers—a big chance. Though they had the permission of the Pittsburgh Steelers to interview Capers prior to the team's appearance in the 1994 NFL playoffs, technically the contact violated the NFL's antitampering policy. Capers was supposed to be off limits to the Panthers until after the Steelers' season was over. It was a rule put in place to keep a team from getting raided in the middle of a run at the Super Bowl. The policy did not, however, apply to college teams, and it was not uncommon for one to hire an NFL assistant coach during the playoffs. The Panthers didn't want to risk the possibility of a major college team hiring Capers before they even got a chance to interview him, so they decided to pursue him despite the league rules.

During Capers's job interview, Richardson placed a printed copy of the NFL's antitampering rules on a table so it was visible to him, McCormack, Polian, Mark Richardson, and Capers. He wanted to make sure everyone understood exactly what was happening—that the Panthers were breaking the rules—and what the consequences could be.

When the Panthers' courtship of Capers was reported in the media, NFL commissioner Paul Tagliabue struck with swift punishment. He stripped Carolina of their picks in the second and sixth rounds of the 1995 draft and fined the team $150,000.

Fans throughout the Carolinas expressed disappointment that team officials had decided to disregard NFL policy in order to get the coach they wanted. Richardson later issued a public apology and promised the Panthers would abide by the rules in the future.

Again, it was Rozelle who put the situation in perspective in a letter he sent to Richardson shortly after the incident: "I felt you handled the little problem with the league as well as possible and now it should be full speed ahead."

FROM THE BEGINNING, RICHARDSON KNEW WHAT THE key words for the Panthers would be: teamwork, harmony, and hard work. "The power of teamwork, harmony, and hard work is huge," he said. "I can't think of many professional sports franchises that have been able to pull it off."

Richardson firmly believes in those words. In fact, he often dreams of a day when the Panthers no longer need contracts for front-office personnel and the head coaching position. He wants the people running the team to be so happy with their jobs and their working environment that a binding legal agreement between them isn't necessary. Of course, that also would require a unique level of loyalty, but Richardson believes it's possible. "The way we do business is unique in sports," he said.

Ask people around the Panthers why that's so and they point all the way to the top—to Jerry Richardson himself. He has worked hard to build close relationships with everyone in the organization, from the coaches to the players to the maintenance staff at Ericsson Stadium. "I couldn't imagine having a better relationship with an owner than I do with Jerry," Capers said. "He's a guy I can just relate to very well. He's very supportive and he's a tremendous people person. You don't have to be around him very long to see why he's been successful."

Richardson and Capers have a tradition of meeting together alone 70 minutes before the kickoff of every Panthers game. "It's very comforting to me," Capers said. "It's a relaxed setting. We talk about themes for the week, any problems that have come up, what we have to do on the field to win the game, and we might laugh a little, too."

Richardson described the meetings as "quiet, peaceful, not stressful"—except once. On October 1, 1995, the Panthers were preparing to play Tampa Bay at Memorial Stadium at Clemson, the Panthers' temporary home for their debut season. That morning in their regular pregame meeting before playing Tampa Bay, Richardson dropped some heavy news on Capers. "I don't mean to put any pressure on you, Dom," Richardson said. "But I've got to go to the bank Monday morning and ask to borrow fifteen million dollars." The team was losing money because of the lack of sellout crowds at Clemson. Richardson needed help to cover the anticipated shortfall, which eventually would reach $23 million before that first season was over.

Richardson hadn't intended to rattle Capers, but the news was unsettling for the coach. The Panthers were already 0–3, and that day, rookie quarterback Kerry Collins was making his first career start. The situation got even worse after the Panthers committed four turnovers in Tampa Bay territory and lost 20–13 to fall to a dismal 0–4.

"That was probably the most pressure I'd felt in years," Capers said later with a chuckle. In late 1996 Richardson happily announced there was no shortfall for Carolina's second season, after the Panthers moved into their new stadium and sold out every home game. It also didn't hurt that the team had sold the naming rights for the facility to the Ericsson telecommunications company for an estimated $25 million, to be paid over nine years.

Apart from his pregame meetings with Capers, Richardson is usually sensitive about not being viewed as intrusive to coaches and players. As much as he would like to attend every practice, he rarely does.

"The truth of the matter is I can show up where I want to show up,"

Richardson said. "I'm one of thirty people who can go where they want to go if it's an NFL function. If you own a team, you can do that. You can go where you want to go, sit where you want to sit, do what you want to do. But I think it's helpful that I don't do that. I don't want to encumber people." Instead, he gives them space to do the jobs they were hired to do.

Cornerback Eric Davis fondly tells the story of a rainy, cold practice during the 1996 season when Richardson was driving the first of a group of golf carts lined up to transport players from the practice field back to the locker room at Ericsson Stadium. The carts were golden to the players, because they turned a seven-minute walk into a one-minute ride after a long, tiring practice. Richardson had gone into the locker room, borrowed safety Pat Terrell's Notre Dame jacket to keep him warm, put a towel around his neck, and headed out to pick up some of the players.

"A lot of owners would have sent someone else to pick us up, but there's only one I know who would do it himself," said Eric Davis. "That right there showed me a lot. It let me know he cares about us as men. He's not out to make money. He wants to win championships."

Richardson knew how it felt to practice on a cold, wet day. Of all the thirty owners in the league, he is the only one who is a former player. The only other NFL owner who had ever played in the league, in fact, was the legendary (and now deceased) George Halas of the Chicago Bears.

Though Richardson's pro career lasted only two seasons before he set out to pursue a business career, he experienced the ultimate thrill: playing for a championship team. He played on the Baltimore Colts 1959 NFL championship team that beat the New York Giants 31–16.

"I think it's been very helpful to our organization to know that the Panthers are owned by a player who played in a world championship game," Richardson said. "There are two hundred million people in America, but there were only thirty-five or -six of us that day who were in the winning locker room. That's a very small percentage. I know what it takes to win a world championship and I know how you feel when you do it. No writer can write the words to describe the feeling I personally had that day. I want our players to have that."

Richardson took the $4,864 he earned in playoff money for his part in the 1959 championship to start a restaurant with a friend of his named Charlie Bradshaw. In October 1961 he and Bradshaw opened a Hardee's in Spartanburg, South Carolina, where they had both gone to college at Wofford. It was so successful that they opened another. And another. Under the umbrella corporation of Spartan Food Systems, they eventually acquired the Quincy's Family Steakhouse chain. As Richardson's company grew and merged and got renamed, it kept expanding. By the time Richardson finally resigned in May 1995 as chairman of Flagstar Companies, Inc., the company had more than 1,500 company-owned and franchised Denny's restaurants, 210 company-owned and franchised El Pollo Loco restaurants, 600 Hardee's, and 211 Quincy's.

Richardson had gotten rich in the food business, but he retained a common man's touch, and he relates to the players better than most NFL owners. Though he never hovers over practices, he stays visible to all the players. They see him working out in the weight room, and he stops by the locker room occasionally to speak with them one-on-one.

During the week before the Panthers' win at home over the 49ers, Richardson had a conversation at the stadium with linebacker Kevin Greene that left a strong impression on the linebacker. Their talk wasn't about football. It was about horses.

"The horse is an incredible animal," Richardson told Greene. "It is smart, intelligent, proud, strong, and highly durable."

"You're right," Greene responded. "Do you have any horses?"

"Yes, I do," Richardson said. "I have fifty-three of them and I love each and every one of them dearly."

"Wow!" Greene said. "You've got a whole stable full of freakin' horses!"

"Do you know what I call them?" Richardson asked.

"No," Greene said. "What?"

"Panthers," said Richardson. "I call them Panthers."

Counting all the players on the active roster, the Panthers had 53 members.

"It felt so great to be a horse in his stable," Greene would later say. "It was because of the way he said it—I knew he meant it. If I didn't see him backing it up by knowing everybody and always asking about their families, I would think he was just shooting into the wind. But he wasn't. He really cares."

IT WAS SATURDAY, APRIL 20, 1996. FOR THE SECOND straight year, Richardson had a seat inside the Panthers "war room" on the day of the NFL draft. He loved watching Polian masterfully maneuver the team's picks to add running backs Tshimanga Biakabutuka and Winslow Oliver, plus wide receiver Muhsin Muhammad to a Carolina offense that desperately needed young firepower. But Richardson's heart wasn't truly into what was happening that day. He was carrying a terrible secret.

"I knew I had cancer," he said. "The other people didn't know it yet. My mind wasn't into the draft as much as it would have been." One week earlier, Richardson had been diagnosed with prostate cancer. "It's a jolt when somebody tells you that you have cancer," Richardson said. "That's a scary thing. . . . It was scary to me."

Given a choice of surgery or radiation treatments, Richardson chose surgery. "I decided I didn't want to have cancer in my body," he said. "I was going to be just as aggressive as I thought the cancer was going to be."

Richardson delayed the operation until after the NFL owners held their spring meetings in Charlotte in early May 1996. His most anxious moments came in the days leading up to the May 28 surgery. He thought of Carl Navarre and Craig Wall, Sr., two close friends and business associates who had died of a cancer similar to what he had. Navarre owned the Coca-Cola bottling franchise in south Florida and lived in Chattanooga, Tennessee. Wall was a businessman from Conway, South Carolina.

"They were two men I greatly admired and respected," Richardson said. "They died of cancer and they died very quickly. Carl got cancer and the next thing I knew, he wasn't living. Craig had cancer in the same area of the prostate as mine. I went to see him at Duke Hospital one day and within twenty-four hours he was dead. So as I was waiting for surgery," Richardson said, "I was thinking about all of that."

Not until after the May surgery, which was deemed a complete success, did Richardson reveal his condition to the public. For his wife, Rosalind, some of the most difficult times during his recovery were the 10 days following his return to their Spartanburg home. He wasn't allowed to climb stairs and thus wasn't able to get to their second-floor bedroom. Since there was no bedroom on the main floor of the house, Richardson slept in the small guest house located on their property.

"It was hard to leave him there at night because he was in a great deal of discomfort," Mrs. Richardson said. "So I got a nurse's aide to come sit out there at night because I couldn't bear the thought of leaving him out there and not being able to hear him."

It was the second time in nine years that Richardson had been confined to the downstairs area of their home because of his health. The first time, in 1987, came after he injured his Achilles tendon playing racquetball; he had to wear a full-leg cast. The guest house, built in the 1930s by the original owners of the property, had not yet been renovated, so Richardson slept in a hospital bed that had been set up downstairs. Obviously, it was not an ideal setup, even temporarily. But on the plus side, it gave Rosalind Richardson one of her favorite stories about her husband.

"I had tucked Jerry in one night and had lain down on the sofa near him and covered up," Mrs. Richardson said. "All of a sudden, I felt this little movement going down my side and then up my arm. I thought something was happening to me, so I threw the cover back. It turned out to be a tiny little mouse that jumped off the sofa. I yelled, 'Jerry, a mouse!' He said, 'Get the broom! Get the broom!' Well, I got up to get the broom and when I came back there was no sign of Jerry except for his crutches. I found them at the bottom of the stairs."

Richardson had somehow made his way up to their bedroom, frantically scurrying away from the mouse as fast as he could. He didn't come back downstairs again until he was healthy enough to walk the stairs regularly.

The two downstairs-only predicaments led the Richardsons to design the new home they're having built in Charlotte with *two* downstairs bedrooms.

As for his cancer, Richardson was able to announce at training camp, six weeks before the start of 1996 season, that doctors had determined his body was cancer-free. He would say later that the experience dramatically changed his life.

"Now that I don't have it anymore, I can say it was a good experience for me," Richardson said. "I'm not quite as hyper about things. I think it made me more patient. It was a very humbling experience for me. It was a reminder to me that you don't know when your time may have arrived and passed."

RICHARDSON OFTEN REMEMBERS PETE ROZELLE TELLing him that by bringing the Panthers to life, he was assured of leaving a legacy in the Carolinas that would outlive him by 50 years or more.

"We've touched everybody in a positive way so far, and our goal is to keep it positive," Richardson said. "It really is a big responsibility for me and my family. Because we have such high standards, we really have to be careful of ourselves in what we say or do."

As owner and founder of the Panthers, Richardson lives in a fast-paced world. Sometimes, he can still get very impatient. Before one game early in the '96 season, Richardson had attended the Panthers' Sunday morning chapel service at the team hotel in uptown Charlotte and was hurriedly trying to drive through the city to the stadium, where he was scheduled to address a group of people before they were given a tour of the facility. On the drive over, Richardson saw a man running down the street. He, too, was in a hurry to get somewhere. So Richardson pulled over and offered him a ride.

"He got in the car but it turned out he wasn't really sure where he needed to get out," Richardson said. "I told him, 'You have to tell me where you want to get out, sir, because I've really got to hustle and I don't want to be late.' So he told me to stop, and I stopped in a hurry. I wasn't driving as safely as I should have been. The car behind me didn't hit me, but it was obviously a distraction to them." Richardson made his appointment on time but he later received what he described as a "scorching" letter from the people who had been in the car behind him when he let his passenger out.

"The letter described from a fan's point of view how I was driving carelessly and how I wasn't being thoughtful and I was setting a bad example for others," Richardson said. "They said how disappointed they were that I did that. Apparently, they beeped the horn when I stopped and when the guy got out of my car, he said something to them he shouldn't have said. So they associated that person with me.

"I wrote those people back and said, 'Shame on me.'"

PANTHERS PLAYERS PAID SPECIAL NOTICE TO THE fact that Richardson chose the Reverend Billy Graham to dedicate Ericsson Stadium. "He could have selected senators or ex-presidents," Kevin Greene said. "He could have selected astronauts or Gulf War veterans. But he selected Billy Graham. That's the kind of power you can't mess with."

The Panthers played the season feeling empowered at Ericsson, especially the players who had strong religious convictions. There were so many of them that Carolina could aptly have been called "the God Squad." "We've got a lot of spiritual players on our team," Richardson said. "They feel like our place is blessed. I do too."

Running back Anthony Johnson said, "There was not—for lack of a better way to say it—any type of voodoo or anything of that nature, but we believed we were blessed and raised by God to have an impact on the league and the country."

Some players noted after the win at home over the 49ers that, because of the upcoming Billy Graham crusade, Ericsson had been one of the most prayed-for places in the world that week.

Kicker John Kasay made a special effort to meet Graham at the dedication during the preseason. Was it coincidence that he started the year by making his first 13 field-goal attempts? "You can't discount a little divine intervention," Greene said.

Ever the realist, Kasay was the first to say the point shouldn't be exaggerated. "A game still requires all the players to go out on the field and do their jobs," Kasay said. "I often think about something I read three or four years ago. It said, 'Don't confuse who you are with what you do.' What I do is play football. What I am is a child of God."

Several of the Panthers' most prominent players were deeply religious and used their platform as star athletes to witness to others during the '96 season. Whenever Kasay was asked about a field goal he made, he'd give "all the glory to God." Running back Anthony Johnson, wide receiver Mark Carrier, snapper Mark Rodenhauser, special-teamer Dwight Stone, Kevin Greene, and others openly discussed their faith throughout the season.

"What really impacted me was being able to rub shoulders with people who loved the Lord the same way I did," Johnson said. "We had a good mix and we could make each other strong. Many of us were at all different levels of our spiritual maturity, but we were able to come together and sharpen each other, as the Bible says."

Some members of the team considered certain players religious extremists. "I thought our ultrareligious people were too nice on the field," cornerback Toi Cook said. "You can be completely fair and still whip somebody's butt."

Johnson disagreed that the team's religious players were soft. "A lot of times people mistake another person's meekness as weakness," Johnson said. "But nine out of ten people who try to walk right are stronger in a lot of areas. I think the notion that you have to get drunk at night, be crazy and wild eyed, and want to tear somebody's head off to play this game effectively is wrong. To play this game, you have to love the part of being physical, hitting, and taking hits. That has nothing to do with religious convictions."

Johnson said having so many players with a strong faith helped make the Panthers a stronger team in 1996. "We had people who loved the Lord on the team who were willing to put personal goals aside for the team and stand firm on the convictions of right and wrong," Johnson said. "And most people who love the Lord, despite the mistakes they might make, usually are people with a strong character."

Billy Graham developed a strong sense of connection with the Panthers and with Richardson during the '96 season. Graham was wearing a sweater vest with a Panther logo in photographs that accompanied a feature article about him and the Charlotte crusade in the October 14 issue of *People* magazine. Richardson knew it was no accident. It was Graham's quiet way of endorsing Carolina.

In a letter Graham would send to Richardson later in the season, he wrote that the times he saw Carolina players gathered in a prayer circle on the field after games "touched me more than anything I can remember." Graham also wrote: "I am not only proud of your football achievments, but [of] the attitude of the team and staff through the printed page and media. You have made me proud to be a Carolinian and as you so graciously said to me—'You are part of the family.' I am delighted and thrilled and honored to be a part of the Panther family. My main contribution will be prayer and friendship."

Graham later pointed out in an interview how pleased he was that the Panthers had so many players that he called "true believers" and that he thought their on-the-field prayers were made in the appropriate spirit. "Before and after the game, they gather for prayer," Graham said. "They aren't praying to win, rather that they won't be hurt, that God's will be done, and that they do their best."

Then Graham paused and smiled.

"But," he added, "I'm praying for them to win."

CHAPTER SEVEN

A Sudden Slump

IF YOU'VE EVER BEEN A LITTLE BROTHER, OR A JUNIOR partner, or a freshman plebe, you know how the Jacksonville Jaguars felt in late September 1996. Carolina had turned into a media darling. With their three-game win streak to begin the '96 season, the Panthers had won ten of the 19 games they had ever played.

Like the Panthers, Jacksonville joined the NFL in 1995 but so far had finished second to Carolina in everything. NFL owners invited the Panthers into the league a full month before they invited Jacksonville. Carolina had a glistening new stadium; Jacksonville had to face-lift an old one. Carolina had won the coin flip for the first pick in the 1995 draft. And when the two teams played in the inaugural Hall of Fame game in 1995, Carolina had beaten Jacksonville 20–14.

Now, the 3–0 Panthers were a slight favorite to win this game—the first time all year Carolina had been favored. Worst of all for the Jaguars, they had a poor 1–3 record in 1996 and a 5–15 mark overall to show for their 1¼ seasons.

So as the two teams prepared for their September 29 matchup in Jacksonville, the first time the expansion rivals had ever met in the regular season, the Jaguars were preparing to be testy hosts. There would be no killing the fatted calf for Carolina, the NFL's prodigal son.

The Jaguars were angry about all the attention being lavished on the Panthers. "I think nationally we are pretty disrespected," Jaguars safety Dana Hall said three days before the Carolina game. "People measure us against Carolina. That's natural, because that's the team we came in the door with. But we are *not* a bad team."

They were just treated like one.

"The Jaguars must feel like a shunned sibling whose twin brother has achieved greatness," the Jacksonville-based columnist Mike Bianchi wrote in the local paper, *The Florida Times-Union.*

Carolina, on the other hand, believed this game was just "another day at the office," according to quarterback Steve Beuerlein. With Collins still out, he would be making his second straight start for the Panthers.

Beuerlein had started the '95 season for Jacksonville, had gone 1–5 in that role, and had gotten yanked in favor of Mark Brunell. Now, he was riding high in Charlotte. Some Panthers fans were even crowding the local radio talk shows with the idea that Beuerlein should be starting for the Panthers full time.

"That bothered me," Collins said. "I can't say it didn't." Collins would eventually have his chance to prove those callers wrong. For now, however, it was still Beuerlein's job.

At Wednesday's practice before the game the Panthers had a surprise visit from former president George Bush. In town to give a speech, Bush had stopped by to watch the last 30 minutes of practice. The irony of the visit: Carolina coach Dom Capers didn't know when Bush was there that one of Bush's sons actually owned a minority share of the Jaguars. Reporters—who aren't allowed to watch most of practice because of Capers's paranoia about having his game secrets stolen—gleefully told Capers about it after practice.

"Hmm," Capers said, puzzling it out. "Well, I think we're safe. He wasn't writing [player] assignments down or anything."

THE JAGUARS AND PANTHERS HAD BUILT THEIR TEAMS far differently.

Jacksonville had hired young front-office people with a rock-and-roll edge to them and little NFL experience. Carolina had stuffed themselves with veterans of the league like Mike McCormack and Bill Polian. Jacksonville had only four players over 30 on its entire roster; Carolina had six 30-something players on their starting defense alone.

Jacksonville coach Tom Coughlin was far more rigid than Capers. He had made headlines his first season for starting training camp earlier than any other NFL team and enforcing a number of dictatorial rules. (One of the more bizarre ones: Both feet had to be kept on the floor at all times during meetings.)

"We are so completely different in our thinking than they are," said Jacksonville's Michael Huyghue, the team's senior vice president for football operations. "They are very traditionally patterned and more prone to take a league viewpoint."

"And everyone," Coughlin growled, "had decided we were on the short end of the stick."

The two teams would have to sort their differences out on the field. That Sunday dawned like many in late September in Florida—incredibly hot. The on-field temperature would creep above 100 degrees and stay there for much of the day. The only people who seemed completely at ease in the sweltering heat were the 71,537 fans who piled into Municipal Stadium, ready to exact a measure of revenge from the Panthers.

"For the fans, this is a grudge match," said Sara Nichols, the 55-year-old president of the Jaguars thousand-member booster club. "We want to beat them up. I'd use stronger language, but I'm a lady."

"I understand that you've got sort of a wine-and-cheese crowd there in Carolina," said Tommy Charles, the programming director for an all-sports radio station based in Jacksonville. "Well, we've got some beer-drinking, hell-raising fans here, and are they excited. . . . They want to beat your butts to a gnarly pulp."

It sure looked that way. Jacksonville scored touchdowns on each of their first two possessions, immediately jumping to a 14–0 lead. Quarterback Mark Brunell befuddled the Panthers defense with his speed. He was doing a better imitation of San Francisco quarterback Steve Young than Young himself had done a week before.

Carolina, meanwhile, couldn't do anything on offense. Beuerlein was plastered several times by his old Jacksonville teammates as the Panthers offensive line did their best imitation of a turnstile. After completing 15 of his first 16 passes against the 49ers, Beuerlein started this game one-for-six for eight yards. And each time Beuerlein got hit, the fans greeted the punishment with a sadistic cheer. "The crowd wanted to see Steve's head on a platter," Panthers offensive guard Greg Skrepenak said.

"I don't know what he did to those players when he was down here playing with them," Panthers center Curtis Whitley drawled. "But they don't seem to like Steve very much."

That first quarter ranked as one of the Panthers' worst all season. And the most disastrous part came not on Jacksonville's two touchdowns, but on a simple two-yard gain by Panthers running back Tshimanga Biakabutuka.

BIAKABUTUKA HAD YET TO BREAK A BIG GAIN FOR THE Panthers—his longest run in 71 carries had been for a modest 17 yards—but the soft-spoken rookie seemed to get a bit better each game. He was making up for all the time he had lost during training camp, and with each carry he became a little more in tune with the Panthers' offensive plan. But then he ran for two yards late in the first quarter, got tackled in a pile, and felt his left knee wrench. He yelled in agony, then quickly got up, and limped off the field. As he approached the sideline, his face told the story. Just as he reached the white line, he fell to the ground and collapsed in pain.

Panthers general manager Bill Polian, watching from the press box, had one thought as he saw his No. 1 draft pick crumple on the sideline: "Uh-oh." He had seen many players fall exactly the way Biakabutuka had. Almost always, they were seriously hurt. This was the player Polian had been so ecstatic to get on draft day, the one he felt would rush for 1,000 yards. Now Biakabutuka was writhing in pain.

"It's a knee," Polian said grimly, surveying the Panthers sideline from his high vantage point. "Who do we turn to now?"

Biakabutuka, unlike Collins, didn't immediately believe his injury would be the "big one" that would end his season, but it was. The

Panthers wouldn't know it for sure until the next day, but the Zaire native who had learned football in high school in Canada was gone for the year. The diagnosis was a torn anterior cruciate ligament—an ACL.

CAROLINA COULDN'T WORRY MUCH ABOUT BIAKABU-tuka in the middle of the Jacksonville game, however. The Panthers and Jaguars were in a catfight, and Carolina was getting clawed up. It was 17–0, Jacksonville, at the half.

Beuerlein was getting blasted. The Jaguars were not only hitting him legally, they also smashed into him late twice in a row, resulting in back-to-back roughing-the-passer calls. Beuerlein, who had a feisty streak, held up his hands to the crowd after the second hit while he was still on the field. "Is that all you've got? Is that the best you can do?" he yelled.

In fact, the Jaguars would do better. They had an answer for everything the Panthers did that day.

"Jacksonville was the only team that physically whipped our ass," Panthers linebacker Lamar Lathon would say later as he reviewed the season. "We went there thinking they were going to lay down. We started slow. And they whipped us."

The Panthers just couldn't mount a successful attack. On one play, Beuerlein fumbled the ball away when Carolina had advanced it to the 17. On another, a mishandled handoff cost them the ball just as they were about to score from the Jacksonville one-yard line. The back who missed the handoff was Biakabutuka's sub, backup tailback Anthony Johnson.

Carolina finally scored in the third quarter when Mark Carrier snared a 24-yard touchdown pass from Beuerlein, but Kasay—who had been near perfect all season—missed the extra point. The Jaguars led 17–6. Then Jacksonville put the game in their pocket with a 15-play, 80-yard drive that consumed almost eight minutes and parts of two quarters. When James Stewart ran for a three-yard TD, the Jaguars led 24–6 early in the fourth quarter and the game was all but over. The Panthers—after three straight Sundays of jubilation—were miserable. The heat was oppressive, and looking at the scoreboard made them feel even worse. Three Panthers players had to get IV treatments for dehydration while the game was still going on.

"That was probably the hottest day in the history of the world," said Carrier, whose eight catches for 124 yards were one of the few bright spots for the Panthers. Carrier caught another TD pass late in the game with 4:07 left. It was thrown by Kerry Collins. Capers had inserted him in for the final 5:41 of the game, after Beuerlein had finally cramped up from sheer exhaustion. Collins's knee was feeling better, and on the very next play, Collins ran for a two-point conversion to make the final score more respectable: Jacksonville 24, Carolina 14.

The Panthers had gotten drilled by a hungrier team. "People tried to downplay it all week, but we were playing for the pride of this town and this community," Jaguars center Dave Widell said.

Lathon hadn't gotten a sack in a game for the first time in the season. His sack total, in fact, sounded like a rocket ship countdown: 3–2–1–0. "Jacksonville had been kicked for so long," Lathon said. "It was like when you back a cat into a corner and it wants to come out fighting."

The Panthers fans who had backed Beuerlein for the full-time starting job quieted down after the Jaguars loss. Collins had come in and quickly led a touchdown drive late, even though he was only playing at about 75 percent. He would be back for the next game though, on October 6 vs. Minnesota. The Panthers needed him.

They also needed a running game. Polian frequently said that one major injury could mean the difference between a 10–6 season and a 7–9 one. Carolina's offense was predicated on a successful running game. Who could the Panthers count on now to carry the ball 20 times a game?

IN CAPERS'S QUIVER OF PANTHERS PLAYERS, ANTHONY Johnson may have been the straightest arrow of all. The player teammates called A.J. rarely watched R-rated movies because he didn't like the blood, the profanity, or the sex. He drove a 1990 Toyota Celica Supra with 67,000 miles on it to practice every day, the same car he had when he broke into the NFL. Other players loved to make fun of that car. It didn't look bad in a mall parking lot, but in a lot full of Mercedes, Lexuses, and sports utility vehicles, it stood out like a wallflower at the debutante ball.

Johnson didn't care. He was a deeply religious man and material things were not of great importance to him. He liked gospel music and movies with a "good moral message," and often during interviews, he would speak of God and his strong faith. He was very thrifty, too.

Johnson, his wife, Shelley, and their four children all lived together in a modest three-bedroom, 1,400-square-foot apartment in Charlotte. The family would have rented a two-bedroom—all the kids except for the two-month-old piled into the same bed at night anyway—but state law required a family of six to lease at least three bedrooms.

The Johnson family was a tight-knit one. Johnson got up early enough to take his son Taylor to first grade before heading to Ericsson Stadium, and he often got tackled by his kids at night as frequently as he did in practice during the day. He didn't feel like his family was large at all—he had grown up in a family of nine kids—and he still appreciated the value of a dollar. He didn't spend his money on hot rods or second homes, like many players. He was 29 years old, had been dropped by three NFL teams already, and was very concerned about his future.

"Football is not bigger than life for me," Johnson said.

That was a good thing. Johnson had once suffered the embarrassment of being cut by the New York Jets, football's worst team in 1996. The Panthers had found him languishing on the waiver wire and had signed him in November of 1995. He contributed a little bit in the Panthers' first season, mainly on special teams. Then, in April 1996, Carolina drafted a quartet of running backs in the NFL draft (Biakabutuka, Winslow Oliver, Marquette Smith, and Scott Greene).

"They picked four running backs—four!" Johnson said. "That sent a little bit of a message."

After Capers denied Johnson's request to be released during training camp—Johnson had figured he might as well get a head start looking for another team to play for—Johnson found a niche by becoming Mr. Versatility. He had roles on all four of the Panthers' main special teams—kickoff and punt coverage, kickoff and punt return—and also knew how to play both backup tailback and fullback.

"I'm not real flashy, but I definitely get the job done," Johnson said.

The Panthers weren't so sure. In the wake of the Biakabutuka injury, they signed Leroy Hoard, a formerly well-known player who had been with the Cleveland franchise and was at the time a free agent. At first it appeared that Hoard would get the start against Minnesota after only a week of practice.

But gradually, the Panthers coaches became more comfortable with Johnson as they watched him work in Biakabutuka's role throughout the week. He was smart (he had a psychology degree from Notre Dame), he found the hole and ran straight at it, and he did whatever you told him, whenever you told him to do it. Biakabutuka's injury had become Johnson's opportunity. The law of the NFL jungle had struck again, and this time a player who hadn't gained 100 yards in a game since 1985—in that year Johnson was a senior in high school in South Bend, Indiana—was the beneficiary. "The circumstances for this are quite tragic—it's tough to see your buddy down and in pain—but what can you do?" Johnson said, shrugging his shoulders. "It's football."

On the first play of the Minnesota game, Johnson sprinted into a hole between center and left guard for seven yards. It looked as if Biakabutuka's understudy would fit into the starring role just fine.

COLLINS, ON THE OTHER HAND, WASN'T LOOKING GOOD. In his first start since September 8, a month earlier vs. New Orleans, he felt strange and out of place. "I went in there and it was almost surreal," Collins said. "I just didn't feel I had a chance that day. I wasn't ready to go."

Collins's first pass was incomplete. So was his second. On his fifth attempt, he fumbled. Minnesota—a playoff-caliber team that sported a 4–1 record going into this game—recovered at the Carolina 49. Eight plays later, the Vikings scored a touchdown when Warren Moon found Cris Carter on a six-yard pass. Minnesota led 7–0.

On Carolina's next series, the Panthers started driving. Hoard had come in for one play in the last series, subbing for Johnson, and gained zero yards on a third-and-one. On this drive, Johnson was back and running well. He sprang a 22-yard run on the surprised Vikings and then a 13-yarder. Then, on third-and-seven at the Minnesota 32, Vikings cornerback Dewayne Washington looked in Collins's eyes and saw something he liked. Washington's coaches had told him all week that Collins was not yet adept at looking off receivers—he had a tendency to "lock" on the receiver he was throwing to before firing the ball to him.

Collins would get better at this later in the season, but for now, he was just trying to get by. He looked at Muhsin Muhammad and then threw to him. Washington grabbed the ball instead at the Minnesota 27. The Panthers defense—particularly the ever-emotional Lathon—was growing tired of Collins's miscues, but they prevented further damage this time when Kevin Greene caused Warren Moon to fumble. The Panthers recovered, trailing only 7–0.

On the Panthers' first play, Collins threw another interception, his third turnover of the game. Capers grimaced on the sidelines, but the thought of putting Beuerlein in for Collins never crossed his mind. The Panthers would sink or swim with their second-year quarterback—Capers had mentally committed to that long ago. The future would be now, even if it looked as bleak as the inside of Minnesota's Metrodome at the moment.

Carolina got the ball back once more before the half. With two seconds remaining, on fourth-and-five at the Minnesota 45, Capers briefly considered having John Kasay try a whopping 63-yard field goal. Instead, he sent Collins back out to throw a Hail Mary. Fittingly, it was intercepted. Minnesota still led at halftime, 7–0.

It was one of Collins's worst halves of football ever. He had completed five passes and turned the ball over four times. Carolina's seven possessions for the half had ended like this: Punt. Punt. Punt. Fumble. Interception. Interception. Interception. Still, Carolina was down by only a touchdown. But that changed on the first drive of the second half, as Minnesota took it 80 yards in 12 plays. It was Moon to

Carter for the TD again—this time from three yards out. That made it 14–0.

Then, the slumbering Panthers offense awoke. Carolina ran off an 80-yard march of its own. The Panthers ran 13 plays, and Johnson carried on eight of them. He got 31 of the yards, including the final four for the touchdown. Suddenly, it was 14–7, Minnesota, and the Panthers sliced the lead even further, when, on the Vikings next possession, special-teams demon Michael Bates sped off the outside corner and blocked Mitch Berger's punt out of the end zone for a safety. Carolina was now only down five points entering the fourth quarter, and they were hot.

On their second possession of the last quarter, they started at the Minnesota 43 after another good defensive series and drove to a second-and-four at the Vikings five. There, Johnson got stuffed up the middle for a single yard. On third-and-three from the four, Collins tried to lob one up to Muhammad in the end zone, but the rookie barely batted it away from the Minnesota defenders. That made it fourth-and-three and Capers decided to go for the field goal. John Kasay nailed the 22-yarder and cut the lead to 14–12 with 6:28 remaining in the game.

Carolina got the ball back one more time, at its own 15, with 3:32 left. On third-and-17, Collins threw—and Minnesota's Washington intercepted the ball again. That was the ballgame. The Vikings had done nothing offensively after the first series of the second half, but managed to hang on for a 14–12 win that would bother the Panthers for months. It especially irritated Lathon.

"How in the hell can you lose a game like that?" Lathon would rage months later. "They [the Vikings] were supposed to be so hot at the time. How can you lose against a team you knew wasn't better than you? Defensively we beat them. We whipped them. Everything was going our way, but this guy [Collins] jumps in and throws *four* picks."

It was Collins's worst game of the season, one reminiscent of a few of his high-turnover games as a rookie. "I was off for four weeks," he said. "I barely had a week of practice. We went on the road to a tough place to play and I was just trying to get my bearings back at that point. I don't think it's uncommon for a young quarterback to feel something like that. . . . It was weird. It was in that dark, dingy dome. It was like I never, ever felt like I was in the football game. . . . All the conditions were there for me to lay an egg, and I certainly did."

Johnson certainly didn't. He had gained a startling 102 yards in 23 carries in his first start as a Panther—his first 100-yard game in 11 years. It looked like Carolina had filled the Biakabutuka void.

"Personally, that Minnesota game might have been my favorite of the season," said Johnson, who had also played on all the special teams during the game. "If I don't start out well there, that certainly changes the complexion of the rest of the season. It was very gratifying."

But still, the Panthers had fallen to a 3–2 record with the loss. It was time for some leadership. As usual, cornerback Eric Davis stepped in with a few words. "We're at a crossroads," Davis told his teammates. "It's time to reassess things here. It's time for guys to ball up their fists and keep them that way the rest of the season. Because the first time you open that palm in the NFL, somebody else is swinging at you. We need to decide what kind of team we want to be."

DAVIS KNEW WHAT KIND OF TEAM HE WANTED THEM to be: a winner. He had spent his whole NFL career until this season on a winning team at San Francisco, and he preached the winning gospel like no one else in the locker room. For Davis, winning was all that really mattered. Giving your best wasn't always good enough. "A coach will say that sometimes, you know," Davis said. "Just give me your best. I say, hey, if you can't get it done, thanks for your best, but we can't use you."

Anyone could have used Davis, one of the best "cover" cornerbacks in the NFL. He had a wonderful sense of balance, good speed, and a knack for playing calmly in big situations. Of his 18 career interceptions, six had come in the playoffs for San Francisco.

He and Anthony Johnson tied for team member with the most children. A.J. had been way ahead until June 14, when Davis's wife, Serena, gave birth to triplets—two boys and a girl. He and his wife already had an eight-year-old son, Kevin. Davis taped pictures in his locker of his three tiny babies in three tiny bassinets.

"It was great," Davis said. "But I wasn't getting too much sleep in the early part of the season. I don't think I really slept at all until October."

Davis had reluctantly signed an $11.4 million, four-year contract with Carolina in the off-season. He had been happy in San Francisco, but the 49ers had been too salary cap–strapped to pay him. "The salary cap breaks up a lot of happy marriages," Davis's agent, Leigh Steinberg, said when his client signed with the Panthers. So Davis had come across the country to Charlotte, put on his do-rag, and set up shop.

As soon as Carolina got him, other teams started throwing at Tyrone Poole. Poole wasn't a bad corner, but Davis had the reputation of being a great one. Davis had joined the 49ers as a second-round pick out of Jacksonville State in 1990 and quickly developed a reputation in 49ers practices as one of the few players who had a shot at covering Jerry Rice consistently. When Davis started alongside Deion Sanders for a year in San Francisco, Neon Deion called him "the best cornerback I've ever played with."

Davis would justify that reputation later in the Panthers season, but in the first few games he had allowed a couple of big plays. Two of them resulted in short touchdown passes thrown over his head in the end zone. "I'd make just one stupid, high-school mistake and then I wouldn't get another opportunity," Davis said. "It was driving me crazy, the way I'd never get the ball."

Like almost all of the best NFL cornerbacks, Davis was cocky. He had some of the trappings of success: A huge diamond earring in his left ear glittered as he spoke. He seemed to have the right mind-set, too. Cornerbacks are supposed to have short memories, because they all get beaten at one time or another. They have to run backward as fast as a wide receiver, and only the wide receiver knows where they are ultimately going to end up.

Inwardly, Davis struggled with himself that first month of the season. "Everybody expected me to be Superman," he said. "For that money, I felt like I had to be Superman, too. Finally, though, I started telling myself, 'Just play football. Who cares what the coaches think or anybody else? Just do your job.'"

He loosened up. When teammates looked like they had "fish eyes" in the huddle—Davis's term for the look players get when they are scared—he calmed them down. By the Minnesota game, he had gotten back his old attitude. "I don't give a damn," Davis said. "That's my attitude. You beat me? So what? I'm coming after you the next time. I'm not backing off. It's not cockiness or whatever—I just don't give a damn."

As Davis started to feel better on the field, he started to let his personality show more off it. He told his teammates that they were aiming too low. He had played on a Super Bowl winner before and this team had just as good a chance as any to be that.

Although the Panthers defense was somewhat unknown nationally because of the team's 3–2 record, the veteran cornerback already understood that this defense had two things many others didn't. One was a lot of talent. The other was a fine mesh of personalities.

"The trick in this game is understanding it takes all types on defense," Davis explained. "You have to have a couple of guys who—if they weren't playing football—might be out stealing your car. Then you need a couple of guys who you wouldn't mind coming home with your daughter." Davis, whose sweet, gap-toothed smile seemed incongruous with his aggressive style, counted himself as one who would probably be out stealing your car.

But it was the Vikings who had stolen the win from the Panthers. So when Davis saw the film of the Minnesota game, he started telling his teammates exactly what he thought about it. It made him angry, but it also made him realize that something special was going on here.

"Guys," Davis would tell his teammates in twos and threes for days after that film session. "I was very, very upset we lost that game. We had our chances to win that game. But you know what? I know we're a good team now. We were on the road, playing a team that was playing well. We had six turnovers and we still should have won! You don't see that, but I do. We've got a good squad."

At San Francisco, Davis was used to the ownership figuring that anything less than a Super Bowl win was a failure. He saw that Panthers owner Jerry Richardson wasn't about to set that sort of goal for the season, so he tried to do it himself. "Your expectations aren't high enough," he said. "Put pressure on yourselves! We're three and two, but we can play!"

Davis's teammates listened closely. Did he know something they didn't?

ONE THING EVERY PANTHER KNEW FOR SURE WAS exactly how they each wanted to be outfitted for every game. After years of playing football, they all had their own idiosyncrasies. From a distance, the Panthers looked uniform—all white and blue and black, their silver helmets gleaming in the sun. But as the season progressed toward Game 6 of 16 regular-season contests, a home game against St. Louis, team equipment manager Jackie Miles already had a feel for how difficult it was to dress the Panthers.

Johnson wore a black, Darth Vader–like face guard because he had taken a thumb in the eye five years ago during a game. "It's not for aesthetic reasons. It's because I'm worried I'll get poked again and go blind in that eye," Johnson said. It was an odd but effective look for him. The shield actually made him look dangerous. Kevin Greene ran shoelaces through the sleeves of his jersey, then tied them tightly, so an opposing offensive lineman had nothing to grab on to. Defensive end Mike Fox got Miles to stretch a size 48 jersey over his size 52 body so offensive linemen couldn't find a place to hold him, either. "I almost lost the circulation in my arms trying to pull that jersey down sometimes," Miles laughed. Like all NFL quarterbacks, Collins had an earphone in his helmet so that coaches could call plays to him. He also had his jersey's sleeves shortened by two inches to keep his throwing arm free.

Most players wore a new pair of shoes for each game, which like all Panthers equipment is supplied for free through deals the team has with NFL-licensed manufacturers. About 30 Panthers players wore Nikes; about 25 wore Reeboks. A good helmet lasted all season for the players—the football equivalent of a baseball glove. The offensive linemen generally had the biggest heads. Miles was stunned to find out that Raghib Ismail's helmet size was a lineman-esque 8⅛. "A huge dome," Miles said of the Rocket, the speedy acquisition that Bill Polian had picked up in August from Oakland for a fifth-round draft choice.

Almost all players wore gloves to protect their hands, but the Panthers quarterbacks didn't. Neither did tight end Walls or cornerback Davis, who liked the feel of a football's pebbled leather against their bare palms.

Capers usually wore a black turtleneck under his gray shirt, but professed to be unaware of this. "I've been wearing black, huh?" Capers said. "I guess I have. Whatever Jackie [Miles] hangs in my locker, that's what I put on."

EVERYONE WORE SHORT SLEEVES FOR THE PAN-thers' sixth game of the season, October 13 at home vs. the St. Louis Rams. Again, the Panthers would enjoy a gorgeous day—68 degrees, with a slight breeze.

The 1–4 Rams weren't very good this season, but they hadn't been very good in 1995, either, and Carolina had lost to them twice. The Rams were starting five rookies on offense, including quarterback Tony Banks. Banks sometimes showed wonderful athleticism, but he seemed to fumble almost every time someone in the stands sneezed. He held the ball down too low too often when running around in the pocket, and at year's end he wound up setting an NFL record with 21 fumbles.

Banks had two things in common with Panthers wide receiver Muhsin Muhammad: They would both start Sunday and they were great friends who used to play together at Michigan State. "We're about as tight as it can get, I guess," Banks said before the game. "We were roommates my senior year. We got pretty close. We were looking forward to this game. We've been talking about it ever since draft day."

Banks said Muhammad still owes him a dinner because on draft day the two had bet which player would go first. Banks was picked forty-second overall by the Rams, one slot ahead of Muhammad at No. 43. "Kind of creepy, isn't it?" Banks said, laughing.

The Rams defense was more proven than their young offense, but not any better. Among 30 NFL teams, St. Louis's offense was ranked dead last in yardage, and their defense was ranked twenty-seventh. It was no surprise, then, that Carolina came out firing. Their first drive was a masterpiece—nine plays, 68 yards, and a nine-yard touchdown pass from Collins to Walls to finish it off.

Quickly, it was 7–0, Panthers. But the Rams rallied. On the following series, St. Louis pushed the ball 57 yards in an effort to tie the game. Then, on third-and-11 from the 18-yard line, one of the most memorable plays in Panthers history occurred. Banks, running backward and looking to throw, circled back all the way to the 34-yard line. Panthers lineman Shawn King grabbed hold of Banks around the ankles; as the panicked quarterback tried to move the football quickly to get it away, he bounced it off his knee and fumbled. He watched, helpless in King's arms, as the ball bounded away.

Charging in at the end of the play was Kevin Greene, who suddenly spotted the loose football. Greene couldn't believe his eyes. No one else around him was upright. He picked the ball up and started running. The crowd started screaming, watching this slow outside linebacker do a dash toward the end zone, 66 yards away. Rams receiver Eddie Kennison, one of the fastest players in the league, was the closest man to Greene, some 20 yards away. He started gaining on him. Greene kept running and running, but he was getting tired. "This old war dog didn't have much left," he said. "I'm not sure I've ever run sixty-six yards in my life."

Kennison kept coming. No one else had a chance. The noise washed over Greene like a wave. He made it to the 20. The 10. The five. And then, with only one or two more steps left in him, Greene jumped.

There was no reason to jump, really. Greene was just exhausted. He kicked out one of his legs in another pose and rolled into the end zone, clutching the ball. Touchdown!

"It was only a belly flop, but it was good for the gold," he said later. "I was on the ground, sprawled out, just thanking the good Lord for filling my lungs with air again." He was totally spent for the next 15 minutes and had to take in oxygen on the sideline, but his 66-yard fumble return for a touchdown had given Carolina a 14–0 lead with a minute still left in the first quarter. More important, it had relaxed the tense Panthers, who broke out in laughter at Greene's dive. "That was the funniest thing I've seen in a long time," Walls chuckled at the end of the game.

Already, Carolina had as many points in this game as it had scored in either of its last two losses, and after Greene's rumble, the floodgates opened. In the second quarter Muhammad sprinted 54 yards for a touchdown, catching the ball 20 yards downfield, breaking a tackle, and coasting in the rest of the way.

But the Rams had a chance to get back into the game when a tipped Collins pass resulted in an interception return for a touchdown, cutting Carolina's margin to 21–7 in the second quarter. The Rams kicked off and Panthers return ace Michael Bates was stopped after a mediocre return. But Bates would get another opportunity.

On that kickoff, the Rams had jumped offside, so they had to kick it again. Bates jogged back in place, knowing that special teams usually let their guard down the second time around. In fact, the punt he had blocked the week before against Minnesota had also been after a penalty.

St. Louis kicker Chip Lohmiller booted the ball, and the kick floated down to Bates at the seven. He grabbed it, took a quick look, and sprinted downfield behind a fine block by Panthers fullback Howard Griffith. No one even came close to bringing him down. After 93 yards, Bates hit the opposing end zone and jumped halfway into the stands. The former Olympic bronze medalist in the 200 meters in 1992 had given the Panthers their third 50-yard-plus touchdown of the first half. He had also made the Rams chasing him at the end look very slow.

"What about that Michael Bates?" Curtis Whitley said. "He had the medal. They didn't. Could you tell?"

The Rams never got close after that. The final score was Carolina 45, St. Louis 13, easily the most points the Panthers had ever put up in a single game. The first five Panthers touchdowns—two by Walls and one each by Greene, Muhammad, and Bates—had been scored by players who hadn't been around for Carolina's inaugural 1995 season.

"It was ugly and it was embarrassing," St. Louis coach Rich Brooks said of the game.

Not for the Panthers. This day had turned out just about perfectly. The Panthers had won by 32, Carolina had had to punt only once, and Anthony Johnson had rushed for more than 100 yards again—126 this time.

Despite the one interception, Kerry Collins had put together a fine game after the debacle against Minnesota. He threw three touchdown passes and ran the team like a pro. After the monthlong break for the injury and one terrible game, Collins's world was back in order.

Eric Davis had known the Panthers were capable of wins like this, but even late in the game, as Carolina ran off the final seconds of this impressive win, he wouldn't sugarcoat anything for his teammates. Greene sidled up to Davis on the sideline in the second half to ask him a question. They watched the offense run a play together in silence, then Greene asked the question: "Did I look like Michael Bates on my [touchdown] run?" Greene asked.

"No," Davis said firmly, shaking his head. "No way."

"Hey, c'mon now," said Greene, pretending to be hurt. "You could have at least thought about it a little bit!"

CHAPTER EIGHT

Kerry's World

THE LAVISH THREE-STORY HOUSE, LOCATED IN ONE OF south Charlotte's most prestigious neighborhoods, had everything a 23-year-old multimillionaire could want: five bedrooms, 6½ baths, a five-car garage, a heated tile floor in the master bedroom, a spiral staircase, a theater room, and a billiards room. And with 6,300 square feet, Kerry Collins had plenty of space for entertaining and housing guests. The stucco and stone exterior gave it elegant curb appeal. Plus, it was brand new.

Collins, who'd been house-hunting for months, decided instantly when he saw it in the fall of 1995 that he wanted to buy it. One of the features he especially liked was the fact that the downstairs bath, located off the hall connecting the theater and billiards rooms, included a urinal in addition to a toilet. "That's like totally a guy thing," he said.

The location was great, too—about 15 minutes from uptown Charlotte, yet still nestled in the heart of the area's urban sprawl. "I'm young and I don't want to be way out in the middle of nowhere," Collins said. "I want to be around restaurants and I want to feel like I'm close to the places where things are going on." So, Collins asked his real estate agent to strike a deal. There was just one problem: The house wasn't for sale.

Don Potter of Potter Builders Inc. was building it for himself and his wife, Susan. They were within three weeks of moving in. Susan loved the place and could hardly wait to get settled in their new home.

But Potter knew he should probably consider Collins's offer for both its monetary and political value. "I figured it would be a good move politically and could help me down the road if Kerry bought a house I'd built," Potter said. So he mentioned to Susan the possibility of selling it and building a new one for his family.

"Absolutely not!" his wife said.

"We had a pretty big blowout over it," Potter said. "Heck, she almost divorced me, but she finally agreed to it."

Collins paid $905,000 for the house, but he didn't stop there. He added even more features after the sale, installing a 100-inch pull-down television screen in the theater room and an in-ground pool and Jacuzzi in the backyard. He also converted an unfinished downstairs room into a large bar.

Collins, who is very friendly and down-to-earth, loved to host parties and get-togethers for his teammates and friends. Players came over to watch *Monday Night Football* each week during the 1996 season. Pals he grew up with would visit and stay for days and weeks at a time in the upstairs guest rooms. Some started calling it Hotel Collins. "They also called it 'the Black Hole' because people come and they don't leave for a while," Collins said with a chuckle. "They get here and just hang out."

Sometimes it seemed like an upscale frat house. Hanging out with Collins almost always meant having fun. It meant playing pool, watching movies or sporting events on the giant TV, listening to music (especially Pearl Jam), eating pizza, and drinking beer—sometimes lots of it. "I'm not going to sit here and say I'm a choirboy and I do everything perfectly, because I don't," Collins said. "I'm a fun-loving guy. That's a real part of me."

Collins didn't always party at home. He liked to go to Charlotte night clubs to listen to live music. Because of his fame and popularity, it was difficult for him to blend into crowds. Sometimes, he didn't try. Instead, he'd occasionally climb on stage and sing with the band. News like that traveled fast. Fans sometimes called the Panthers offices, area newspapers, and local television stations to tell on Collins—some because they were concerned by his actions, others because they liked to gossip.

"I wish I could sit here and say I was everything everybody wants me to be, but I'm not," Collins said. "I try to be as good a role model as I can, but I've still got to be true to Kerry Collins. Am I going to give up my life because I play professional football? No.

"This job is stressful. You've got to be crazy to stand out there on the field and let three-hundred-pound guys dance all over your face. So, am I going to go out sometimes? Yes. It's a way for me to blow off steam, let loose for a while, and just get away from it. But I don't hurt anyone. I don't drink and drive. I don't make trouble for anybody. I don't think there's a problem as long as I do it in a responsible manner, and I think I do."

That, as Collins would find out later, was a matter of opinion.

COLLINS'S ROLE IN HIS SECOND SEASON AS AN NFL quarterback was made clear by coach Dom Capers: Concentrate on efficiency rather than on trying to become a star. "You don't have to do that many great things if you can eliminate the downside of things," Capers told Collins before the season. "Most teams in this league lose because they beat themselves. Before you learn to win, you have to learn not to beat yourself.

"When you're young and the expectation level is high, sometimes you feel like you have to go out and win the game yourself. If you have that mentality, it's going to backfire on you most of the time. Don't have a gunslinger mentality, because the downside of that for us could be field position, and field position is critical."

Those were the rules, and Collins knew it. Capers figured the Panthers defense and special teams were good enough to keep the team in games, as long as the offense didn't self-destruct.

Except for his miserable four-interception performance at Minnesota, Collins was carrying out Capers's orders well, especially for a second-year quarterback. His big day against the Rams gave him eight touchdowns and six interceptions for the season.

Collins tried hard to satisfy his coaches, but deep down inside he wanted more. It bothered him that he was being so restricted. He was being handled so carefully that at times he almost felt he was being asked to play with one hand tied behind his back.

"I don't think I'd be a quarterback if I said it wasn't difficult," Collins said. "Quarterbacks have egos. I have an ego. Everybody likes the stats. Would I like my role to be a little bit more? Eventually, yeah, I'd like to see it get to that point, but right now we're winning, and that's the most important thing. As long as we're winning, I couldn't be happier."

Collins, who led Penn State to a 12–0 record in his senior college season while making first-team All-America, certainly didn't lack confidence—a confidence that sometimes bordered on downright cockiness.

"I tell him he hasn't been beaten enough yet not to have confidence," said tight end Wesley Walls. "He thinks he can beat anybody at anything. A lot of guys are competitive and confident out there, but Kerry takes it to an extreme. He's got an inner strength."

Without his self-assurance, Collins might not have made it through an emotionally trying, physically draining rookie season. He started the Panthers' final 13 games in 1995, compiling a 7–6 record that was the best by an NFL rookie quarterback since Miami's Dan Marino went 7–3 in 1983. But he also plagued the Panthers with rookie mistakes, throwing 19 interceptions and fumbling 13 times.

"I'm the kind of person who always tries to find the positives in any situation, but everything last year was just so new and so crazy," Collins said. "There were times when I thought, 'Man, this sucks.' There were times when I didn't want to go out on the field. When you feel you don't have a chance to do well, it's the worst feeling in the world. And I didn't have a chance to do well. I didn't have the maturity and I didn't have the knowledge. Sure, I had the ability, but I didn't know enough about the game or this offense."

Collins also struggled as a rookie in his relationship with offensive coordinator Joe Pendry, who had a reputation for developing conservative offenses for winning teams. Pendry had spent five seasons as the offensive coordinator for the Cleveland Browns and Kansas City Chiefs under coach Marty Schottenheimer, accentuating a balanced offense that mixed the running and passing games at both stops.

Pendry was demanding of Collins, to the point that Collins sometimes went home muttering to himself that Pendry was "impossible" to deal with. Collins once delicately described his relationship with Pendry as "a process of two people getting to know one another." The two of them had numerous one-on-one discussions about their differences during the Panthers' first season.

"It's something most quarterbacks and their coaches have to work through," Pendry said. "Especially with young guys, our job is to get them to understand their role, and that the most important thing is to get us in a position so we can win. Sometimes the relationship takes a while for the understanding part to be there. But it happens."

Collins and Pendry were getting along better so far in the '96 season, though they still clashed sometimes. "Kerry doesn't always like Joe's coaching and what he tells him," Panthers general manager Bill Polian said. "But he has learned from it and he's receptive to it."

POLIAN KNEW WHEN HE WAS SCOUTING THE 1994 COL-lege football season that the Panthers would likely choose a quarterback with the first draft pick in team history. "Very few teams get very far without a top-flight quarterback," he said.

Polian knew he could have the best quarterback available, since the Panthers owned the No. 1 pick in the 1995 draft by virtue of a coin flip with the other expansion team, the Jacksonville Jaguars. Polian and the rest of Carolina's scouting department focused on two players: Penn State's Collins and Alcorn State's Steve McNair.

Collins was bigger and more of a prototype NFL quarterback. McNair was more athletic—a multidimensional passer, scrambler, and runner often compared to San Francisco's Steve Young.

"Because of what we wanted to do in our offensive system, Kerry was a better fit for us," Polian said. "He had tremendous arm strength, great competitiveness, great leadership, and much better athletic ability than the so-called experts thought. As far as negatives, he did not have the quickest delivery in America. There was no hitch [in Collins's throwing motion, as was widely rumored before the '95 draft], but he doesn't get rid of the ball really fast. Quite honestly, he wouldn't fit into a West Coast system because of that."

The West Coast offense features a short, precise passing game, usually employing three receivers. It requires a quarterback to have an extremely quick release because most of the pass routes are based on split-second timing.

The 49ers were the masters of the West Coast offense, so even though Polian wasn't sure Collins could have been a star for San Francisco, Collins was the man he picked to lead the Panthers' efforts to try to challenge the 49ers' supremacy in the NFC West.

Even though Carolina had the No. 1 pick in the 1995 draft and could have used it to select Collins without fear that another team would take him, team officials believed they could drop down a few spots in the first round and still get him. If they did that, they'd be able to acquire extra picks via a trade. So they pulled off a deal with Cincinnati, swapping the No. 1 choice for the Nos. 5 and 36 selections. The gamble paid off. No other team drafted Collins before the Panthers' turn to pick arrived.

Moments after Collins was officially drafted, owner Jerry Richardson telephoned him, reaching him where he was sitting on a couch at New York's Marriott Marquis Hotel, where the draft was being held.

"Son," Richardson said to Collins, "do you know what the Lombardi trophy is?"

"Yes, sir, I sure do," said Collins, fully aware that the trophy is presented each year to the team that wins the Super Bowl.

"Well, good," Richardson responded. "You're going to be the guy to take us there."

Instantly, at age twenty-two, Collins was anointed the Panthers' franchise player. It was as if Richardson had taken a sword and touched a kneeling Collins on both shoulders.

"That set the tone right off the bat," Collins said. "I knew Mr. Richardson was serious and committed. I could tell he had a lot of pride in his voice. I could tell he was convinced he was going to do it."

Collins was convinced, too.

"Oh definitely," he said. "I believed it in my heart right from the beginning."

As excited as he was to be a first-round pick and to be going to a team with an owner who was committed to winning—he knew that many NFL owners weren't—Collins wasn't thrilled to get selected by an expansion team he'd never seen play before.

He grew up in West Lawn, Pennsylvania, near Philadelphia, going to Eagles games at Veterans Stadium and dreaming of playing for an NFL team steeped in tradition, like the Eagles or the Chicago Bears.

"I've always considered myself a traditional kind of person, and to go into something with no background at all was a little disappointing," Collins said. "But, on the flip side of that, it's a lot of fun being part of something brand new and getting a chance to establish a great tradition."

Still, even during a second season that already looked very promising, Collins sometimes struggled with the idea of playing for a team that hadn't existed during his childhood. "Sometimes when we're playing and I look out there on the field, it's different to see our team and our uniforms because I'm not used to it," Collins said. "It has kind of a surreal overtone to it. It's almost like I feel, 'Am I really in the NFL?'"

COLLINS MIGHT NOT HAVE BEEN IN THE NFL HAD HE not transferred from Lebanon High to Wilson High midway through his sophomore year in 1986. The move was a pivotal factor in his athletic development, but one that will haunt him forever in other ways. He believes it contributed to the divorce of his parents and that it permanently altered his relationship with them, dividing his family instead of bringing them closer together. "It hasn't been a typical father-son, mother-son relationship since then," Collins said. "We did it because of sports. It was like they looked at me and said, 'Okay, we've done this. He's an athlete now.' That's how they treated me after that."

For the rest of his teenage years, he felt more like a star-in-development than a son. "I probably lost some of my adolescence," Collins said. "But the goal was to get me in a better athletic environment, where I'd be able to earn a college scholarship."

The move came after a rift developed between Collins's father, Pat, and the Lebanon High School coach, Hal Donley. One of the factors was that Donley's son, Ed, had competed with Collins for the team's starting quarterback position. Collins won the starting job, but neither he nor his father was convinced that Donley was looking out for Collins's best interests.

"I got really beat up in a game on a Friday and we came right back with a full scrimmage the following Monday," Collins said. "I ended up getting a broken ankle in that practice. I'm laying there on the field and he [Donley] didn't even come over. It was like, 'He's hurt. So what?'"

Ten years later, Donley still bristled when asked about the subject. "There are going to be different opinions and different stories about what happened," Donley said. "He went down at the line of scrimmage and a guy accidentally rolled on his ankle. But there was a lot of background stuff people don't even know about. It's just not worth rehashing."

When it happened, Pat Collins thought he had no choice except to move Kerry to Wilson High in West Lawn, 30 miles from Lebanon, even though it required a change of residence. According to Kerry, his mother, Roseanne, opposed the move and stayed in Lebanon with their other son, Pat Jr., while Pat Sr. and Kerry began living in an apartment in West Lawn.

"The bottom line was, I thought Kerry was being abused," his father said. "It wasn't easy for him to leave all his friends at school. He had second thoughts, but I had more insight into the situation and knew it had to be done."

Suddenly Collins, 14, not only had to get used to a new set of friends at a new school, but also found himself in the middle of a full-blown controversy after school officials in Lebanon tried to block the move. "Basically, they were saying that I had moved him down there and left him there by himself, which was utterly ridiculous," Pat Collins said. "It got to the point where the school administrators were harassing him, trying to make him ineligible for the team. It really woke Kerry up to the real world. He got hard because of it. He developed some thick skin."

For Kerry, a multisport standout, it was a nightmare.

"The last thing you want to do as a fourteen-year-old is make any enemies," he said.

There was a formal hearing on the case, but eventually the matter was dropped. Collins's eligibility was not affected. He went on to become an all-state star at Wilson High, quarterbacking the football team to the state championship game during his senior year and earning a scholarship to Penn State.

Pat Collins said that he has never questioned the decision to move Kerry to another school, but that he regrets the emotional toll it took on his son. "My only goal was to give him a good shot in a fair situation," Pat said. "It's easy to second-guess. I don't regret the decision on moving, but I might have done a couple of more things to be a little bit more sensitive to his needs emotionally. I'm sure he feels to a certain extent he lost out on some of the family's closeness and togetherness. But life is tough and you've got to make decisions. It's always a tradeoff."

Those words sound as cold as a winter day to Kerry, but he never let the fact that he didn't feel close to either of his parents stop him from fulfilling the athletic destiny his father had foretold at an early age. "Let's face it, I moved to get to the pros," Collins said. "My dad thought I had a gift and that was the ultimate goal. Now that I'm here and I've made it, maybe I can forget about it and go back to being myself.

"I think I kind of lost touch with reality for a long time. Athletics has given me a great life and a lot of great things, but I was so much more before. I was a good person first, then I was an athlete. Then, when we moved, it was like I became just an athlete. I think I lost some of the interpersonal things you lose when people put you on a pedestal. It's only been very recently that I started to get those things back."

WHEN HIS ROOKIE SEASON WITH THE PANTHERS CON-cluded, Collins found himself searching for his place in this new world. Life in the NFL was much different from being a college quarterback and the demands on him were greater than he'd ever imagined. "Everything changed so dramatically," Collins said. "I asked myself, 'Where do I as Kerry Collins fit into all of this?'"

So much was happening so fast, he had to stop and get off the merry-go-round. He needed a period of introspection. In less than a year, he had become richer than he'd ever imagined after signing a six-year, $21.6 million contract. He had also been thrust into a starting quarterback job in the fourth game of his NFL career and because of it, had emerged as a blossoming sports celebrity not only in Charlotte but around the country. Female fans screamed hysterically when they saw him. Magazines called him one of the country's most eligible bachelors. Young children begged for autographs. Some even found out where he lived and rang his doorbell. Almost always, Collins signed whatever they brought—a football, an item of clothing, a picture, a trading card, or even just a piece of paper.

Yet he grappled with how he really should be reacting to all the attention he was getting. Was it really so important to be accommodating? That was his nature, but the demands seemed unending. When was it okay to say no?

"I was a little skeptical of being open to people who wanted my autograph," Collins said. "I enjoy meeting and talking to people, but I wondered if I should just be cold. Should I take the approach that it's no big deal? I wondered, 'Is it just an autograph or does it really mean something?'"

Two things gave Collins his answer. First, there was the young boy who rang Collins's doorbell a few days before Christmas and immediately exclaimed 'Great!' when Collins signed something for him. Second, there was the Pearl Jam concert in Charlotte in October 1996, when Collins got a chance to go backstage and meet the group's lead singer—his rock hero—Eddie Vedder. "You've got to understand, this guy is like an icon," Collins said. "When I was going through college, Pearl Jam was like *the* band. They were the identity of my college years."

Collins knew Vedder was a sports fan and brought one of his number 12 Panthers jerseys to the concert to give Vedder.

"I took a little bit of a chance," Collins said. "I gave him my jersey and he took me back into his dressing room. He got out a T-shirt like he wore on stage that night. It was the coolest thing: Down in the corner, he wrote 'number twelve' in a black magic marker and on the back he wrote 'Eddie Vedder.' He put his initials, 'E.V.,' on the inside tag. To me, it was so cool. It wasn't a signature. It meant so much more than an autograph. To this day, it's one of the greatest experiences of my life. I called my friends from college the next day and said, 'Wait till you hear what happened to me last night!' "

HOWIE LONG, THE FOX-TV COMMENTATOR AND FORmer star defensive lineman for the Raiders, once said he thought Collins looked so big he could "eat a sandwich off the top of my head. He makes Terry Bradshaw look like Doug Flutie."

Flutie, the former Heisman Trophy–winning quarterback from Boston College who later became a star in the Canadian Football League, is 5′ 9″. Bradshaw, 6′ 3″, weighed 210 pounds when he quarterbacked the Pittsburgh Steelers to four Super Bowl titles in the 1970s. At 6′ 5″, Collins is built like a tight end. He's the new prototype, a giant, strong quarterback able to take the punishment handed out by today's faster and bulkier defensive linemen and linebackers.

It took him less than two seasons to gain the respect of Bradshaw, who joined Long on the set of Fox's NFL pregame shows.

"The most important thing for me is when I watch a quarterback in the pocket," Bradshaw said. "I look at a guy's feet and I've got to see if he's comfortable. If he's comfortable then, man, he's automatically got a big check with me." When Bradshaw looked at Collins's feet, he saw calm and poise.

"The second thing is, I want to see a quarterback throw," Bradshaw continued. "And this kid Collins can gun it—tight spirals all day long."

Someday Collins would like to join Bradshaw in the select group of quarterbacks who have led their teams to more than one Super Bowl title. As the 1996 season neared its midpoint, he was already thinking about trying to win the first football championship of his life.

As successful as he was at West Lawn High and Penn State, he had narrowly missed winning championships at both places. He quarterbacked West Lawn to the 1989 Pennsylvania Class AAAA state championship game as a senior, but threw a critical second-half interception in the end zone in a 12–7 loss to Upper St. Clair.

"We were right in front of the goal line, getting ready to get into the end zone and score," Collins said. "We ran a little rollout pass play. A guy stepped right in front of me and picked it off."

Collins led Penn State to a 12–0 record during his senior season in college in 1994, but the Nittany Lions finished second in the national rankings, behind 12–0 Nebraska. If ever there was a case for a playoff tournament being added to big-time college football to replace the poll system, Collins thought the Penn State–Nebraska argument was it. The national title should be decided on the field, not by the polls of college coaches and sportswriters. Penn State vs. Nebraska that year might have been one of the great matchups of all time in college football. Penn State's offense had three players selected in the first nine picks of the 1995 NFL draft: running back Ki-Jana Carter (No. 1 to Cincinnati); Collins (No. 5) and tight end Kyle Brady (No. 9 to the New York Jets). Nebraska, a team that featured running back Lawrence Phillips and quarterback Tommie Frazier, would go on to win a second national title in the '95 season.

"It was a shame we didn't play those guys and settle it once and for all," Collins said. "If they beat us, fine. At least they'd always know and we'd always know and Joe [Paterno, Penn State's head coach] would always know. But now, none of us will ever know. That really bugs me. I'd play them out in the street today if I could."

So the Panthers had drafted a hungry quarterback when they selected Kerry Collins—just the kind of ultracompetitive leader Jerry Richardson needed to head the chase for the Vince Lombardi Trophy. But as Polian would say many times, the process of developing Collins into a superior quarterback—and the Panthers into a championship-caliber team—was a marathon, not a sprint, and some of the toughest miles the Panthers would face in 1996 loomed just over the horizon.

CHAPTER NINE

Problem Child, Problem Season

PANTHERS STARTING CENTER CURTIS WHITLEY STARED at the single line of the "crystal meth" amphetamine he had neatly arranged in front of his nose. The powdery drug—"poor man's cocaine," some called it—just lay there on the bathroom counter in the women's room of an exclusive Charlotte restaurant in October 1996. Whitley had already rolled a hundred-dollar bill into a tiny tube, preparing to snort it.

This was wild, Whitley thought to himself. *Wild!* This was the real him—not the watered-down version that three years in the NFL alcohol and drug program had forced him to become. This was Curtis "I-Don't-Give-a-Damn" Whitley, the guy who once got stopped by a cop in San Diego and ate the marijuana cigarette he was bringing to a friend before the policeman could get to the car window. This was the friendly partier everyone liked, the guy who seized the day—and the night—and let someone else worry about tomorrow.

Whitley, 27, said he had never bought drugs in his life. Not once.

But ever since his college days at Clemson, he had experimented with drugs occasionally when someone else had them. "I don't believe there are many drugs that I haven't done at one time or another," Whitley said, reflecting on his actions. "When they're around, it's like there is some devil on my shoulder."

Whitley had experimented with crystal meth "quite often," he said, in the off-seasons while playing for the San Diego Chargers from 1992 to 1994. The drug, used widely by many fighting men in World War II to combat fatigue and enhance performance, often caused a temporary sense of elation much like cocaine. Some researchers now call it "the drug of the '90s."

When Whitley had used it before, he felt euphoric and ready to move, ready to *do* something. One night he had stayed up until the wee hours building a picnic table while high on the drug. Now, kneeling in the bathroom of a restaurant, Whitley was about to do it again. A female friend of Whitley's wife had offered him the crystal meth, and he had quietly agreed to take her up on it. No one else at the table noticed. The rest of the group, including his wife, Tracy, had no idea that the woman and Whitley had actually ended up in the women's room with the baggie full of crystal meth. They had no idea what was taking place on the bathroom counter near the sink, where Curtis Whitley was thinking about whether to walk the tightrope one more time.

It was early in the week, several days before the 4–2 Panthers were to host New Orleans in a game they needed to win to put some more distance between themselves and the .500 mark. Whitley knew he would get drug-tested at least once or twice more during the week (as a member of the NFL alcohol and drug program, he usually got tested three times a week). He was only one mess-up away from a four-game suspension.

He had already lost $164,705—nearly one quarter of his salary—in April 1996 after botching a set of directives handed down from the NFL. The league had said they couldn't find Whitley in Arizona when they wanted to test him. It was a big deal, because the NFL always needed to test Whitley. For three years, he had lived with a rigorous

10-times-a-month testing schedule, which had started back in San Diego. The Chargers had required Whitley to enter the NFL alcohol and drug program because he had run a stoplight in July 1994 while legally drunk and had caused a traffic accident.

The woman whose car Whitley collided with eventually filed a civil suit against him. Because he had no auto insurance at the time, Whitley said, he had to buy the woman—who suffered minor injuries—a new car and pay her $100,000 in the ensuing settlement.

The Chargers wouldn't let him back on the team unless he went to an alcohol rehabilitation center and entered the NFL drug program. General manager Bobby Beathard said Whitley needed to learn that the NFL wasn't "adult nursery school." Whitley desperately needed his job and would do anything to keep it. So, he did everything the Chargers asked, spending 26 days at the Betty Ford Clinic in Rancho Mirage, California, soon after the accident. Because he had caused a wreck while driving drunk—Whitley's blood-alcohol level was .10—Whitley was diagnosed with an alcohol problem and told not to drink anymore.

He did anyway.

But he was fairly careful. Since joining the Panthers in 1995 and almost immediately becoming the anchor of their offensive line, Whitley had made sure not to "throw my drinking in their face," as he said. But he had drunk beer a number of times—at Collins's Monday-night parties with the team, at his own home, and at restaurants.

"If I want to drink, I'm going to drink," Whitley said. "I don't give a shit. . . . After a long hard day or something, a nice cold beer sounds so good."

Whitley had found out that alcohol wouldn't show up in a urine specimen unless you drank some that morning right before you got tested. And even if you were cutting it too close, theoretically you could drink a gallon of herbal tea and mask the alcohol in your system. "Or so I've been told," he said with a wink.

Even though Whitley kept passing the tests, he had gotten sick of them. He had a stormy relationship with Dr. Lawrence Brown, the man in charge of the NFL's drug-testing program. Whitley had cursed out Brown a number of times on the phone. "I want my life back!" Whitley would scream, interlacing his speech with profanities.

But rules were rules, and Whitley was required to be in the program for at least another 18 months because he had missed a test in April. He also had to tell the NFL where he was staying at all times—phone number, address, the works—so they could randomly test him whenever they wanted to.

Whitley had gone to Arizona to take a horse there to breed. He had told the NFL he was staying in a Holiday Inn, but had accidentally given them the wrong name of the Arizona city. Unable to locate him for a test, the NFL had fined him four games' pay. Whitley appealed the fine, but he couldn't get the NFL to see his side of the issue in the course of a telephone conference call that had been held in training camp—Whitley in Spartanburg and NFL officials in New York. So Whitley, a spontaneous sort who hated the idea of being held on such a tight leash, was one mistake away from a very major problem.

His tangles with the NFL authorities were in stark contrast to the Panthers' clean image, and Whitley knew it. "Maybe I'm the example," he said. "Maybe I'm the guy *not* to be. Maybe that's my value to this team. . . . Don't be that guy. That may be my place in history for the Carolina Panthers. Who knows?"

Maybe so? Who knew?

Whitley looked down once more at the line of crystal meth. Then he bent his head forward, stuck the hundred-dollar bill into one nostril and inhaled the drug straight up his nose.

THE 2–5 NEW ORLEANS TEAM THAT VISITED ERICSSON Stadium on October 20 was closer to collapse than anyone knew. Coach Jim Mora had grown increasingly frustrated with his players and the organization. More than any other single team, New Orleans had lost player after player to the Panthers in the free-agent market: Carolina tight end Wesley Walls, safety Brett Maxie, cornerback Toi Cook, and linebacker Sam Mills were all former Saints who had jumped ship.

Most of all, Mora hated losing Sam Mills, who was now the 37-year-old heart of the Panthers defense after playing the same role for years in New Orleans. Before the game, Mora said that Mills was "the favorite player I've ever coached—absolutely the best. I coached him for twelve years, and I never saw him loaf through a single practice or a single game. I can't say that about any other player I've coached."

Mills—whose off-the-field behavior was about as polar opposite of Whitley's as you could get—always had a special feeling when he faced his old team. Some of that feeling evaporated quickly early in the first quarter on a sunny, 62-degree day, when Mills, on New Orleans' first play of the game, thought he had an angle on Saints running back Mario Bates after Bates caught a short pass. Instead, Bates, the brother of Panthers kick returner Michael Bates, zipped right around Mills for 15 yards. It made Mills feel old. And slow.

The Panthers held off New Orleans on that first series anyway, and Mills jogged to the sideline and sought out Michael Bates, who is faster than his brother Mario and has that 1992 bronze medal to prove it. "Did you see your brother cut around the corner on me?" Mills asked Bates as the two watched the offense. "And he doesn't even have a medal."

The first half settled into a low-scoring game—two Panthers field goals from John Kasay and one New Orleans touchdown run from Ray Zellars provided all the points. New Orleans left the field feeling pretty good at halftime, ahead 7–6.

The Panthers needed a play, and they got it late in the third quarter from Mark Carrier—who had almost been forgotten in the previous two games. Carrier still led the Panthers in receptions, but if you believed his locker, that wouldn't last for long. Carrier altered the nameplate on the top of his locker with adhesive tape and Magic Marker before the New Orleans game, changing it to read "Mark Casper." As in "the friendly ghost." As in disappearing from the Panthers offense.

"Hey, you've got to laugh to keep from crying," Carrier said.

Carrier hadn't caught a pass the week before against St. Louis—only the second time in his 22 games as a Panther that he had been shut out. But on third-and-eight from the New Orleans 13, Collins looked for Carrier cutting over the middle. He found him, and Carrier scored. That pushed Carolina to a 16–7 lead late in the quarter.

Carrier bent down briefly to offer a prayer after the TD, and then he spied Greg Good, a 39-year-old social worker from Winston-Salem who was wearing Carrier's jersey and sitting in the front row of Ericsson Stadium the way he did every week. Carrier didn't know Good's name, but the two had talked some during warmups, and Carrier had been impressed by both Good and Greg Jr., his eight-year-old son.

"I thought about giving him a TD ball for a while," Carrier said. "He's always there for me. But I'd never scored in the end zone where he's been sitting." Carrier jogged over and carefully tossed the ball to Good, who showed good reaction time and snagged it. "I just wanted Mark to jump up here or something," Good said excitedly. "But he did me one better than that."

New Orleans's last chance at coming back faltered on fourth-and-one from the Carolina 31 early in the fourth quarter. Mora disdained the field goal and decided to go for the first down.

"I figured they were going to run the ball inside," Mills said. "And if you were going to guess, you'd figure they'd run behind Willie Roaf and Jim Dombrowski [on the left side]."

That's exactly what New Orleans did. The Panthers and New Orleans lines locked up, with no forward or backward movement. "I knew pretty much right then it was going to be him and me," Mills said.

Zellars didn't try to jump; instead, he tried to run right through Mills. Mills came with everything he had, filling the one gap he thought Zellars would hit.

"He lowered his shoulder," Mills said. "I lowered mine. We met."

Mills won. That was the last chance New Orleans had.

MILLS HAD BEEN MAKING PLAYS LIKE THAT ALL HIS life. Generously listed at 5′ 9″, he had been told he was too short to become a football player time and again. In college, he played football at Division III Montclair State—he was the first of Sam and Juanita Mills's 11 children to obtain a college degree, so his family already thought of him as a success at age 23. The pro career he had hoped for at college didn't look promising, however. He didn't get drafted. He got cut by the Cleveland Browns and the Canadian Football League's Toronto Argonauts, so he got a high school teaching job in New Jersey, instructing students in woodworking and photography for $13,600 a year.

But the football flame wouldn't die, and in 1982, Mills went to an open tryout with the USFL's Philadelphia Stars. Joe Pendry, now Carolina's offensive coordinator, was a Stars coach and liked what he saw. In the back of Pendry's beige Chevrolet van, he offered Mills a contract on the spot for $25,000.

Mills was ecstatic. "I would have played for a lot less than that," Mills said later.

Mora was the coach of that Stars team, and Mills was his defensive stud. He brought Mills along with him to New Orleans in 1986 when Mora got the head coaching job there. For nine years, Mills patrolled the middle of the Saints defense, earning a reputation for never being out of position and for hitting incredibly hard.

"Just once I'd like to get a hit like he does," New York Giants linebacker Lawrence Taylor once said of Mills. "It has to be better than sex."

With a wife and three children—18, 13, and 13 during the 1996 season—and a good life in New Orleans, Mills seemed likely to stay there for the duration of his career. But Carolina lured him away by making him feel more wanted in the 1995 off-season. The money was the same—$2.8 million over two years—but Mills felt that New Orleans only grudgingly matched the deal the Panthers had been so eager to give him. He left for Carolina and has been the "heart and soul" of the Panthers, as Polian said, ever since.

Team owner Jerry Richardson said of Mills, "Sam is extraordinary. In my mind, he is the greatest representation of what we're trying to do. He's selfless. He never complains. He does his job. The players are impressed with him and follow him. He is one of the most unusual people I know."

Mills rarely raised his voice and enjoyed the locker-room give-and-take. With his gold-rimmed glasses and squat build, he looked more like an accountant who knew his way around a YMCA weight room than an NFL player. The players loved to kid him about his diminutive stature, too. Hardly a Panthers game went by where some defensive player wouldn't scan the huddle, look right over Mills's helmet, and yell, "Where's Sam?"

They teased him even more about his age. Mills was relieved when punter Rohn Stark joined the team just before the season, because Stark was also 37 years old—in fact, one month older than Mills. They were the only two players in the Panthers locker room born in the 1950s.

Stark was just a punter, though, and kickers rarely engage much in the interplay in NFL locker rooms. So Mills was still the butt of all the "old" jokes.

"What did it feel like to play with leather helmets?" Panthers wide receiver Willie Green would sometimes ask. "What was it like to play before television was invented?"

Mills would laugh—then go out and do his job. He was a stickler for preparedness. Mills was the only Panthers player who always came in on Tuesdays—the players' off day—to get a head start watching film on the following week's opponent. On the field he was always making sure his gloves were dry, just in case a ball came his way. Fox-TV analyst Matt Millen once said that on the day of Mills's birth, he "came out in the hitting position." Capers, who had coached the defensive backs in New Orleans while Mills was playing linebacker, loved him.

Mills had once thought he would play only until he was about 32, but he kept improving. His son Sam III, a high school senior, was closer in age to most of the Panthers players than Mills was. Mills didn't like the rap music many of the Panthers liked to play while working out in the weight room, so he would often put Marvin Gaye or *Greatest Hits of the '70s* on the stereo instead. Every Christmas, Mills had to play Nat King Cole's Christmas CD before any of his three children got to open their presents.

He was a good man in a hard business. And he was having a Pro Bowl–caliber year well before he decked Zellars.

"It doesn't bother me," Mills said of the talk about how he is getting old. "I am. Actually, I think that's the nice side of it—*getting* old. They could just say he *is* old."

MILLS'S PLAY HAD CEMENTED CAROLINA'S WIN, AND, in retrospect, helped seal the fate of his old coach, Jim Mora.

Carolina tacked on one last field goal to make the final tally Carolina 19, New Orleans 7. The Panthers had improved to 5–2.

Mora was furious. He flew into a profanity-laced rage after his team lost Sunday at a postgame press conference, stunning the reporters who held tape recorders near his red face. In just six minutes with the press, he uttered 25 curse words. He started off with "Well, what happened was, that second half we got our asses kicked." He progressed to "I'm totally embarrassed and totally ashamed. Our coaches did a horrible job. Our players did a horrible job. We got our asses kicked in the second half. We stunk. The second half was an abomination. Terrible, terrible, terrible." And: "It was a horseshit performance by our football team. Horseshit! It was an embarrassing, shameful coaching and playing performance by the New Orleans Saints. I couldn't be more upset. . . . We just lost patience [with the running game]. It's stupid. Stupid! That's why we're two and six."

The next day, Mora stunned the NFL further. He quit. Capers and Mills—both old friends of Mora's—had inadvertently forced him out of his job.

WHITLEY HAD PLAYED WELL IN THE NEW ORLEANS game, helping the Panthers rush for 159 yards against the Saints. He was the first person mentioned in *The Charlotte Observer*'s lead story on the game, in which he was described as "puffing a victory cigar" and chuckling at the Saints' ineffectiveness against Carolina. The game had been the twenty-third consecutive start for the Panthers center—he and fellow offensive lineman Blake Brockermeyer were the only two offensive players to start every game in Panthers history.

And so far, so good on the crystal meth. Whitley had given a drug tester a urine specimen two days after doing the single line of the amphetamine and had heard nothing about it.

Perhaps his carefree attitude stemmed from the fact that football had always come easy for him. He had always been a good football player. "For me, playing football has been easy," he said. "I've never really had to train hard for it."

Whitley grew up a southern boy with an affinity for horses and farming. The bumper sticker on the back of the RV that he sometimes took his family camping in read HAVE YOU HUGGED YOUR HORSE TODAY? A big, sloppy player with a natural wit, he was the closest thing the Panthers had on their team to the movie actor and former *Saturday Night Live* star Chris Farley.

He was raised in Smithfield, North Carolina, on a 200-acre farm just three hours from Charlotte. His father planted tobacco and beans, and Whitley sometimes used to jog in place beside his father's tractor, dreaming of making the NFL.

He was given a Miami Dolphins football uniform when he was four and he wore it until it could practically stand up by itself. He had always loved the game, and he had the size and the skills to play football at the highest level. Whitley could figure out an opponents' pass-rush scheme in a second and call it out to his teammates, but his decision-making ability off the field was always questionable.

In college, Whitley had gotten thrown off Clemson's team by coach Danny Ford, who was not a strong disciplinarian. As a sophomore, Whitley and another Tigers player had beaten up a Clemson student in the restroom of a Clemson bar in early 1989 and that caused his dismissal from the school. So he transferred to Chowan, a small school in North Carolina, but begged for another chance when Ken Hatfield took over the head coaching job at Clemson in 1990.

Hatfield gave Whitley another chance, and Whitley actually managed to get through three years at Clemson—drinking beer and tequila on and off throughout his stay and playing some fine football—with only one incident when Hatfield sent Whitley home early from the Hall of Fame Bowl game for violating team rules.

In 1992, San Diego drafted him in the fifth round.

Way out on the West Coast, far away from his checkered past, Whitley had another opportunity.

"I've always been good with fresh starts for about a year and a half," Whitley said. "Then the wheels start coming off."

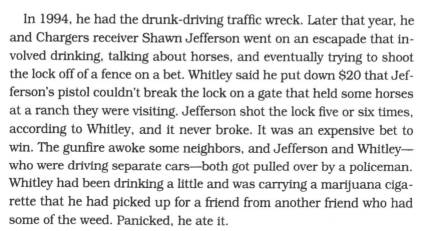

In 1994, he had the drunk-driving traffic wreck. Later that year, he and Chargers receiver Shawn Jefferson went on an escapade that involved drinking, talking about horses, and eventually trying to shoot the lock off of a fence on a bet. Whitley said he put down $20 that Jefferson's pistol couldn't break the lock on a gate that held some horses at a ranch they were visiting. Jefferson shot the lock five or six times, according to Whitley, and it never broke. It was an expensive bet to win. The gunfire awoke some neighbors, and Jefferson and Whitley—who were driving separate cars—both got pulled over by a policeman. Whitley had been drinking a little and was carrying a marijuana cigarette that he had picked up for a friend from another friend who had some of the weed. Panicked, he ate it.

"It didn't taste good at all," Whitley said.

A few days later, his NFL drug test showed up positive for marijuana. Whitley claims the NFL let him out of that one, reasoning that his story sounded too strange to be anything but true. (The NFL and the Panthers are prohibited from commenting on Whitley's specific problems due to confidentiality guidelines in the NFL drug policy). He was not charged by the California police in the incident, either.

WHITLEY AND HIS WIFE, TRACY, HAVE TWO CHILDREN, A daughter, Hannah, and a son, Curtis Jr. Whitley has said he is happiest either with them or with his horses. He grew up around the graceful animals and liked to dabble in all sorts of equine pursuits—breeding horses, riding them, and raising them. He sometimes spent off-days during the Panthers season in Clover, South Carolina, about 40 miles away, with the four horses he owned and stabled there.

As the season neared its midway point, Whitley was feeling good. He was playing well and his one recent brush with possible disaster—the single line of crystal meth—appeared to have gone by unnoticed. The morning after he snorted the drug he had wished that he hadn't done it. But now, Whitley was happy.

But several days before the Panthers' seventh game of the season against Philadelphia, the phone rang. Whitley's world was 10 seconds from crashing in on him. The call was from the NFL.

The crystal meth had shown up on the test. Whitley was about to get suspended for four games and lose four more paychecks. The NFL would announce the suspension the following week. Whitley could play in this game, but then he would be lost for a month. One more positive test, and Whitley would be banned from the NFL for a year. One more after that, and he would be banned from the league for life.

The news shook Whitley badly, but he knew he was guilty. When the NFL asked him what he had to say about the test, he said tiredly, "You're right. You got me." Later Whitley would say, "If I want to do something, I do it. That's kind of how I live. And my daddy always told me, 'If you're going to play, you've got to pay.' I played and I paid."

Financially, Whitley would lose $329,410 of his 1996 base pay of $700,000—$164,705 for this penalty and $164,705 for the missed test in April. He would also lose his games-started streak, and many of his friends on the team as well.

He had one more game before the suspension, so he stayed out of trouble and quietly tried to prepare himself for Philadelphia.

KERRY COLLINS HAD GROWN UP LOVING THE PHILA-delphia Eagles. When he was young, he had an Eagles helmet that he loved to wear—indoors. "I used to put it on and run around the house, trying to go through doors and stuff," Collins remembered.

A typical autumn Sunday before Kerry was a teenager followed a pattern. "I'd have a midget football game first," Collins said. "Then we'd go to my grandma's and she'd cook this huge dinner for us. Then we'd go and crash on the floor and watch the game. Dad would fall asleep.

"At halftime, we'd wake my dad up and make him go out and throw some passes to us. Then Patrick [Collins's older brother] and me would just go out and beat the heck out of each other."

Collins's father had taken his two sons to a couple of games at Veterans Stadium, noted for its "700" level upper deck, one of the most blue-collar, nastiest upper decks in all of sports.

"We sat in the nosebleed section," Collins said, "so we got the full effect. What I mainly remember is all these big old fat guys, all of them drunk, yelling at people. I'm a little kid, just taking it all in."

The Carolina Panthers' endless source of inspiration:
the "Indomitable Spirit," guarding an entrance to
Ericsson Stadium.

1

2

The man responsible for building the Panthers franchise: general manager Bill Polian, greeting punter Rohn Stark before a game.

Head coach Dom Capers, the mastermind behind Carolina's successful second season.

Team president Mike McCormack, who helped build the organization from the ground floor up, poses inside Ericsson Stadium.

Opening day at Ericsson Stadium, August 3, 1996: an exhibition game between the Carolina Panthers and the Chicago Bears. The Panthers would christen their new stadium with a 30–12 win.

5

6

The Reverend Billy Graham (right) dedicated the Panthers' inaugural season at Ericsson Stadium while team owner Jerry Richardson looked on.

"Salt & Pepper": Kevin Greene and Lamar Lathon, two distinct personalities whose initial differences off the field translated into immediate success on it.

Defensive team captain Sam Mills headed a stingy Carolina defense that allowed a miserly 13.6 points per game.

Tight end Wesley Walls hauls one in against his old team, the New Orleans Saints.

"Franchise" quarterback Kerry Collins—the first player drafted by the organization.

11

Anthony Johnson
(#23) filled in with
over 1,000 yards
rushing when first-
round draft pick
Tshimanga
Biakabutuka went
down with a season-
ending knee injury.

Offensive
tackle Blake
Brockermeyer
leads a cheer
on the
sidelines.

Two key components of Carolina's secondary: cornerbacks Tyrone Poole (left) and Eric Davis.

13

Free safety Chad Cota. Poole and Davis could afford to cheat a little on their coverage, knowing that Cota roamed the open field behind them. Here he celebrates his game-clinching interception against the Pittsburgh Steelers in the last game of the regular season.

14

Problem child Curtis Whitley— fined $329,410 and suspended for four games after violating the NFL's substance abuse policy.

15

Placekicker John Kasay drills yet another field goal on his way to an NFL scoring title and a Pro Bowl season.

16

17

Linebacker Kevin Greene was all smiles after nailing 49ers quarterback Steve Young in Game 1 of the team's two-game series. Carolina's sweep of the 49ers showed that the Panthers were for real.

Lamar Lathon
tried unsuccess-
fully to intimi-
date Philadelphia
Eagles quarter-
back Ty Detmer.
Detmer carved
up the Panthers
defense for 342
yards—one of
the few defen-
sive lapses of
Carolina's 1996
season.

18

Rocket Ismail, the
Panthers' eccentric
wide receiver, scored
his only touchdown
on this 35-yard
reverse against the
New York Giants.

19

Willie "Touchdown Machine" Green celebrates after the second of his two touchdown catches against the Houston Oilers late in the season.

Kerry Collins holds a football high as he walks off the field after Carolina's nail-biting home win over Pittsburgh in the final regular-season game. The win clinched the NFC West championship and a first-round playoff bye for Carolina.

Ho! Ho! Ho! Kevin Greene and Lamar Lathon celebrated Carolina's undefeated December in their own unique way.

23

Sporting wide receiver Mark Carrier's #83 jersey, Panthers fan Greg Good cradles the ball given to him by Carrier after the wide receiver scored a touchdown during a 19–7 midseason win over New Orleans.

Defensive lineman Les Miller drops Dallas quarterback Troy Aikman for a loss during Carolina's playoff victory over the Cowboys.

24

Lamar Lathon sported a somewhat friendlier attitude after comments he made sparked controversy at a midseason team meeting.

25

A familiar gesture from Coach Capers and the Carolina Panthers organization: acknowledging the dedication of their fans.

26

The ever-exuberant Kevin Greene, whooping it up for the fans in Carolina.

27

28

A season of contrasts: Above, Sam Mills celebrates Carolina's
early-season whipping of the San Francisco 49ers. Below, Mills is
consoled by Packers wide receiver Andre Rison as Green Bay sends
Carolina home without that coveted trip to the 1997 Super Bowl.

29

30

The Panthers' magical season came to a cold end in the NFC Championship Game when Green Bay's Dorsey Levens (right) outbattled Eric Davis for a 29-yard touchdown that sparked a 17-point second quarter for the Packers.

The Eagles had made a point of cleaning up the "700" section since Collins had been there, but there would undoubtedly be a few drunk, fat guys left, and this Sunday they would all be yelling at Collins.

Collins would have his own cheering section there, too. About 200 of Collins's former coaches, teachers, friends, and family made the 90-minute ride (in three charter buses) from his hometown of West Lawn to see him play against his boyhood team.

They saw a great quarterback performance that day—but not by Kerry. Instead, Philadelphia quarterback Ty Detmer stole the hometown crowd's hearts.

At 6 feet and 194 pounds, Detmer was a slightly built quarterback who had taken over for the Eagles after Rodney Peete had gotten hurt. The week before he had thrown four touchdown passes—all to Irving Fryar—and Philadelphia fans were wondering if he shouldn't be their full-time starter.

Panthers linebacker Lamar Lathon saw Detmer on the field before the game and could barely stifle a laugh. "They built Detmer up to be a world beater," Lathon said later. "They were saying things like 'Oh this team has taken off since he was the quarterback.' I just looked at this little guy and I was, like, 'How in the hell is he doing all this stuff?'"

Lathon knew what he would do. "Man, I'm going to whip his ass," he said to himself. "The tackle they had playing in front of me, I knew there was no way that guy was going to block me."

Lathon would get a chance to back up his talk after Carolina's first drive stalled. On fourth-and-one from the Eagles 15, Capers decided to go for it. The Panthers ran a play called 25 Ben Jab—a basic run play to Anthony Johnson up the middle—but Eagles linebacker Ray Farmer knifed in from the weak side and caught Johnson before he got up any steam, stopping him cold.

The Eagles took over at the 15, and Detmer started firing. He threw seven yards to Ricky Watters, then 16 to Irving Fryar. After two run plays, he completed another pass for eight, then a 42-yarder to Fryar. Two plays later, Philadelphia scored on a short run by Watters, driving 85 yards in only eight plays for a 7–0 lead.

It would be like that most of the day for Carolina. Lathon was indeed beating left tackle Barrett Brooks, but Detmer was taking three-step drops and throwing short slants with the accuracy of a jeweler. "I was in the backfield so many times, man, it was ridiculous," Lathon said. "I would hit Detmer, and that guy was *tough.* He was the toughest quarterback I've ever faced."

Early on that first drive, Lathon growled at Detmer, "I'm going to be bringing it all day."

"I'll be here all day," Detmer shot back. "So keep bringing it."

Five months after the game, Lathon was still amazed at Detmer's ferocity. He had gotten so angry at Detmer's success that for one of the few times in his life he actually tried to hurt an opposing player. "He's just a little runt," Lathon said. "When I would take him down, I was trying to hit him, bend him, or do anything to try to hurt him. But the last time I hit him, he grabbed my face mask—and kissed me! I thought I hit him just enough where the ball was going to be off, but it was a touchdown. He grabbed my helmet and blew a kiss at my face. I knew the guy was slamming on me. But what are you going to do, rough him up because he slammed on me? Hey, he beat me."

Detmer ended up throwing for 342 yards against Carolina—the most the Panthers had ever allowed.

"Sometimes I wouldn't even see him in there, the pocket was closing in on him so much," Mills said of Detmer. "And then, suddenly, somehow, the ball came out of there."

An outplayed Carolina team never led in the game, getting only three John Kasay field goals for points. Four times the Panthers got inside the Eagles 20. Four times they failed to score touchdowns. Carolina ran nine plays inside the red zone, totaling minus-six yards.

The Panthers' last chance to stay close came with eight minutes left in the game. Trailing 20–9, Carolina had the ball, second-and-goal on Philadelphia's four-yard line. Collins rolled right, saw no one open, and started running for the goal line. As cornerback Troy Vincent came sprinting up toward him, Collins tried an odd fake—a complete 360-degree turn. Vincent didn't buy it and slammed into Collins, who promptly fumbled the ball. Philadelphia recovered. The Eagles won 20–9.

At the midpoint of the season, Carolina was 5–3 and still in the playoff race. But the Panthers had played mediocre football for much of the past five weeks, and in the locker room, cornerback Tyrone Poole decided he couldn't take it anymore.

POOLE, AT 5′ 9″, WAS A SECOND-YEAR PLAYER WITH big dreams. He wanted to be the best cornerback in the game. He drove a black Grand Cherokee that read TOTAL PACKAGE across the spare tire mounted on the back. "That in itself is a little something that says I consider myself a complete player," Poole said. It was also a wordplay on his initials, T.P.

Poole had all the right tools for a cornerback—the memory of an amnesiac and the speed of a gazelle—but he got penalized too often and rarely picked the ball off, so teams threw at him all the time. A small-school player from Fort Valley State in Georgia, Poole was still adjusting to the fact that practically every NFL receiver was better than the best ones he'd ever faced in college.

"I feel like I can become one of the top covermen in the NFL, but it will take time," Poole said. "It's like driving a stick shift. When you're first learning, you try to avoid every hill you can. You'll go out of your way to avoid them. But after you get good at it, no hill is too high for you. You can climb anything."

Poole was the recluse of the defensive backfield, rarely hanging out with what was otherwise a very tight group. He liked to keep to himself. His fourth-grade teacher in LaGrange, Georgia, had once told him, "Better to be thought of as ignorant than to open your mouth and erase any doubt," and that lesson had stuck with him for 15 years.

Like most of the other young players, Poole relied on veteran corner Eric Davis for advice. "He's the teacher, I'm the student," Poole said. On this day, neither the teacher nor the student had done very well. And before reporters entered the locker room to interview the players, Poole flew into a self-directed rage, screaming about how badly he and the defense had played. Davis would eventually have to calm him down.

"We had gone out as a team and played horseshit football," Poole said later, explaining his outburst. "This game has so much pressure in it, and every player has his own way of relieving stress. That was mine. Those things are like an eclipse for me—they are rare, and you don't know exactly when they are going to happen."

THE PLANE RIDE HOME FROM PHILADELPHIA WAS quiet until Whitley told a couple of his teammates about his upcoming suspension. They were sorry to hear about it, but not terribly shocked. Whitley's drinking had been an open secret on the team. And since he wasn't telling anyone that the suspension was actually for drug abuse, not alcohol, most simply assumed he had been caught drinking again.

Still, it was a blow, mainly to the offensive line. It was time for another major offensive adjustment, and no one knew how the line would handle it.

Whitley had already checked into a local drug and alcohol rehabilitation center in Charlotte by the time the NFL and the Panthers concurrently announced his four-week suspension on Wednesday, October 30. The NFL announced the suspension was due to "substance abuse," but the Panthers said in a press conference that Whitley's suspension was alcohol related. Technically, this was true: Whitley was in the NFL alcohol and drug program in the first place because of alcohol abuse. Because there was no mention of the crystal meth, reporters and fans couldn't guess the true nature of Whitley's latest problem.

For two weeks, Whitley had to stay day and night in the local treatment center. Since he had already done a stint at the Betty Ford Clinic in California—"Betty's house," as he sometimes called it—he was familiar with the structure of group meetings. "You sit in there for a week and it's the same story," Whitley said, a touch of sarcasm creeping into his voice. "Everybody's life is over. Everything is messed up in their life. They can't do anything without having a drink or a drug or a pill. . . . But I've never had that. I've never been to the point where it's all just out of control, where my life is over or I feel like killing myself."

Outside the meetings Whitley said that he never *needed* alcohol or drugs. He just *wanted* them sometimes. But in the meetings he tried to listen. Some of what he heard he agreed with, some he didn't. Mainly, he just wanted to go home, so he tried to play along. "I was trying to say all the right things to get out of the treatment facility," Whitley said. "Yes. Yes. I'm a drunk. I lost control of my life. Whatever."

THE ATLANTA FALCONS HAD LAST WON A GAME ON Christmas Eve 1995. Their home game with Carolina was November 3, 1996—315 days since their last win. Nevertheless, the 0–8 Falcons had looked dangerous the last two weeks, nearly upsetting Pittsburgh and Dallas. In recognition of that and Carolina's road woes—the Panthers entered the game 1–3 on the road in '96—Carolina was only a slight one-point favorite. Whitley's absence didn't help.

The Panthers had to readjust their offensive line. Rookie Norberto Garrido, one of the few Hispanics in the NFL, took over at right tackle for Mark Dennis. Left guard Matt Elliott took over at center, and reserve Matt Campbell moved to a starting position at left guard. Neither Campbell nor Garrido had ever started an NFL game.

"We just have to press on," Capers said. "We want Curtis to get better, but we can't have this be a distraction to our football team."

Of course it was, but the Panthers thought they could still beat Atlanta, the same team they had trounced by 23 in the season opener.

The Falcons had other ideas. They got a field goal on the opening drive of the game and on the ensuing kickoff, recovered a fumble.

"The kickoff is the most violent play in football," Panthers kicker John Kasay once said. "You've got two-hundred-fifty-pound guys running full speed and slamming into each other. Just think of the physics of it. Things are going to get broken."

This time, nothing got broken, but Michael Bates fumbled the ball away at his own 32, starting what would become the worst special-teams performance of the year for Carolina.

On the very next play, Atlanta's Jamal Anderson scooted those 32 yards around left end for a touchdown, and with only 6:40 gone in the game, Atlanta was ahead 10–0. The Panthers had yet to run a play.

The Panthers offense looked sharp when they finally did get the ball, and on their first offensive snap, wide receiver Rocket Ismail ran right by former Panthers cornerback Tim McKyer, and gained 51 yards on Collins's throw.

Collins then directed the Panthers to a third-and-one at the Atlanta 22. This situation called for a play the Panthers had worked on all week, a play-action pass to Muhsin Muhammad straight up the seam of the field, but Muhammad had hurt a hamstring Friday before the game and couldn't play. His backup was Dwight Stone, who never got the ball thrown to him but was a special-teams terror. Stone ran downfield. No one paid any attention to him. Collins lofted a perfect pass to him at the goal line.

And Stone dropped it.

That was the story of Carolina's day. The Panthers never seemed synchronized, despite Collins's efforts. They missed out on another short-yardage situation in the second quarter, running the same play up the middle twice in a row with one yard to go at the Atlanta 34 and getting turned back each time. On the second one of those plays, Panthers left tackle Blake Brockermeyer got hurt and had to leave the game. Mark Dennis, who had been ineffective enough to be removed from the starting lineup before the game, would now go back in at the crucial position of left tackle to protect Collins's blind side.

Collins kept completing almost everything he threw. By Carolina's first drive of the third quarter, he had thrown for 222 yards. If he kept up the pace, he would throw for an astonishing 403 yards—far and away the best game of his career.

Then, on first-and-ten from the Atlanta 35, Collins faded back to pass. Atlanta's Chuck Smith came after him, circling around Dennis's block. Collins completed the pass to Wesley Walls for 13 yards, but Smith kept coming. The Falcons defensive end hit Collins late and low, right on his left knee. Smith got penalized for roughing the passer, but Collins was still down.

Smith's illegal hit had strained the same knee ligament that had forced Collins to miss two starts earlier in the season. Smith stood over the fallen Collins briefly before returning to his huddle.

Collins had never been angrier in his life about a play. "He knows what he did. He knows it was cheap!" Collins said afterward in the locker room. "He's trying to take me out of the game, trying to end people's careers. . . . Then he stood over me like I was some prize."

The quarterback called for Smith to get fined and accused Smith of also cheap-shotting Pittsburgh quarterback Mike Tomczak and Dallas quarterback Troy Aikman in earlier games.

Smith, though, was unrepentant. "I didn't try to hurt the man," he said. "It wasn't a late hit, and it wasn't a cheap shot." Smith further suggested that the Panthers offensive line—specifically left tackle Dennis—should do a "better job of blocking. When I'm coming off that corner, the lower you are, the faster you go," Smith said. "I'm going to keep coming. . . . What am I supposed to do? Grab a flag? Is this touch football?"

Some Panthers players thought Dennis or some other offensive linemen should have retaliated with a blow to Smith's knee, but no one did. The NFL fined Smith $15,000 a week later.

Carolina never could make up the early 10–0 deficit. The scoreboard read ATLANTA 20, CAROLINA 17 as the Panthers players walked silently off the field. There had been a few bright spots, though—wide receivers Willie Green and Rocket Ismail had both caught more than 90 yards' worth of passes—but the Panthers had still managed to lose to what had been the only winless team in the NFL.

"It was so terrible," Walls said in a locker room that seethed with bitterness and frustration. "It was public. A zero and eight team beat us. It's embarrassing."

WHITLEY HAD WATCHED THAT GAME FROM THE TV room of the substance-abuse treatment center in Charlotte. The patients weren't supposed to watch TV on Sunday, but a friendly counselor had flicked the game on and let Whitley watch the Panthers go on the field for the first time without him.

"I had mixed feelings about it," Whitley said. "For one thing, I felt that the outcome might have been different. But I couldn't have made Stony [Dwight Stone] catch that ball. . . . I was sad the team lost, but deep down I also felt, 'Hey, maybe they do miss me.'"

Later that week, four of Whitley's teammates came to visit him one night—Kerry Collins, Wesley Walls, Toi Cook, and Brett Maxie. Whitley took this as a very good sign: When he got out of treatment, he thought, his friendships would strike up again just as they had before.

They didn't.

Five months after getting out of treatment, Whitley said, "Everybody kind of doesn't want to be around me." He was still on the Panthers team in early 1997, but he believed his time with Carolina was drawing to a close. "Before, the damn phone was ringing off the hook," he said. "Now they don't want to lead me astray, or else they don't want to think they have a problem themselves."

For two weeks Whitley stayed in the center full time, then for another week after that he went in for outpatient treatment. His life would never be quite the same in Charlotte after his stay. He knew that. "When someone recognizes me in a restaurant, they look to see what I'm drinking," Whitley said. "I mean, you feel the look. Every time."

Whitley went to linebacker Lamar Lathon's Christmas party toward the end of the season. While standing near the bar, but not drinking, a lady he didn't know began "preaching to me, saying, 'You really don't need to be drinking, you know.' Instead of beautiful women coming up to me, I've now got old drunks coming up to me, talking about, 'Hey man, let's go to a meeting.' And there's no way to explain this now," Whitley said, frustrated. "If I try, people just say, 'You're in denial of your problem.' "

Without mentioning names, Whitley said that a number of Panthers players drank "immensely more than I would. So they see I'm in a treatment facility and they're stopping and looking at themselves. A lot of guys came up to me, asking me about this and that—like I'm some guru-o-alcoholic."

After the suspension, Whitley would not be a factor for the Panthers again in 1996. Later in the season, the Panthers stuck the feisty Frank Garcia into Whitley's spot permanently, and Whitley could never get his starting job back once he returned in late November. By the end of the season, Whitley felt fairly sure he would never play for the Panthers again, although he remained under contract at the time.

"I think it's over for me here," he said bluntly.

Polian, who had signed Whitley to a three-year, $4.5 million contract after the center's strong 1995 season, said, "What happened to Curtis Whitley was bad for Curtis Whitley. I don't think it ended up harming our team one iota. . . . Frank Garcia proved he could be a championship center."

Polian continued, "It was Curtis's own doing. He knew what the stakes were. He knew what the discipline would be. And even with that, he kept drinking. He was deserving of some public brickbats after that. He was deserving of scorn from his teammates. He let his teammates down and he let his family down."

Whitley understood that much of that was true. "Obviously, I'll never get to the Hall of Fame," he said ruefully. "Maybe the wall of shame." He took the blame for most of what he had done wrong—and asked for forgiveness for his errors. "I wish people would understand—I'm human, just like everybody else," Whitley said. "But I know I'm not at all a poor innocent victim here." Then Whitley smiled, letting a touch of his wild side surface again. "I'm a wild child," he said. "I've done some bad things. But I've had a good time."

THAT GOOD TIME HAD COST THE PANTHERS DEARLY IN the Atlanta game. The reshuffled offensive line had given up six sacks. Carolina was 5–4 and teetering on the brink of meltdown. Their center was in a treatment facility. Resentment brewed between the offense and the defense. They had just suffered the most embarrassing loss in team history. Most worrisome of all, the Panthers were mired in a six-week slump. After that scintillating 3–0 start, they had lost four of their past six games.

"This thing could get real ugly," fullback Howard Griffith said solemnly. "It would be real easy for this thing to start into a tailspin and head down real quick."

Carolina needed a cure—no matter how rough or nasty it might have to be.

CHAPTER TEN

The Turning Point

THE PANTHERS WERE LIKE A PIPE READY TO BURST.

Something had to be done to relieve the pressure. Something had to change. The loss to Atlanta was a sure sign that a once-promising season was on the verge of becoming a flop.

Linebacker Sam Mills, the most respected player on the team, had wanted to call a players-only meeting the Thursday before the Atlanta game but changed his mind after discussing the possibility with coach Dom Capers and safety Brett Maxie.

"We decided not to have the meeting at that point because it was too close to game time," Mills said. "But we decided, regardless of what happened against Atlanta, we were going to have the meeting the next week because I just thought the team wasn't playing up to its capability."

Even before the Atlanta game was over, Mills was more sure than ever that a meeting was necessary. He conferred with Capers again and scheduled it for Monday morning, the day after the Falcons game, while the anger and the embarrassment of losing to the only winless team left in the NFL were still fresh.

Kerry Collins sensed that a meeting was forthcoming, but certainly not what was going to take place once it began. "We were in a state of disarray," Collins said. "You could tell there were a lot of feelings, overriding things, everybody knew needed to be addressed. It was probably affecting the way we were playing." Little did Collins know that Monday was going to be a day in his career that he would never forget.

Lamar Lathon knew what was coming, too, and he could hardly wait. There was a lot he had been wanting to say to certain high-profile teammates for a long time.

Mills had an idea of what most of it was. "In the position I'm in with this team and the respect these guys have for me, when there's a problem with the players getting along with a coach or another player or any part of the organization, there's a good chance I might hear about it," Mills said. "Some of those things, I try to help solve." The solution in this case, Mills decided, was an "air-it-all-out" meeting, in which players, including Lathon, could say whatever was weighing heavily on their minds.

Mills had the full support of Capers. "I knew our team was extremely down," Capers said. "We were five and four, and when you're five and four, you can go either way. But I had total confidence in what was going to happen. If I hadn't known our team, then I would have felt uncomfortable about it, but I know the character of our team. The challenge for each of our guys was to look in the mirror. And the biggest thing is whether you have the belief in the guy next to you, if you believe he's making the same sacrifices you are."

That's exactly what the meeting was going to be all about. And if some feelings got hurt along the way, or some egos got stepped on, so be it. The overall good of the team was at stake. The season teetered atop a tightrope.

Mills thought it was worth the risk. So did Capers.

THAT MONDAY BEGAN AS USUAL. THE PLAYERS DID their normal morning running drills and then they came inside for a quick 12:30 P.M. meeting with Capers. From there, the routine usually called for the team to split up into position groups to look at film of the previous day's game. That day, Capers made an exception. "Sam has asked me to give you guys some time for a meeting,"

Capers announced. With that, Capers and all of his assistant coaches left the room, leaving the 53 players alone together for the first time all season in the team auditorium. The door was closed for total privacy.

Mills stood up and talked from his spot near the front of the amphitheater-style room, which sparkled with silver, black, and blue accents. Mills called no names in his opening remarks, but his message was firm. He urged every player to examine himself. He said some players could be doing more—much more—to help the overall team cause.

"We have guys who are thinking of themselves and not concentrating on the goals we set for ourselves as a team back in August," Mills said. "In order for us to get this team turned around, we've got to look within ourselves. If what we're doing as individuals is hurting the team, we have to be willing to admit that and correct it. All of us need to look at ourselves."

Then Mills invited players to take part in an open discussion. He cautioned that everyone should remain calm, yet he urged open communication.

"I love you guys and I know all of you love me. We all love one another," Mills said. "But as happens in a family sometimes, there are disagreements and bad feelings for one another that need to be aired out. This is the time."

Mills reminded everyone that whatever was said, it wasn't personal and should be perceived as constructive criticism.

Eric Davis, the cornerback who knew what it was like to win a Super Bowl with the San Francisco 49ers, was quick to speak out. Davis was one of Carolina's wisest, most vocal leaders. He had learned much from playing with former 49er great Ronnie Lott, his mentor, and was about to say many of the things Lott probably would have said if he were a Panther.

"Ronnie was a torrid team-meeting guy," said tight end Wesley Walls, another ex-49er. "You ducked when Ronnie Lott got started. It was the same with Eric." Especially that day. "Eric had about ten points to make and he made all ten of them," Walls said.

"Look at all we have here," Davis said, panning his gaze around what had to be the plushest meeting room in the NFL. "It's not this way everywhere. Look at this facility. Look at this locker room. Look at this stadium. Some people have put out a lot of money for this team. They're not putting pressure on us here, but the pressure is there. They're not happy. They expect to win.

"We can't go and lose to a team we're supposed to beat. We have to go out and win those games. We can't keep saying, 'Next week, we've got next week,' because sooner or later you'll run out of next weeks and that hammer is going to fall. You don't want to be the guy it falls on.

"Fellas, what we've got to keep in mind is, we're not sitting around playing on some expansion team that's willing to wait around five or six years to win. They expect to win now."

Collins was fast to stand up and speak, too. He was not a happy guy. Not only had Chuck Smith infuriated him with the "cheap shot" hit the day before, so had his own offensive linemen because none of them made any attempt to retaliate. Collins figured at least one of the five linemen on the field, who were assigned to protect him, should have charged Smith and made it clear that such treatment of Collins would not be tolerated under any circumstances, from any player on any team at any time. Wouldn't the 49ers linemen do that if an opponent put a dirty hit on Steve Young? Wouldn't the Packers linemen sacrifice themselves to defend Brett Favre?

Collins was especially mad at Mark Dennis, who had failed to successfully block Smith on the play. "Mark, you saw the whole thing and didn't do anything," Collins said. "I'm not asking for anything huge here. Basically, I just want you guys to respect me enough to defend me."

Collins had plenty of support on the issue, and Dennis felt bad that he hadn't done more to make sure Smith knew the hit was unacceptable.

Lamar Lathon's anger was building to the boiling point as he listened to Collins. He was almost ready to bust loose on the quarterback in front of the whole team. He'd been saving his thoughts, waiting for the right time to unleash them. Although Lathon agreed with Collins's basic premise that Dennis or one of the other linemen should have—in Lathon's own words—"put a foot up Chuck Smith's ass," he thought it was pathetic that Collins was having to stand up and plead for respect. He had been watching Collins closely and didn't like some of the ways Collins had been conducting himself, especially off the field.

Collins completed his minispeech on how the team should be playing better and should get recommitted for the remainder of the season. Then, he unintentionally gave Lathon the opening the linebacker had been waiting for. "If anybody in here thinks I've been fucking up, I want somebody to tell me," Collins said.

It was a noble, sincere invitation, the kind Collins believed a leader should make as a sign of his intended accountability to the rest of the team.

Lathon reacted sharply, swiftly, and with no mercy. "You *are* fucking up!" Lathon barked.

Everyone in the room was shocked, especially Collins. "What?!" he asked, astonished.

"You heard me!" said Lathon. "You're fucking up! You need to get your shit together!"

"What do you mean?" said Collins.

And there it was, the moment Lathon had been waiting for. The room was pin-drop quiet. Lathon stood in the back of the room, but he might as well have been on center stage with spotlights pointed directly on him. He could say anything he wanted. There were no coaches around to intervene. Everyone was watching and listening, turning in their seats to see what would happen next.

As intrasquad confrontations go, this was as potent as it got: Lamar Lathon, the Panthers franchise linebacker, on the attack against Kerry Collins, the Panthers franchise quarterback. The gloves were off now and it was obvious that no one was untouchable.

"Kerry, you're our quarterback," Lathon said. "You're a franchise guy. You come from a winning program at Penn State. Everybody knows what you accomplished there. But what have you accomplished *here?* You're riding a horse from last year. You're supposed to be this and you're supposed to be that.

"You go to these night clubs. That's great, because I do the same shit. But there's a time and a place for that. We've got seven months in the off-season for stuff like that. But you're going now. That's wrong. I'm committed to this team and this season. Are you?

"All people around town want to talk about is you throwing up in clubs, passing out in clubs, sleeping in your car. How can you do that and expect these guys to block for you? They know what's going on. Everybody around here knows what's going on.

"But, yeah, you're Kerry Collins and nobody wants to say anything. Well, I'm saying it. I don't care if you get mad. I don't care if any of you guys in here like me or not. I'm going to tell the truth!"

Lathon's attack stunned Collins, who had no idea Lathon or anyone else on the team thought his partying was such a problem that it could hurt the team.

Collins was furious. He thought if Lathon had a concern, it should have been delivered in private, not in front of the whole team. He thought Lathon's way was as tactless and inconsiderate as it got.

Listening to Lathon, Collins was incredulous. "Where in the hell is this coming from?" he thought. "What is this? It's unbelievable, absolutely unbelievable." Collins knew he liked to have fun, drink beer, and, as he has said, "blow off steam." But he certainly didn't consider himself a problem drinker. And Collins was certain that he played as hard and wanted to win as much as any player on the team. As mad as he was, though, Collins knew his teammates would judge him by how he responded, so he tried to stay calm. "If you're going to single me out, at least get your facts right," Collins said.

One of Lathon's charges was that Collins had gotten so drunk on a recent Wednesday night that he had gotten sick and vomited in a Charlotte bar. It sounded bad to the rest of the team, not only because it was embarassing to think of the starting quarterback being so publicly intoxicated, but also because it was in the middle of the week, just four days before a game.

Collins was quick to try to set the record straight, telling his teammates the incident to which Lathon was referring actually happened on a *Sunday* night, just hours after the Panthers beat the St. Louis Rams at home on October 13. He had gone out with some of his college friends from Penn State to the South End

Brewery, a trendy Charlotte microbrewery that was a popular hang-out for many of the players. "I got sick," Collins said. "I'm not proud of it, but it wasn't on a Wednesday at all. It was a Sunday night, seven days before our next game. Like about seventy-five percent of the team, I was there ordering shots and celebrating our win." Collins couldn't believe he was having to defend himself in front of his teammates.

At 23, he really was still just a big kid, still getting used to being out on his own with more money than he'd ever dreamed of having. He was still learning about life and about what it takes to be a successful football player. Who could blame him for wanting to live it up?

But the truth of the matter—as evidenced by what was happening in the team meeting—was that he was going to have to mature at an accelerated pace. Unlike most young NFL quarterbacks, Collins didn't have the luxury of growing into his job or his postcollege life as a low-profile backup player. He became a starter in the fourth game of his rookie year and now, midway through his second year, was on a team with playoff aspirations that expected him to perform, behave, and lead like a veteran.

Despite his mistakes, Collins believed he had played amazingly well for his age and experience level, and he was quick to remind his teammates of that: "Does anybody think I'm not playing good?" he said. "Didn't I just have one of my better games against Atlanta before I got hurt? Does anybody have a problem with the way I'm playing?"

Collins had a point. He'd completed 14 of 21 passes (66.7 percent) against the Falcons for 222 yards, no interceptions, and no touchdowns.

Wesley Walls, Collins's favorite receiving target and good friend, spoke out in Collins's defense. "I don't care what a guy does Monday through Saturday as long as he's accountable to me and the rest of the team on Sunday," said Walls. "If Monday through Saturday is causing him to do a bad job on Sunday, then that's a problem. But that's not the case.

"We can all watch over each other and babysit each other if you want to, but the fact is, everybody gets ready for a game differently. Some people watch more film than others. Some people drink water all week. Some people drink beer all week. What I'm telling you is I think Kerry is there for us every Sunday."

Lathon's reaction was predictable: *"Bullshit!"*

IT WAS SURPRISING THAT COLLINS WAS THE PLAYER being called out for criticism, but it was no shock that Lathon was the one on the rampage. Lathon had spent the week before the Atlanta game being purposely nasty to the Panthers offensive linemen in practice. In his mind, however, he had the good of the team at heart.

Lathon felt he had played superbly the previous week against Philadelphia—despite Ty Detmer's big day—and that the main thing that kept the Panthers from beating the Eagles was the line's failure to block well enough for the offense to convert a couple of short-yardage plays into first downs.

"I told some of my teammates on defense that I was going to make those linemen pay," Lathon said. "They're going to block somebody this week because I'm going to go out there and whip their butt every day. And I did it. I went out there like a man possessed. And I whipped some ass. I'm talking about fist fighting with the whole offensive line. I called them pussies. I called them fat and said they couldn't block." Lathon purposely lined up on the defensive scout team in practice. "You can't even get one damn inch!" he shouted at the offensive line. "Block me then!"

His best fight was with center Frank Garcia, the toughest and scrappiest lineman on the team.

His choicest words were saved for guard Greg Skrepenak.

"How can you have Skrepenak on one side of the line and you can't gain half a yard?" Lathon said. "Skrep, what's it saying about you if they have to take the play away from you and run it behind [Matt] Elliott and Garcia?"

When Lathon put his mind to it, he could be as relentless with his mouth as he was in a game when he pursued quarterbacks. And his mind was set on it that week in practice. "I figured when players saw they were being disrespected, that would make them get their act together," Lathon said. Wrong.

The Panthers had the same short-yardage problems against the Falcons that they'd had against the Eagles. They drove to the Falcons' 33-yard line late in the second quarter, but couldn't pick up the necessary inches for a first down on consecutive third- and fourth-down running plays.

"Everything I said and did that week in practice didn't do any good," Lathon said. "We went to Atlanta and those guys did the same thing. Then they let the guy hit Kerry and nobody put their foot up Chuck Smith's ass. So that's kind of what set this whole thing off."

In the Georgia Dome locker room after the Falcons game, Lathon seethed. He didn't want to ride home on the team plane. He sulked as he showered and dressed. As he was leaving the locker room, he heard Collins complaining about Smith's late hit. He wanted to stop and rip into Collins right there. "No," he thought to himself. "Not now. I'm saving it."

So he stomped onto the team bus for the ride to the Atlanta airport, his mind racing the entire way. "If you carry yourself like this stud quarterback you're supposed to be, you wouldn't have to be in here bitching to your linemen about protecting you," Lathon imagined himself telling Collins. "If you didn't do the crap you do around town and if you didn't throw all these interceptions and if you'd just work your butt off, you wouldn't have to make this speech. I'm through with this bull. We're letting things slip away from us. We have too much talent for that. We've gotta do something fast."

The stage had been set and Lathon was ready to explode. He knew he wasn't going to have to wait much longer to do it.

THERE WERE TWO PRIMARY TARGETS IN THE TEAM meeting: Collins and the offensive line.

Collins actually had plenty of support for his complaint that nobody struck back against Smith. "If you see somebody doing something to Kerry, A.J. [running back Anthony Johnson], or any of those guys, you've got to step up and stop it," Eric Davis said. "We've got that on defense. If a guy cheap-shots me, I know somebody's going to do something about it. You have to have that on offense as well. And this isn't the first time this has happened."

Wide receiver Mark Carrier agreed, and he did so with more anger and emotion than any of his teammates had ever seen from him before. Some even said it was the first time they'd ever heard Carrier, a devout Christian, utter a curse word.

Once the play of the offensive linemen became the focal point of the meeting, criticism poured down on them. Not only did Collins, Lathon, Davis, and Carrier get tough about the Chuck Smith incident, but the short-yardage failures were hammered on, too. Two of the linemen got singled out in particular: Dennis and Skrepenak.

Wide receiver Willie Green said he was embarrassed that Smith, an acquaintance of his, had told him the Panthers offensive line was one of the weakest in the league. Then Green let loose on Skrepenak. "Skrepenak, you're a big man," Green said. "When you first came to this team, there was no way I wanted to meet you in some dark alley. But right now, the way you're playing, I'll take my chances."

Green's shot drew laughs from some players, but not from the offensive linemen. None of them said much of anything the entire meeting.

"We were all stunned at that point," Skrepenak would say later. "We didn't say a word. We were in such amazement that the meeting had turned into an offensive line bashing."

Skrepenak was especially disappointed by Green's insult. Just one day earlier, Chuck Smith had told him how well he'd played the last time the two teams met, so Skrepenak didn't put much stock in the putdown Green attributed to Smith.

"The first thing that crossed my mind when Willie Green said what he did about me was, he probably didn't know any more about offensive line play than I did about playing wide receiver," Skrepenak said later. "All he knows about my position is we block. I couldn't believe he was bashing me. I felt it was unfair. But that's Willie Green. He's never one that shies away from saying what he thinks."

There were 53 players in the room. Nine of them were offensive linemen. Of the other 44, only one stood up and spoke in defense of the way the line had been playing. That person was Anthony Johnson, the team's starting running back. Johnson had strung together three consecutive 100-yard rushing games in the first half of the season. They were his first 100-yard games since high school. "These guys are opening big holes for me," Johnson told the team. "They're the reason I'm running the way I am. I believe in those guys. I'd go into battle with them anytime."

At that moment, the bond between Johnson and his blockers became inseparable. "Our goal already was to help A.J. gain a thousand yards," Skrepenak said. "And when he said what he did on our behalf, I decided if he got to one thousand, we were going to do something special for him." It was a vow Skrepenak would keep.

NATURALLY, WALLS WASN'T THE ONLY PLAYER WHO IN-terjected an opinion in Lathon's bashing of Collins. Eric Davis backed most of what Lathon said, but he also made a point to note that Collins was still maturing as a quarterback and a pro athlete. "Kerry is twenty-three years old," said Davis. "He's a youngster. Some of us in this room forget about what we used to do when we were that age. He's a kid. When we were that age, we didn't have the responsibility he has.

"But I'm not saying anything is right. If it's hurting our team, you can't do it. It's that simple. That's the bottom line. And with all the guys sitting around here talking about this right now, it's obvious it's affecting the team. So you've got to cut it out. It's not your problem anymore. It's the team's."

Among the players backing Collins was one defensive player, cornerback Toi Cook. "I realize this is a source of concern for all of us, but there's a long history of successful players in sports who have run the streets on their own time," Cook said. "There was Jim McMahon and Babe Ruth. The list just goes on and on. Some guys can drink a twelve-pack every night and still produce Hall of Fame numbers.

"Kerry is twenty-three years old. He's a multimillionaire. He's got a big fat crib, whatever car he wants to drive, and he's The Man in this town. C'mon, fellas. You don't think he's going to go out? That's like giving somebody ten thousand dollars, sending them to Las Vegas, and saying, 'Don't bet.' Look, guys. Kerry's got the goods. It's that simple."

Carrier defended Collins, too, but there were plenty of players who sided with Lathon, including some who chose not to speak in the meeting.

Defensive end Gerald Williams, an 11-year veteran and perhaps the team's most popular player, shared some of his teammates' concerns that Collins was showing up at too many Saturday morning walk-through practices with beer on his breath. "He would come in on Saturday mornings sometimes and you'd think he'd been out all night drinking," Williams said. "He would just reek of alcohol and he'd have bloodshot eyes. So I think what Lamar said to Kerry was needed. Sometimes if you sugarcoat things, they don't hit home as strongly as they need to. But if you have an abrasive personality, as Lamar can have sometimes, that gets the point across a little stronger.

"Kerry is our leader, so if he's not taking care of himself, whether it's mentally or physically, the team is not going to flourish."

Lathon felt his biggest ally in the meeting was fellow outside line-backer Kevin Greene, who didn't accuse Collins directly but instead gave a gripping personal testimony that many players would later say was one of the most memorable speeches anyone gave all season.

"What Kevin said broke everything down into the simplest of forms," said safety Pat Terrell. "He had his soft-tone, high-intensity, fist-in-the-palm thing going."

Though Greene has a reputation as a showman on the field—and in the wrestling ring—his teammates respected him for his dedication and for how hard he played. "What Lamar is talking about is commitment," said Greene. "You have to be committed in this game. I am one hundred percent committed to you, you, you, and you." Greene pointed around the room.

"I watch film on Tuesday, our day off, because I want to win. I watch film after hours. I tell my wife when we go to training camp that everything except football is going to take a backseat until the season is over. When the season starts, I am *totally committed!*"

The second half of Greene's spirited message was something that many players found especially useful for the remainder of the season.

"Football is not a complicated game," Greene said. "It's very simple. It's a one-on-one battle—you against the person in front of you. One of two things is happening out there. Either you are kicking his ass or he's kicking your ass. There's no in-between. And everybody in here knows who's getting their ass kicked and who's kicking the other guy's ass."

SAM MILLS NEVER DISCUSSED THE SPECIFICS OF THE meeting with anyone except his teammates after it ended, just as he'd promised in his opening remarks. However, he did admit later that "the meeting went as planned." While Mills felt good about the potential the meeting had to help solve some of the team's problems, some of the other players were concerned.

"I was worried it might have an adverse effect," said fullback Howard Griffith. "Some guys left that meeting feeling very alienated."

The offensive linemen felt terrible. As soon as the team meeting broke, they immediately filed into their group meeting room, which was down the hall and around the corner from the team auditorium. The linemen hadn't spoken out in the team meeting, but they let loose when they gathered together alone.

Skrepenak went ballistic, railing on and on about what Willie Green and the others had said. "We just played a pretty damn good game, if you ask me," he said. "Except for a few mistakes, we came off the ball aggressively. If there's anything wrong with us, it's that we're a young unit."

Line coach Jim McNally mostly listened as his linemen talked. For once, they were leading a group meeting, not him. He, too, was hurt that the line had received so much criticism from the rest of the team.

"We discussed the things you'd expect us to discuss after getting abused," said Dennis. "We needed to circle the wagons. We decided if no one was going to respect us, then we were going to play for ourselves."

As much as it hurt to play the scapegoat, the line was able to use the criticism as something to rally around for the rest of the season. "For a lot of the guys on the line, it became us against the world," said tackle Blake Brockermeyer. "It woke up a few guys, too."

Collins found plenty of motivation amid his frustration and anger. That night, he and Wesley Walls sat on a couch in the family room of his opulent south Charlotte home, discussing their thoughts about the day's events. It seemed clear to them that the Panthers were separated by a rift pitting the defense and offense against each other.

"We were a team divided," Collins said. "That's what happens once people start calling you out. It was about as bad as it gets."

Collins and Walls were so steamed at what they'd considered a "we're superior" power play by the defense that they found themselves calling certain defenders about every name in the book. "We were *pissed!*" Collins said. "It was such an overriding theme in that meeting that the defense thought it was the offense doing everything wrong. Maybe I felt it more than some other people. That's probably because I got called out in the meeting.

"Hey, I realize the reason we win games is because of our defense. But I'm a quarterback. I've got an ego. I'm not a guy who likes to be just a role player who doesn't make waves. I want to be The Guy. I don't think there's a quarterback in this league who doesn't. But I said, 'Fine, if the defensive guys want to think what they think, they can. We'll just sputter along as an offense and try not to screw things up for everybody.'"

There were—and there would continue to be—strongly differing opinions about how much that Monday team meeting would mean to the remainder of the Panthers season. But with each passing week it became more and more obvious that something changed in the Carolina Panthers that day when they sat together and unloaded their innermost thoughts. Mills, Davis, and Greene thought it was a vital turning point. Collins later admitted he did, too.

The offensive linemen were more reluctant. "I've never been a big fan of those types of meetings," Mark Dennis said. "There's always a scapegoat, and it was us. I lost some respect for some of my teammates in that meeting—the ones who pointed the finger and said, 'You're why we're not winning.'

"As far as I'm concerned, it's a team sport. You can say a team is only as good as its weakest link. But if you ask me, you become the weakest link when you start blaming somebody except yourself."

Despite the division that existed that day in the meeting room, the Panthers were determined to become a stronger, better team when they showed up two days later for Wednesday's practice.

Lathon thought he instantly noticed a change that day.

In the weeks ahead, Skrepenak's teammates thought he was clearly practicing and playing harder. Lathon and other Panthers began to notice that Collins seemed much more aware of how he was presenting himself to his teammates. He no longer showed up for team functions with beer on his breath. He didn't stop partying, but he was certainly more careful. "People got their act together because they knew their butt was under a microscope," said Lathon.

Davis had been saying since training camp that the Panthers would not become a good team until the players took over. Now, they had. "I don't mean breaking rules and being late for meetings," Davis said. "But there comes a time when you realize that you're the one that has to get it done. Nobody else can do it for you. In that meeting, guys were letting one another know, 'Hey, I'm watching you and I know you're watching me. You owe me and I owe you.'"

The first big test came six days after the meeting in a nationally televised Sunday-night game in Ericsson Stadium against the New York Giants.

The Panthers couldn't afford to lose. Another defeat would mean disaster, but a win would be the start of something big.

CHAPTER ELEVEN

Start of the Streak

PRIME TIME WAS A VERY RARE COMMODITY FOR THE Carolina Panthers in 1996. The Panthers game at home vs. the New York Giants on the evening of November 10, a Sunday, would be the one time all year when the Panthers' NFL peers could watch Carolina.

Every NFL team got at least one Sunday- or one Monday-night game per year, so once per season the NFL's version of not-ready-for-prime-time players all crawled out from behind the woodwork. NFL schedule makers, figuring the Panthers would be far out of the play-off race in '96, had slated them for the bare minimum of prime-time exposure. It would be Carolina's only chance for three hours of fame—unless they could make the playoffs.

In the NFL prime-time games are partly for showing off, for demonstrating to the national television audience that you belong in this league. "It's the one night of the season that you want to make sure your uniform looks just right," Panthers wide receiver Mark Carrier said.

The Panthers needed a lot of things to look right, of course. Whether the team meeting had helped or hurt so far was hard to say. For the first time all season Carolina coach Dom Capers varied his schedule during the week, holding a Friday late-night practice in the stadium to get used to the lights. The 5–4 Panthers practiced well all week, knowing that a loss to the 4–5 Giants would turn them into an average team. "We are in real danger of getting real mediocre real fast," linebacker Sam Mills told his teammates.

The game started at 8 P.M. on an unseasonably cold November night, as the fans shivered in 40-degree weather. Since ESPN was televising the game, the Panthers brass decided to pass out 60,000 masks of ESPN sportscaster Chris Berman. The sight during the first quarter, of many fans wearing the masks was unsettling—a stadium filled with eyeless clones sipping hot chocolate.

After the opening kickoff, Carolina struck first. On the Panthers' first drive, the team moved down the field in small increments until they reached the New York 35. It was time to launch "the Rocket." Raghib Ismail, the Panthers' speedy but inconsistent wide receiver, was inserted into the game on the right side. He quickly circled back on first-and-10, took a handoff from Kerry Collins, and flew around left end. Giants cornerback Phillippi Sparks had a shot at him, but Ismail showed one of the moves that made him so feared at Notre Dame and darted past Sparks. Suddenly he was in the clear—the Panthers had blocked the play well and no one was going to catch the Rocket. He high-stepped into the end zone for a 35-yard touchdown—his first (it would be his only) TD of the season.

ISMAIL WAS ONE OF THE PANTHERS' MOST UNIQUE characters. Intelligent and giddy, spectacular and strange, flaky and fast, Ismail had befuddled the Panthers for most of the season. First off, he had almost quit football rather than accept a trade to the Panthers in August from Oakland. The Panthers had given up only a fifth-round pick for Ismail, who didn't want to leave the West Coast, even though the Raiders didn't want him anymore. "I was devastated," he said. "I was about to say football is for the birds."

Only a calming talk from Bill Polian had quieted Ismail down. Polian told Ismail to take his time making whatever decision he had to make. It was an adept handling of the situation by the often tempestuous Polian. "If he had been callous and had said, 'Look, get your butt here now!' my butt would *never* have been there," Ismail said.

Then, once Ismail did get to Carolina, he was slow getting into the lineup because of nagging injuries and was slow to make an impact once he did. The other wide receivers, particularly veterans Carrier and Willie Green, grumbled that Ismail's salary of $935,000 (highest among the receivers) was quite a price to pay for someone who ran a reverse or two every game and sat on the bench the rest of the time.

Ismail perplexed his teammates. He didn't fit in any specific locker-room group. He sometimes called himself a "man of God in a hip-hop industry." He was very articulate but dodged reporters. And at times, you couldn't tell whether he was joking or not. A couple of games before the contest with the Giants, he had begun screaming at Panthers mascot Sir Purr because Sir Purr was wearing a red-devil outfit.

"Down with the devil! Down with the devil!" Ismail yelled every time Sir Purr came near him.

But the incident that stuck in most of the Panthers' minds was the Friday that Ismail had been overcome by fumes on the practice field. At every practice the Panthers use a large tower, powered by a portable generator, to lift up two men to videotape the practice from about a hundred feet up. On this day the generator had malfunctioned and spilled gas all over the grass. Some practice groups moved away from the tower to get away from the smell of the gas. Only Ismail, though, seemed badly affected. "I know my teammates thought I was hallucinating or something, but those fumes—they just got to me," Ismail said. "I was looking at the ball, but I couldn't focus. I felt queasy."

Ismail asked for permission to sit out the rest of practice and got it. Dwight Stone—whose description of Ismail as a "kaleidoscope" was probably the best anyone gave all year—took his place in the wide receiver drills. "I thought I would die [with laughter]," Stone said.

Fullback Howard Griffith said, "That was the strangest thing I've ever seen in football. . . . He sat there and got away with it. Guys really get on you at this level if you're not out practicing with them. Guys can start to take that personally. You've got to do your job, too."

Ismail was so fast, though, that much was forgiven. He was the only player on the team who would have been able to challenge kick returner Michael Bates in a footrace. And he had scored a touchdown to start off this game—a game Ismail would later call his favorite of the season.

"I remember, in the pregame, stretching out and looking around and thinking, 'Man, this looks professional!'" Ismail recounted. "There were banners on the wall. That was one of the coolest moments of the season. It felt like the home team was about to be loved."

THE CROWD LOVED ISMAIL'S TOUCHDOWN, BUT THEY weren't so hot about the Giants' tying touchdown on their first series of the game. And they didn't much like New York marching straight down the field for another TD on its next possession, taking a 14–7 lead late in the first quarter.

In the second quarter Carolina got a field goal from John Kasay, but still trailed 14–10 at halftime. Collins was playing, despite his strained knee, but he had not been very good so far. Capers, who had backed the team meeting all the way, now wondered what sort of effect it had had. "There wasn't any great revelation," Capers said. "In the first half of that Giants game, we were getting our butts kicked."

New York opened the second half the same way. Led by quarterback Dave Brown, the Giants—who were supposed to have one of the NFL's worst offenses—blasted down the field again. They had a first-and-goal on the Carolina four almost immediately. It was then, Panthers defensive coordinator Vic Fangio said later, that Carolina made its most important (and most overlooked) goal-line stand of the season.

The year before, most had remembered Sam Mills's interception return for a touchdown against the New York Jets as the pivotal defensive play of the season. For Fangio, this was comparable. "We were losing fourteen-ten already," Fangio said. "We knew we had to go out and play real good in the second half and not give up any more. . . . If they had scored that touchdown, they might have won the game. We could have fallen to five and five. Who knows what happens then?"

But on consecutive plays, Panthers reserve defensive lineman Les Miller stuffed a run, linebacker Kevin Greene forced an incompletion, and safety Chad Cota, coming on a third-down blitz, forced another. The Giants had to take the field goal and a 17–10 lead with ten minutes left in the third quarter.

Carolina's defense made another big play on its next series. Safety Pat Terrell picked off Brown's pass and returned it six yards to the New York 30, giving the Panthers ideal field position.

On four of the next six plays, Collins handed to Anthony Johnson and A.J. bulled into the end zone from one yard out for the tying touchdown.

But Collins, unbeknownst to the fans, had gotten hurt again. On a seven-yard scramble to the right sideline, Collins had refused to do a quarterback slide and instead tried to run over a defender. "Kerry sticks his head into a lot of situations where it doesn't have any business being," fullback Griffith said bluntly.

Collins got upended and slammed his shoulder and his face into the ground. He suffered a slight separation in his throwing shoulder, and even though he threw one more pass on the drive—an incompletion notable only for the fact that when he threw it, "It was like, 'Oh, God. Somebody shot me in my shoulder!'"—he was done for the game. Or so he thought.

Collins managed to finish off the series with handoffs, but then left the game for the locker room for what he would later call "the miracle of modern medicine."

Despite Collins's absence, suddenly, the crowd was alive—and so was the defense. Nose tackle Greg Kragen—a steady, underrated force game after game—punched the ball away from Giants running back Rodney Hampton and recovered it at the Giants 14 on the next series.

Carolina only managed a field goal behind backup quarterback Steve Beuerlein, but that was good enough to get the Panthers a 20–17 lead over New York late in the third quarter.

Collins, meanwhile, had gone to the Panthers locker room with team doctors. It was time for another one of the NFL's quiet rituals—the painkiller shot. Collins's shoulder wasn't in danger of permanent damage, and as for the gashes on his face from an earlier spill in the same game, well, they were unsightly but manageable. The doctors put six medical staples in Collins's face to hold it together, then gave his right throwing arm the painkilling shot.

"About twenty seconds later it was like, 'Wow, this feels great! I'm healed!'" Collins remembered. "Modern medicine, man. It's awesome."

Actually, Collins was as beaten up as he had ever been. He had six staples in his face. His knee still hurt from where Chuck Smith had hit him late the week before. His shoulder was partially numb, but he could feel the pain just under the surface.

"One thing I know—we've got a tough quarterback," Carolina coach Dom Capers said admiringly.

The tough quarterback wanted to play. He returned for the next series—Carolina's first of the fourth quarter.

On first down, Collins threw 10 yards to Griffith. Two plays later, he laid a sideline pass in perfectly to Wesley Walls for 13 yards on a critical third-and-seven play. Then, it was nine more yards to Willie Green. On second-and-seven from the 17, Griffith took a short pass from Collins and rumbled for a touchdown. Carolina led 27–17 with 11 minutes left in the fourth quarter, and that would be the final score.

The Panthers defense—on fire after that goal-line stand—got another interception from Terrell and one from Toi Cook to clinch the game.

Terrell was later named NFC Defensive Player of the Week for his efforts, a nice honor for one of the classiest players in the organization. Cook—a brash player who sometimes called himself "Deion Lite" in honor of cornerback Deion Sanders—had a knack for making major plays in a limited time on the field. The Panthers had earned this 27–17 win and had stopped the momentum of a two-game losing streak. Their record was 6–4, and when they left the field the scoreboard flashed: THE PANTHERS' PLAYOFF DRIVE CONTINUES!

Collins felt great about his role in the win—until about 3 A.M. That's when the shot wore off.

Collins bolted up in bed in intense pain. Sitting up with his arms wrapped around his chest, he moaned. His knee hurt. His shoulder felt even worse. Doctors had replaced the staples with stitches after the game, but now the stitches itched. The pain pills weren't doing a thing. He tried to get back to sleep, but his body hurt too much. This was one of the secret prices of being a quarterback in the NFL.

COLLINS WOULDN'T BE CLOSE TO READY THE FOLLOW-ing week. It turned out that he had played the rest of the Giants game on adrenaline as well as the painkilling shot, but his shoulder wasn't going to let him off the hook against St. Louis.

The Rams, already whipped once by Carolina, had rebounded from that defeat. They had scored an astonishing 59 points against Atlanta the week before—the most points any NFL team would score in a game all season. But the Panthers, exuberant after their defeat of the Giants, were also seeing something emerge on their team—the offensive line. Without Whitley the unit had rallied. Collins had given each starter $250 after the Giants game, the reward he had promised for each time the offensive line didn't allow a single sack. It was the first time all year that Collins had had to pay.

Ironically, Collins had still gotten hurt. But the scramble and re-fusal to duck was not the offensive line's fault—it was the fault of a reckless 23-year-old quarterback who believed he was indestructible. "I figure I'm twenty-three, I can still do these types of things," Collins said. "I'm not supposed to get hurt."

The line—now featuring Blake Brockermeyer, Matt Campbell, Matt Elliott, Greg Skrepenak, Norberto Garrido, and Frank Garcia in vari-ous roles—was supposed to work together. And they *had* banded together tighter after the team meeting that had used them as a scapegoat. The players weren't naturally friendly with each other—they were too competitive for that—but they were trying. Their meet-ing room was in sharp contrast to the bland ones that the rest of the position units worked inside every day. Its walls were covered with photos—of John Wayne, Janis Joplin, Elvis Presley, Muhammad Ali, Richard Nixon, and Lucille Ball. There was a Norman Rockwell illus-tration, a *Wizard of Oz* poster, and an advertisement for the Barnum & Bailey circus. There was a map of the United States and an aerial view of New York City. But, mostly, there were pictures of the linemen themselves and their personal mementos, some dating back to child-hood.

"The stuff is on the wall because we want to make the room more personal than the cold place meeting rooms usually turn out to be," Elliott said. "An offensive line is a very tightly knit group. It's a lots-of-little-private-jokes-and-secrets kind of group. We bring things to put on the wall so we can get to know about each other better, because when it comes to being out there on that field, you've *got* to know the guy playing next to you."

THE TEAM HAD TO TRAVEL TO ST. LOUIS FOR ITS eleventh game of the year and play in the Trans World Dome, a state-of-the-art facility that had lured the Rams franchise from Los Angeles to St. Louis the year before. It would come in handy on this cold, drizzly November day.

The Rams had begun that 1995 season in St. Louis with a 4–0 record, but they had faded fast since then, finishing that season with a losing record and now starting '96 with a 3–7 mark. Their worst loss in those two years had been the 45–13 plastering Carolina had laid upon them a month earlier. Before this game, St. Louis coach Rich Brooks called that win "a total ass kicking" and the most "inept performance" the Rams had ever had in his two seasons with them.

This one would be much closer. Neither team could move in the first quarter, and St. Louis finally dented the scoreboard in the second with a field goal that made it 3–0. Carolina's John Kasay matched that, but St. Louis then got an 11-yard pass from rookie Tony Banks to fellow rookie Lawrence Phillips for a 10–3 halftime lead.

Again, Carolina was in trouble on the road. The Panthers were 5–0 at Ericsson but only 1–4 on the road so far, and now they were losing again. Beuerlein, replacing Collins, had thrown an interception that led to the first half's only touchdown. His wife was eight months pregnant at home in Charlotte, and he was supposed to be making it easy on her watching this game. So far, no good.

If Carolina was to win this game, the Panthers would have to grind it out and rely on the defense. The team's first drive of the second half was just what they wanted—runs to Johnson mixed in with short passes to four different receivers.

The final throw, a nine-yarder to Wesley Walls for the touchdown, was controversial. Just as Walls's feet touched the ground after a jump to catch the ball, Rams safety Keith Lyle banged into him and dislodged the ball. At first the pass was ruled an incompletion. "I was trying to yell, to protest, but my breath got knocked out so I couldn't at first," Walls said. "I knew I had it. There was never a doubt."

There was doubt on the Rams' part, however. They believed that Walls had dropped the ball and that the pass should be ruled incomplete.

The officials conferred. Coincidentally, the man who made the critical call lived just north of Charlotte. Head linesman Ron Phares wasn't playing favorites, though. Phares was one of the best in the NFL at his position, having worked for the league since 1985 and officiated in two Super Bowls. Phares said after the game: "He [Walls] had possession of the ball with both feet down. Then there was a time delay and then he got hit and then the ball came out."

Head referee Tom White agreed: "That meets the requirements of a touchdown."

Walls's TD made it 10–10, and, again, the Panthers defense got cranked up in the second half, denying St. Louis on their first possession. Again, Carolina rushed down the field to score. This drive was almost all Anthony Johnson. He started it with a four-yard run, kept it going with a seven-yarder, and finished it with another seven-yarder for the touchdown. It was Carolina 17, St. Louis 10, with one minute left in the third quarter.

The rest of the game was dominated by Carolina's defense. The Panthers ended up sacking Banks six times, led by Kevin Greene's 2½ sacks. The Rams' longest second-half drive was 26 yards, and they never scored again. Kasay added a field goal for Carolina's final 10-point margin.

After the game linebacker Sam Mills when asked about Greene, joked, "Number Ninety-one? I don't know. Does he play for us or for them? It seemed to me like he was lining up in their backfield on every play."

"I'm grateful for our best friend—the defense," Beuerlein said after the game.

Banks looked "like he was being pulled down by sharks back there," Panthers safety Terrell said.

Carolina punter Rohn Stark got a rare moment in the spotlight in the fourth quarter. Stark—he pronounces his first name "Ron" and jokes that the silent *h* stands for "hangtime"—was a 15-year veteran who had punted all over the NFL. In the fourth quarter, he hit a 39-yarder that made him the NFL's all-time leading punter in yardage.

Johnson and Ismail, close friends off the field, did something endearing as they left the field with Carolina's 20–10 win secured. Ismail grabbed Johnson's hand and swung it high repeatedly as they ran off the field together, yelling "Wheeeee!" Johnson didn't try to pull away. NFL players are just as prone as high school players to tease their teammates for anything other than macho behavior, but neither player worried about that. These were two solidly religious men—good friends who were married to pretty wives and were fathers of five children between them. They were not afraid to hold hands in public if the mood struck them. Who cared who got teased?

A.J. and Rocket accounted for every one of Carolina's 147 rushing yards that Sunday: 123 for Johnson and 24 for Ismail (on three reverses). Combined with Beuerlein's 130 yards passing, it turned out that Notre Dame alumni had something to do with every single offensive yard Carolina came up with.

Johnson wasn't satisfied, though. "I should have had fifty more yards with the sort of holes the offensive line was opening," Johnson said. "I'm going to be sick when I watch the film. I stumbled several times with a lot of space in front of me."

It was that sort of game—one of the Panthers' ugliest wins of the season. Few Carolina players would remember it as more than a blur after the year was over.

But it counted. Carolina was 7–4, smack in the middle of the play-off race, with five games to go.

LAMAR LATHON LOUDLY PREDICTED AFTER THE RAMS game that his next performance, against Houston, would be the best of his career.

"Mark it down!" Lathon said.

Lathon desperately hoped that would be true. He had grown up near Houston, gone to college in Houston, and started his pro career in Houston. The Oilers were deep in his blood, although he had left the team with mixed feelings to sign a huge contract with the Panthers before the 1995 season.

Now he was coming home. He had bought 57 tickets for friends and family for the game in the Astrodome. More than anything he wanted his old team to miss him. "Man, a part of me still loves the Oilers," Lathon said. But a bigger part of him wanted to "go out and kick their ass. I wanted [Oilers owner] Bud Adams and [Oilers GM] Floyd Reese to be looking at each other real uncomfortably," Lathon said later. "I wanted Bud to be telling Floyd, 'How in the world did we let this guy get away?'"

The Oilers were a decent team—6–5 and in the playoff race in the AFC. But they had hardly any crowd support in Houston because they were a lame-duck franchise. Adams was going to move the team to Nashville, Tennessee, as soon as he could get out of his lease with the Astrodome.

As usual, the Panthers left Saturday afternoon for the Sunday road game. The charter flight was scheduled to leave at 3 P.M., which everyone knew except one Panthers player—quarterback Kerry Collins. Somehow, Collins had gotten the idea that the flight was at three-thirty. He pulled up to the airport at about three-fifteen with reserve Panthers center Bucky Greeley (a former teammate of Collins's at Penn State) in tow. "I got there in time to wave bye-bye to the plane," Collins said.

Capers knew that Collins wasn't on the plane, but he signaled it to take off anyway. The rules were the rules, in Capers's book. Collins got fined $1,000 for missing the plane and also had to buy his own one-way ticket from Charlotte to Houston on Delta Airlines, for about $600 more.

It wasn't looking like much of a weekend for Collins. He wasn't going to get to play again because of his injured throwing shoulder and now he was stranded at the airport, watching the Panthers' plane take off with quarterback Steve Beuerlein and all of the other players safely aboard.

As Collins stood by his car wondering what to do, his car phone suddenly rang. He answered it.

It was Beuerlein, calling Collins from the air. Collins couldn't even make out what was being said, there was so much noise in the background, but he knew he was being teased.

"I just heard a lot of laughing in the background," Collins said. "The guys killed me about it all weekend."

CAPERS HADN'T BEEN ABLE TO CALM LATHON'S STEW of emotions all week, so he tried to capitalize on them. Before the game, the coach told Lathon that he could represent the Panthers in the pregame coin toss.

Lathon immediately started crying. Tears streamed down his face.

"I have never, ever in my life been this emotional before!" Lathon told Capers.

Lathon won the coin toss, with his knees wobbling slightly. But he would not be a major player in the game after all.

"I got totally too hyped," Lathon said. "I couldn't sleep. I played a game I can't win at. Football is an emotional game, but I was in it playing for pride and for the wrong reasons—me showing them what I've become. Anytime you put personal goals ahead of the team, it never works out."

Other teammates would have to step up for Carolina to win in the Astrodome. The game had attracted only 20,107 fans to a stadium that could hold 64,000, just 25 fans more than the all-time Astrodome low. Had it not been for the 57 tickets Lathon bought, it would have *been* the all-time low.

"When the cheerleaders were doing their cheers, you could hear it on the field," Panthers nose tackle Greg Kragen said. "It kind of felt like a high school game."

"Crowd? There was no crowd out there," wide receiver Willie Green said. "That looked more like a family reunion."

It was Green who made the game's biggest play. After a scoreless first quarter, Carolina had the ball with a third-and-five at the Houston 30. Green knew what the call would be—this was where he usually slanted into the middle for six or seven yards. It was one of the Panthers' signature plays—or had been, anyway, until first Muhsin Muhammad and then Rocket Ismail had replaced Green in the starting lineup.

"Everyone in the world knows that I'm going to run a slant on third down," Green said, "because I've done it so often."

Houston cornerback Darryll Lewis had studied game films of Green and expected it. He jumped toward Green's inside shoulder as if he had been in the Panthers huddle, but Beuerlein made the throw in the only place he could make it—throwing the ball slightly behind Green and away from Lewis.

"If he had thrown it in front of me, it would have been eighty or ninety yards the other way," Green said.

Instead, Green caught the ball on his outside shoulder. Then he spun away from Lewis, headed toward the sideline, and outraced everyone else into the end zone. Touchdown, Carolina! It was the first time Carolina had scored first in a road game all year, and it gave the Panthers a 7–0 lead.

GREEN WAS ONE OF THE PANTHERS' MOST INTERESTING players. He was a Muslim in a locker room mostly full of Christians. He was a single parent who always talked about his son, Dontellis, and what the two of them were going to do next.

He had been a huge surprise for Carolina. Out of the league in December 1994, Green had been available when the Panthers wanted to sign their first ten players on December 15 of that year. Polian thought that only a few of that group would make it. After all, no one had wanted them in 1994. But Green had become a dazzling big-play threat for Carolina in 1995, once scoring on an 89-yard touchdown. He was a big talker who genuinely enjoyed conversation with everyone he came in contact with—fans, teammates, and reporters. He had one of the tiniest heads you would ever see, perched on top of a lanky 6′ 4″, 188-pound frame. He had gone to high school with John Kasay in Athens, Georgia, and occasionally argued theology with him in the locker room.

A thoughtful, honest man, Green also had an occasional bite to him. He sometimes answered his home phone with "What do you want?!" and often complained about his lack of playing time.

"He's always the guy who's getting slighted and all the forces are working against him," Collins said with a laugh. Yet he could play, and the Panthers kept him around despite what Green conceded was his "locker-room lawyer" reputation.

He hadn't scored a touchdown all season, though, and that was making a mockery of the nickname he loved so much: Willie "Touchdown Machine" Green. He liked it so much that his computer screen name on America Online was a shortened version of the nickname. Now, he was getting another chance, for Muhammad was hurt and Ismail's play was inconsistent. Green made the most of it. He scored another TD in the third quarter, pushing Carolina's lead to 17–3 on a 12-yard touchdown pass from Beuerlein.

Meanwhile, the Panthers defense was having a surprisingly easy time with a good Houston offense. The Panthers were stuffing rookie running back Eddie George, and the pass rush was overwhelming quarterback Chris Chandler.

Twice, Lathon thought he might grab hold of Chandler. Once, though, Chandler stepped up in the pocket just as Lathon flew around the right side and Greene flew around the left. The two men banged into each other at full speed. The impact was scary and knocked both to the ground. "That's the hardest I've ever been hit," Lathon said. "It was like I'd been hit by a freight train."

"All I saw was his head coming to my head," Greene said. "The next thing I knew there were tweety birds flying around."

They both recovered from that and kept playing. Another time, Lathon burst into Houston's backfield, but overran Chandler. Greene, who had not beaten his blocker as cleanly, worked free to get a late sack.

On the sideline after the series, a hyped-up Greene started screaming at Lathon. "Hey, when you've got him in your hands, you've got to make that play!" he yelled good-naturedly. "I don't want your scraps, man. I want to earn them on my own."

The Panthers were earning this one in every way. Chandler got hurt early in the fourth quarter and was replaced by second-year quarterback Steve McNair, the QB whom Carolina had considered drafting over Collins. It looked like Carolina had made the right move. On McNair's first series, he fumbled on fourth-and-five. Linebacker Sam Mills saw the ball on the ground, zoomed in to pick it up, and ran 41 yards for another touchdown.

"I had a bunch of teammates taking me into the end zone," Mills said in his self-deprecating style. "When I looked over and saw all those guys, I was wondering, 'Are they all running that fast? Or am I running that slow?'"

Ahead 24–6, Carolina piled it on with another score with five minutes left, when Beuerlein threw a 40-yard touchdown pass to Walls. That one angered Oilers cornerback Cris Dishman, who thought the Panthers should have kept running the ball when they had an 18-point lead.

"I'd better not catch that offensive coordinator here in Houston or I'll whip his ass," Dishman said, referring to Carolina offensive coordinator Joe Pendry. "That was bullshit—a second-and-four, play-action pass when the game's over! He's just trying to run up the score."

Walls happily egged Dishman on after scoring. When the two were lining up for the point after Walls's touchdown, Walls caught Dishman's eye. "Wasn't that just a great call?" Walls asked Dishman gleefully. "Just great!" Dishman scowled at him.

Carolina ended up with a resounding 31–6 win—one of their most impressive of the season. The only negative was Blake Brockermeyer's badly injured thumb. Everything else had worked out splendidly.

"I am *still* Willie Green, touchdown machine!" Green said in the locker room after his two-touchdown day.

"We played awful today and got our nose rubbed in it," Houston coach Jeff Fisher said. "We got our butts kicked by Carolina. It's the worst I can remember."

Beuerlein was now 3–1 as a starter and had thrown three touchdown passes, but he still had to give the offense's keys back to Collins the following week—the second-year quarterback was going to be ready against Tampa Bay.

No NFL team had ever made the playoffs in its second season, but Carolina was getting close. With its second straight road win—and third straight win overall since the team meeting—Carolina (at 8–4) had put themselves in an excellent position not only to play in a play-off game, but to host one.

AFTER FIVE GAMES OF NICE WEATHER FOR HOME games, the odds finally caught up with Carolina in their next game. The December 1 home game at Ericsson vs. Tampa Bay was more suited to snorkeling than football. The field was a mudbath, and because East Carolina and N.C. State had played a college game on it the day before, it was in pretty bad shape. For fear of further damaging the field, the Panthers' groundskeeping crew left the end zones as they were, so they read "Wolfpack" and "Pirates" the whole game.

Tampa Bay, like Carolina, was hot. The Buccaneers had won three straight games to improve to 4–8. But this was the sort of day the Panthers defense craved.

Defensive end Mike Fox responded rapturously when asked what was most fun about playing in the rain: "Just being out there, smelling the earth on your body, just kicking up some dirt," Fox said.

Linebacker Carlton Bailey said the game reminded him of days in Baltimore when his mom would say, "Don't bring those muddy shoes back in the house!"

"We were rooting around having fun, like a hog going after a sweet potato," Kevin Greene said.

The Panthers had to shuffle the offensive line around again for the fourth and final time in 1996 as a result of Brockermeyer's thumb injury. Matt Campbell took Brockermeyer's place at left tackle. Matt Elliott switched to left guard. Frank Garcia went in at center.

The Panthers offense started the game slowly, but Carolina still led 10–0 at halftime because of a great defensive play. The Panthers' zone-blitzing defense flustered Tampa Bay quarterback Trent Dilfer badly on one play deep in his own territory. He had no time to react as cornerback Toi Cook rushed from the left side. Dilfer, trying to get the pass off, instead got stripped of the ball by "Deion Lite." "I believe in the Muhammad Ali style—talk some shit and back it up," Cook said. "And if you don't back it up, you crash and burn."

Panthers defensive lineman Shawn King had lined up on the other side and had knocked his man almost all the way back into Dilfer's face. When Cook forced the fumble, King merely had to look down, pick it up, and ramble in from 12 yards out.

"I hadn't scored a touchdown since my junior year in college," King said. "It was a sweet day. After a while, I didn't even notice the mud."

King jubilantly threw the ball into the stands after the TD—and almost immediately wished he hadn't. He later sent a Panthers official up there to ask the fan if he would mind swapping that ball for another. The fan was kind enough to grant the request.

THE PANTHERS LET THE DEFENSE DO THE HARD labor on this day. Collins, running a very conservative game plan, threw for only 83 yards. But Carolina's defense kept plastering the Bucs. Cornerback Davis, who now seemed to make an interception every game, read a route perfectly and ran a pickoff back 39 yards to the Tampa Bay ten in the third quarter. Three plays later Howard Griffith scored from the one, and it was 17–0.

King intercepted another pass from his defensive-line position in the fourth quarter, and Johnson turned that into points, too, with a 25-yard scoring run. Carolina had a 24–0 lead, and was close to its first shutout in team history.

The week before Carolina's defense had allowed only two field goals, and now this. Former Pittsburgh quarterback Terry Bradshaw was one of the many devotees of the zone-blitz concept the Panthers often seemed close to perfecting. "I would have hated playing against their defense," said Bradshaw, who led four Steelers teams to Super Bowl wins in the 1970s. "I think a quarterback leaves the game with a migraine after facing them. With the zone blitz, you're wondering who's zoning, who's coming? Then they get in those eight-man fronts and people pop out of there like, 'Whoa! What was that?!'

"Sometimes during a game a quarterback gets so frustrated trying to figure them out, he says, 'The heck with it.' Maybe that's what I would have done, just said, 'See you later.'"

Tampa Bay hadn't quit, but Carolina's fourth straight win was assured. Regardless of the victory, the fans and the players badly wanted the goose egg. Tampa Bay's last drive started against Carolina's second-string defense, and the Bucs moved from their own 20 to the Carolina 11 with 39 seconds left. Buccaneers first-year coach Tony Dungy, one of the classiest men in the game, still didn't want his team to get shut out. He would call three timeouts in those final 39 seconds, trying to get Tampa Bay into the end zone.

And suddenly—in what should have been a meaningless series—the Panthers and Bucs had what Capers would later call a "showdown" on their hands. The first-string Panthers defense, angry that Tampa Bay was trying so hard to put up points, started begging to get back into the game. The coaching staff relented. The crowd shook off the damp chill and started yelling again.

Said Mills: "Everybody was cheering for that shutout. You could see the killer instinct come out in not only the players, but the fans. They didn't want to beat you, they wanted to beat you badly. They wanted to prove who's the best."

"They were challenging us," Greene said. "Even though the game was out of hand and in the bank, they were saying, 'We're going to put some points on the board.' What we were saying was, 'We don't think so.'"

Tampa Bay got a two-yard pass from the four. Then Gerald Williams stuffed a run for minus-one. It was fourth-and-two from the three-yard line when Dilfer faded back for the last time in the game. His pass was batted down by Eric Davis, and the Panthers players started hugging each other like they had won the game rather than just kept a zero on the scoreboard.

Dungy said after the 24–0 loss to Carolina that the Panthers looked like "a playoff team" and would be a squad that "no one would want to play" in the playoffs, primarily because of the Panthers' strong defense. The shutout had lowered the Panthers' scoring defense average to 12.6 points per game, padding their NFL lead in that statistic.

Suddenly, the Panthers boasted a 9–4 record heading into another huge game with San Francisco, the first-place team in the NFC West at 10–3. Carolina couldn't have had a better four-game run leading up to the 49ers, and the defensive stand that had preserved the shutout provided an extra dollop of motivation as the team entered the month of December.

Mills said of the shutout, "It was sort of like not only were we the Panthers, but we realized we had teeth, too. And we could bite pretty hard."

CHAPTER TWELVE

Beauty by the Bay

WILLIE GREEN COULDN'T SLEEP ANYMORE.

He blinked several times, trying to clear his head. He cut his eyes around the room, searching for a clock in his San Francisco hotel room. It was 5:15 A.M. Pacific time. Carolina wouldn't kick off against San Francisco for another eight hours, but Green was restless. He wouldn't be able to get back to sleep, and he knew it.

The lanky wide receiver slid out of bed, threw on a sweatsuit and hat, and started down to the lobby of the San Francisco Airport Westin hotel. Maybe the gift shop would be open, he thought. He could buy a newspaper.

The sign on the gift shop read CLOSED when Green got there. It didn't open until 6 A.M. In the lobby, he ran into the Panthers director of security, Ed Stillwell. He couldn't sleep, either. By the two men's body clocks, it was 8:15 A.M. Eastern time, and they both usually got up long before that.

They talked awhile, muttering the way people do at 5:15 in the morning, even when no one else is nearby who might wake up. But then Green started getting itchy again. He had to do *something.* "See you later, Ed," he said, and stepped outside into the cool morning air.

Across the street from the Panthers' hotel was the shoreline of San Francisco Bay, and Green crossed the street to get closer to the water. Planes were parked at gates across the bay at the airport. Green had always loved planes, ever since he was a kid growing up in Georgia. Here was something he could do. As he strolled along the boardwalk by the bay, he tried to make out the shapes of the planes and figure out what they were. "Northwest 747," he said softly to himself. "Northwest again. Qantas. Delta."

Seagulls bedded down for the night occasionally lifted a head from under a wing and gazed at the 6' 4" Muslim. Green had a superstition about always wearing sweatsuits in the team color of the opponent when the Panthers were on the road. That's why he had on this red Reebok sweatsuit at the moment.

Other than Stillwell, no one knew Green was out here. He liked that. The air was cool on his face, and he wanted time to think about what was about to happen. Green had felt good all week—bold, even. Earlier in the week, he had said that the San Francisco–Carolina winner would go to the Super Bowl. Capers had gently called him down for that one. It wasn't the smartest thing to say, since Dallas or Green Bay could get pretty offended, and Green had backed off the statement later in the week. But out here, with a breeze blowing in off the bay, no one could get angry with anything Green had to say. Out here, no one was listening. The water lapped against the shore. Green's tennis shoes thumped against the boardwalk. He felt oddly peaceful. "Today I'm going to play the best game I ever have," he said softly.

He would certainly get that chance. He knew that. The Carolina coaches had stressed all week that Green and Mark Carrier had to win one-on-one matchups against the San Francisco cornerbacks or else the Panthers weren't going anywhere. The 49ers played an aggressive "press coverage"—placing cornerbacks Tyronne Drakeford and Marquez Pope within two yards of wide receivers most of the time, rather than the customary five to eight yards. San Francisco believed Pope and Drakeford were good enough that they could afford to play riskily.

Green thought otherwise. But for once he kept quiet about it.

CAROLINA–SAN FRANCISCO, THE SEQUEL, HAD SHAPED up to be the game of the year in the NFC West.

Since Carolina had last met San Francisco, pounding the 49ers 23–7 at home nearly three months ago, the 49ers had found a groove. They had avoided Carolina's midseason slump and had meanwhile surpassed the Panthers in the standings. San Francisco would enter this game 10–3, one game ahead of the 9–4 Panthers. A 49ers win would clinch the NFC West division title for the fifth straight year. San Francisco was a 10-point favorite to do exactly that.

A Carolina win would push the teams into a 10–4 tie at the top of the NFC West, but the Panthers would take over first place because of a season sweep of the 49ers. Carolina was about to take either the passenger's seat or the driver's seat in the division—no one was quite sure which.

The 49ers talked big before and during the game, but it would be a mistake to boil the game down to just a verbal clash. For one thing, Carolina knew that San Francisco's five Super Bowl titles gave the 49ers some right to say whatever they wanted.

"I would have chosen a different tack," said Carolina cornerback Toi Cook, who had once played for San Francisco. "But if anyone had the right to talk some shit, it was the 49ers."

For another, Carolina would have to do much more than get steamed about a lack of respect from the 49ers to win the game. The Panthers were about to face a healthy Steve Young, and few sights in the NFL looked more dangerous than that. "Three or four weeks ago people were talking that Steve Young was going to retire, and now he's out there running around again," Panthers coach Dom Capers said wryly.

Carolina's players had watched on TV Monday night as Young ran for two touchdowns in an easy win over Atlanta, once on a designed quarterback draw from five yards out, and once on a 26-yard scramble. It worried them.

"Young creates another whole dimension for us," Panthers defensive end Gerald Williams said. "Guys get a little more apprehensive on their pass rush. It makes you real cautious as a pass rusher when he's been able to run the ball as effectively as he's been able to do the last couple of weeks."

Young, 35, had played at full strength only once in three previous games against Carolina. In the two teams' first meeting, in November 1995, Young had sat out in favor of backup quarterback Elvis Grbac. Carolina won 13-7 in San Francisco. In Game 2—in December 1995 at Clemson—Young was playing very well. He threw for 336 yards and two touchdowns, ran for another one, and obliterated Carolina almost by himself, 31-10. Then came September and Game 3. Young played with a constant grimace from a groin injury. He later said he felt he played that game "on one leg." The Panthers pounded San Francisco 23-7.

Now Young was 100 percent again. It seemed inevitable that the Panthers would get hit up for more than seven points against the 49ers this time. But all wasn't well in 49ers world. For one thing, Jerry Rice was unhappy. Rice, possibly the best NFL player at any position ever, had scored an NFL-record 163 touchdowns in his career. To put that in perspective, the Panthers had scored only 59 touchdowns as a team entering the game. But in 1996, the 49ers kept throwing Rice short ball after short ball. He was embarrassed about having a lower yards-per-catch average than 49ers tight end Brent Jones (12.6 for Jones, 11.9 for Rice).

"I'm frustrated," Rice said. He wanted more passes—especially more deep passes thrown to him against Carolina. It irked him that in each of his three games against the Panthers he had gained more than 100 yards receiving but had never scored a TD vs. Carolina. The only other NFL team Rice had never scored against was Jacksonville, and that was only because he had never played against the Jaguars.

"If we plan on making a run for the Super Bowl, this is the game," Rice said. "It comes down to this."

FOR KERRY COLLINS, THE IMPORTANCE OF THIS GAME could not be overstated. It was the Panthers' first big game since the infamous team meeting. What he did here would be remembered not only by fans around the country but, more significant, by teammates who wondered what Collins could do under this sort of pressure. Collins, always self-confident, believed he would be fine. He told one of his agent's assistants Saturday night before the game, "This isn't hard." He felt ready.

For Jerry Richardson, the *unimportance* of the game suddenly became apparent. His close friend and NFL mentor, former commissioner Pete Rozelle, had died at the age of 70 of brain cancer two days before the game. In Rozelle's last note to Richardson, after the first San Francisco game in September, he congratulated the owner he had helped shepherd into the league. Rozelle always typed his notes and signed most of them "cheers, pete," in all lowercase letters. Richardson had planned to visit Rozelle the day after the game. Instead, he would soon be attending Rozelle's memorial service in New York. "I knew it was getting sort of to the end," Richardson said somberly. "When he passed away, I really wasn't into the game, even as important as it was."

The Panthers players were confident all week. Green had noticed the team's precision and thought it was the best week of practice Carolina had ever had. Cornerback Tyrone Poole felt like he knew what was going to happen an hour before the game ever started.

"It was like an aura you could feel throughout the whole week," Poole said. "It was like God had given me a vision of what the outcome was going to be. I felt all week we'd win."

Poole, who normally let his brashness out in small doses, felt so good that he told a TV cameraman before the game, while walking onto the field, "Big game today, baby, big game! We're going to do it today! Nobody believes what we're going to do today, but you'll find out at seven o'clock tonight."

By the time the game started—at 1 P.M. Pacific time, 4 P.M. Eastern time—the 49ers already knew they had made the playoffs. Washington's loss earlier in the day had clinched their spot. A San Francisco victory would also guarantee that the 49ers would get a first-round playoff bye. Carolina had no such guarantees, win or lose.

The Panthers would probably be in the playoffs in some fashion, but only a win vs. San Francisco would give them a chance at the division title.

Carolina won the coin toss and took the ball. Immediately, Collins started in with Walls. He hit him for five yards on first down. Sure enough, the 49ers were playing the coverage that Carolina expected—close-up "press" coverage, with eight or nine men near the line of scrimmage to stop the running game.

On third-and-six, Mark Carrier showed his value to the Panthers. He reached behind him to catch a Collins pass, well thrown but not perfect, then spun away from San Francisco safety Tim McDonald before McDonald could react. Suddenly, Carrier was racing free down the middle of the field. Before anyone caught up, he had sprinted 39 yards to the San Francisco 30.

Johnson ran twice again before San Francisco even caught their breath. McDonald got an unnecessary roughness penalty. And before the sellout crowd of 69,000 had settled in, Carolina had a second-and-goal at the San Francisco five.

In the huddle Collins winked at Walls. Then, he sold the 49ers on a pump fake to the left. He glanced back at Walls, who was covered decently by Merton Hanks in the end zone. With a sliver of space, Collins decided to throw the ball anyway, right at Walls's left hip.

Walls trapped the football on his hip and held it as carefully as a baby, even with Hanks grabbing him. Carolina led 7–0 with only 3:21 gone in the game. If San Francisco had any hope that this would be a cakewalk, that notion quickly disappeared.

On San Francisco's second offensive play, fullback William Floyd took a pitch to the right. Lamar Lathon slammed toward Floyd and smashed him at the San Francisco 15 for no gain. As Lathon got up, he yelled at Floyd and then straddled him briefly. Panthers linebacker Carlton Bailey, who loved to play angry, jawed with Floyd, too.

The 49ers had to punt on that series, and on Carolina's next possession John Kasay had a rare miss from 45 yards out, so the score remained the same. Floyd botched a handoff from Young on the next San Francisco possession and Lathon recovered the ball at the Carolina 48. Again, Carolina couldn't move the ball and punter Rohn Stark came on to blast one to the San Francisco eight.

San Francisco's Dexter Carter waited on the ball there—and Andre Royal waited on Dexter Carter.

ROYAL WAS THE PANTHERS' LITTLE-KNOWN CHAMPION OF special-teams collisions. The thing he did best was brutal: he would run 40 yards straight down the field and look for someone coming the other way. The impact often clanged into the upper deck. "I don't think I've had any concussions," Royal said. "Or if I did, I didn't know about it."

No one else on the team was nearly as good at "selling out," as Panthers special-teams coach Brad Seely described it. Royal would sell his body for a one-yard gain in field position. And then he'd get up and do it again. He was a kamikaze from Mobile, Alabama, with a passion for football and the ongoing restoration of his 1968 Buick convertible.

Carter caught the ball at the San Francisco eight and made it six yards before Royal hit him with the force of a thunderclap. *WHAM!* The ball popped loose, and starting fullback Howard Griffith fell on it.

Later, Royal would collect almost $3,000 of his teammates' money for that hit. The normal $100 payment per starter for a big special-teams play had been voluntarily increased by some players for this game. Griffith would also get a chunk for his recovery. "I'm a poor man," Royal claimed, "at least compared to these guys. I need it."

With a first-and-goal at the seven, Carolina ran Johnson over left guard for two yards and Collins couldn't get in on two runs—a scramble for four and a sneak for zero. But Kasay made Royal's hit count for something, nailing an 18-yard chip shot to give Carolina a 10–0 lead with two minutes left in the first quarter.

Young wouldn't get his game on track until early in the second quarter, but then he found a rhythm for the 49ers. A 26-yard pass to Terrell Owens. A couple of 15-yarders to Terry Kirby and to tight end Brent Jones.

The 49ers sprinted to the Carolina seven. On first down, Young found tight end Ted Popson on the right side. Popson, hurtling toward the end zone, got upended and landed horribly head-first; his head was bent backwards at an inconceivable angle. Officials stopped the game for three minutes with San Francisco at the Carolina one. Amazingly, Popson walked off the field. San Francisco didn't need him to score. Young rolled out on second down and surveyed the field. Panthers linebacker Carlton Bailey ran into cornerback Eric Davis while trying to keep up with Jones. That break allowed Young easily to fire to Jones for the touchdown, and Carolina's lead was sliced to 10–7 with 10 minutes left in the first half.

And what a 10-minute session it would be.

MICHAEL BATES, QUIET SO FAR IN THE GAME, WAS A great momentum changer on kickoffs. He did it again on the 49ers' ensuing kickoff, sprinting 58 yards before kicker Jeff Wilkins's desperation shove knocked him out of bounds at the San Francisco 37.

At first Carolina struggled. Collins threw an incompletion. Griffith carried the ball for one yard, then got hit so hard by 49ers linebacker Ken Norton, Jr., that his helmet flew off. But on third-and-nine from the San Francisco 36, Carolina got a break from the player who would soon become one of the Panthers' most valuable in this game, San Francisco cornerback Tyronne Drakeford.

Drakeford illegally held Carrier as he tried to run a slant route up the middle, giving Carolina a first down on the penalty. The Panthers, spying a lack of confidence in the 49ers cornerback, threw at him again on the next play. This time it was Green down the sideline, blocking Drakeford with his body. Green gained 26 yards to the San Francisco five.

Carolina kept throwing. A first-down pass was incomplete. On second down, the call came for a Walls play, the Y-Corner.

Y-Corner was one of Walls's favorite plays. He usually got room to work and then got to break outside after a certain number of steps, depending on how tight the coverage was. Most NFL teams used a variation of the play for their wide receivers, but Walls was quick enough to make it work at tight end.

This time, though, it looked hopeless. San Francisco's Tim McDonald covered Walls closely on his break. Collins lobbed the ball into the corner, five yards in front of Walls, where it looked like it would fall incomplete. "When he threw that ball, I knew he threw it too far," TV announcer Jerry Glanville said on-air.

But Walls dove, reached . . . and somehow got it.

Several months later, Walls, reflecting on the season past, would say that this was the best catch he made all year. It also pushed Carolina to a 17–7 lead with 7:05 still to go in the first half.

Suddenly, points were flying onto the scoreboard, and Young wanted some of the action. He ran 17 yards for one first down and threw twice to Rice for another. On second-and-ten from the Carolina 46, Young watched Terrell Owens working on Poole and fired it to Owens at the San Francisco 37. Poole, jumping in front to try for a deflection, miscalculated. The ball got through and Poole was on the ground, looking for help. Owens started motoring down the left sideline as Pat Terrell came over to meet him.

Owens stiff-armed Terrell at the 22 and just kept going, jogging into the end zone.

It had taken San Francisco only 3:41 to go 86 yards. The crowd roared. Backup quarterback Elvis Grbac got so excited that while congratulating Young he accidentally poked him in the right eye.

Young's vision blurred only for an instant, but then sharpened. He was sick of being hurt, and a thumb in the eye wasn't about to keep him out of this one. The home team had just gotten to within three points of Carolina, at 17–14, and at this rate even more points seemed a sure thing.

They were.

Green knew he had the upper hand on Drakeford as he ran onto the field. The 49ers corner had been victimized twice on Carolina's last possession. But in football, there is never time for sympathy. The weak link is hammered at incessantly until it breaks.

Drakeford was about to break. After a one-yard Johnson run to keep the defense honest, Green was supposed to run his trademark slant pattern. But Collins glanced to the right and saw that Drakeford, trying to guard the slant, was within two yards of Green.

Collins caught Green's eye and stuck out his thumb—"almost like a hitchhiker," Collins would say later. It was the Panthers' secret signal for a "go" route, as in go straight up the field. Green faked short, went long, and mystified Drakeford. Green sped downfield with a two-yard lead on his pursuer. Collins's throw spiraled right into Green's hands, and for a second it looked as though Green would score. Instead, San Francisco's safety came over and barely got enough of Green to push him out of bounds at the 49ers 20.

That play had been the "fade." Now offensive coordinator Joe Pendry went for the home run—the "fade stop." This time Green would run exactly the same route, and San Francisco, oddly, would play exactly the same coverage. But as Drakeford adjusted to take away the outside, at the last second Green would cut inside, stop his pattern, and catch the ball in front of Drakeford—if it was there.

It worked beautifully. At the two, Green planted his right foot and cut in front of a surprised Drakeford. Collins's throw was precise. Green had to leap to reach the ball and fell at the one, but with Drakeford out of the picture going the other way, all Green had to do to score was roll his body into the end zone as if he were simply turning over in bed.

"I'm in a zone!" Green exulted. "I can't miss!"

Collins felt the same way.

Glanville, who normally can't stop talking, just kept saying, "Wow, wow" on television. Panthers center Garcia ran over near Drakeford and started fanning him as if he had gotten burned.

Carolina, where scoring outbursts often meant two Kasay field goals within a quarter, had racked up another TD. The Panthers led 24–14 and had scored in just 84 seconds, leaving 2:50 in the half for San Francisco to try and match the TD.

Drakeford wouldn't have to worry about the rest of this game, however. Disgusted, San Francisco coach George Seifert yanked him from the game after the TD. Drakeford sat on the bench, his head buried in his hands, for much of the rest of the game. "I just didn't make the plays," Drakeford said later. "I haven't gotten an interception all season, but at least I've been there to defend the deep ball. Today, I didn't do it. I don't know what happened."

More fireworks remained for the players on the field, though. Lathon's sack of Young meant the 49ers had to punt on their next possession. Two fights broke out on that punt. Panthers safety Damon Pieri blocked San Francisco cornerback Curtis Buckley so hard that he went 10 yards out of bounds. Then an enraged Buckley came back in bounds to give Chad Cota, the nearest Panther, a fierce head slap.

Farther downfield, San Francisco linebacker Gary Plummer got into a bitter argument about downing the punt. "Bullshit!" Plummer said to side judge Laird Hayes. The word got picked up by one official's microphone. Then Plummer briefly brushed Hayes while screaming at him.

By the time everyone calmed down, three unnecessary roughness penalties had been called: two on the 49ers and one on the Panthers. Plummer got ejected for his bump.

Carolina, with 1:43 left, a 10-point lead, and touchdowns on two straight possessions, wanted more. The 49ers refused to leave their "press" coverage, and soon Collins and Rocket Ismail had burned it for 32 yards to the San Francisco 16. Green caught another one in the end zone, but just barely out of bounds. Eventually, it was Kasay time, and his 26-yard field goal gave Carolina a 27–14 lead with 28 seconds left in the half.

But that wasn't the end of the scoring. With 14 seconds left, Young saw Kirby running a sideline route against Davis, who occasionally had trouble guarding backs going deep. Kirby sneaked behind him and scampered 52 yards with the ball, ending up at the Carolina 13 before Davis could finally force him out of bounds. The 49ers' Jeff Wilkins kicked a 31-yard field goal, and it was 27–17, Carolina, at the half.

There had been four touchdowns, six scoring drives, and 34 points combined in the second quarter. Collins had 213 yards passing by halftime; Young had 237. No way this was going to keep up.

IT DIDN'T. SAN FRANCISCO DEFENSIVE COORDINATOR Pete Carroll, who had stubbornly clung to the close coverage the entire first half, backed off it during the second. Carolina would add only one more field goal to its scoring total in the entire second half, leaving it up to the defense to hold off the 49ers.

Carolina had a 30–17 lead midway through the third quarter, and kept it after Cota intercepted a Young pass at the Carolina one and ran it back 34 yards to the 35. It was Young's first interception in 146 throws. But the Panthers would get no more points in the fourth quarter. Kasay's missed 31-yard field goal was a chance that eluded them. They could have used three insurance points.

Midway through the fourth quarter the 49ers inspired their fans with a 12-play drive that ended with Rice snagging a five-yard worm-burner pass just before it hit the ground. Finally, Rice had scored against Carolina. San Francisco had pulled to within 30–24 with 6:22 left in the game.

Carolina's offense was in a rut. A three-and-out series sent the ball right back to San Francisco at the 49ers 32 with five minutes to go.

Young had thrown for all sorts of yardage, but he hadn't run very much. But on this down that would change. Young sprinted up the middle for 33 yards, immediately getting the 49ers to the Carolina 35.

Whether the 49ers could navigate those 35 yards would probably decide the champion of the NFC West. Carolina's offense, for all its first-half firepower, had been quiet in the second half, and a San Francisco TD would probably seal the game.

Young threw one incompletion. Then he threw another. But on that play, Poole was penalized for defensive holding, giving the 49ers a first down at the 30.

On the next play, Terrell Owens, the San Francisco rookie, got open on the sidelines—but not open by much. Young didn't care. He was hot. He had already thrown for 393 yards and rushed for 63 more—easily the most yardage the Panthers had ever allowed one individual in a game. He would fit the ball into Owens. "I thought I put it in a spot where either Owens or nobody could get it," Young said. "I tried to put it high and away." But he didn't. The throw was high, for sure. Owens got only one hand on it, and the deflection magically floated near Eric Davis, who gracefully swooped it up just inside the sideline and sealed the victory for Carolina. "I better have done something to help this club, the way I'd been stinking up the field," Davis said later.

The Panthers celebrated on-field. The offense got three first downs and held the ball the rest of the game.

Carolina had beaten the 49ers again.

Collins had been sensational. He had thrown for 327 yards, three touchdowns, and no interceptions. It seemed like almost every time he came off the field, somebody was congratulating him—including Lathon, who shouted "Helluva job!" to Collins several times.

For Collins, this was a personal redemption after Lathon's verbal attack in the team meeting. "It just erased everything," Collins said. "It was almost like everyone felt, 'If this guy can play this well in a game like this, everything is fine. We don't have to worry about him. We think he's okay.'

"That definitely had a lot of closure to that whole [team meeting] incident, the whole wondering of, 'Am I serious enough? Did I have it? Am I the guy everybody thought I was going to be in the big game?' It really went a long way."

Lathon said, "Kerry went out there looking like 'This is my deal and I'm going to prove to everybody nationally that I'm The Man.' And he did that."

Greene said, "That was a definitive moment in Kerry's career."

In the locker room, before the reporters arrived, the players gathered in a makeshift huddle. "We did something that no one thought we could do!" Collins said. "Feels good, doesn't it? Feels good!" It did.

"We've had to muzzle ourselves and zip our lips for so long, but now we can say it: playoffs, playoffs, playoffs!" Lathon said in a jubilant locker room afterward.

"I feel unbelievable, remarkable, great!" said Walls, who had scored four touchdowns against the 49ers in 1996. "How many adjectives can I use in one sentence? If I could think of a hundred, I'd use them all."

Green had caught seven passes for 157 yards. Indeed, it had been the best game of his life—his silent, secret early-morning walk had helped.

Only Richardson had mixed feelings. How much Rozelle would have enjoyed this game. The former commissioner was always first and foremost a fan. Richardson would loved to have gotten a "cheers, pete" note after this one. "I'm happy for the players and coaches that we won the game," Richardson said. "But I'm grieving right now because of my friend Pete Rozelle's passing away."

The Panthers would only have to win their final two games, at home against Baltimore and Pittsburgh, to win their first-ever NFC West title.

The headline in *The Charlotte Observer* screamed the next day: ANY QUESTIONS?

There were still a few.

CHAPTER THIRTEEN

"There's No Place like First Place"

AFTER SHOWING UP SAN FRANCISCO, CAROLINA HAD pushed their way into the driver's seat of the NFC West, but two possible wrecks remained: home games against Baltimore and Pittsburgh on December 15 and December 22. Carolina needed to win both to "finish it off," as Capers kept repeating to his team. Baltimore would be first.

The Ravens weren't very good. Their 4–10 record was the reverse of Carolina's 10–4, but Baltimore had a dangerous quarterback in Vinny Testaverde and one of the best offenses in the NFL. The Ravens had led in every single one of their last nine games at some point during the second half, but had gone only 2–7 in those games. They were experts at gaining—and then losing—leads.

The Panthers needed a battle cry this week. Baltimore wasn't the sort of opponent to inspire a healthy respect, as Pittsburgh would do the following week. The Ravens were more of an annoyance. If the Panthers started to slouch, Baltimore could be trouble.

"Remember Jacksonville!" became the quote of the day. It didn't quite have the ring of "Remember the Alamo," but Panthers players knew what it meant. The last time Carolina had won an emotional game over San Francisco, in September, the Panthers had played their worst game of the season the following week in a loss to Jacksonville.

Game week was quiet this time compared to the electricity generated by the San Francisco game the week before. The one burst of emotion came on Thursday, when the NFC and AFC Pro Bowl teams were announced. After not placing a single player on the team in 1995, the Panthers had seven named to the squad this time—second only to Dallas in the entire NFL.

Kevin Greene, Lamar Lathon, and Sam Mills would start at the three linebacker spots, giving Carolina a starting sweep of that position. Cornerback Eric Davis, kicker John Kasay, special-teamer Michael Bates, and tight end Wesley Walls also had been chosen in voting by players, coaches, and fans.

"It's awesome, man, awesome!" Walls exulted. He had slept badly the night before, worried about whether he would make the squad for the first time.

"That's a heck of a statement," Greene said. "Maybe the respect factor is finally coming."

Lathon was so happy when Dom Capers and Bill Polian gave him the news that he hugged both of them. Then he started crying.

The Pro Bowl would be Mills's fifth. He became the oldest non-kicker ever to be elected as a starter to the game.

With the good Pro Bowl news cascading on top of the San Francisco upset, everything was going wonderfully for the Panthers. That scared Collins. "If we were going to have a letdown, it was going to be that game," Collins said. "I was worried, very worried."

The Panthers were workmanlike in practice, but try as they might, they couldn't inspire themselves emotionally as they had for the 49ers. This would be a tricky game.

Shortly before kickoff, a television report on NBC claimed that Panthers general manager Bill Polian might be leaving Carolina soon for another GM job, possibly at New Orleans. "It was completely untrue,"

Polian said later. "I wish in retrospect I had called up [NBC Sports chief] Dick Ebersol and asked him either to substantiate it publicly or retract it. Prior to that, there had been no real problems. But then this [story] had a life of its own."

For the rest of the season, Polian would be dogged by "Will he go?" rumors. But on December 15, he tried to ignore them and simply watch the game like the rest of the 70,075 fans enjoying a clear, 54-degree day at Ericsson Stadium.

Carolina struck first that Sunday with a 29-yard field goal from John Kasay. But Testaverde—who entered the game with 29 touchdown passes and only 15 interceptions—showed the Ravens' talent when he hit Michael "Thriller" Jackson for a 23-yard touchdown six minutes later. Jackson outmaneuvered Eric Davis for the ball on the play, which gave Baltimore a 7–3 lead with 6:50 left in the first quarter.

"I flat-out dropped it," Davis said ruefully. "It hit me in the wrong place—right in the palms."

Carolina retook the lead with a two-yard touchdown run from Anthony Johnson early in the second half; he would go over 1,000 yards rushing on this afternoon. But Baltimore used two Matt Stover field goals to go back up, 13–10.

At halftime the Panthers were trailing by three points to a 4–10 team. The division lead—theirs for only a week—was already in danger. Capers showed no signs of panic in the locker room, however. "We've been here before," he said. "In four of our ten wins, we've been down at halftime."

This was true, as was the fact that the Panthers had developed into the NFL's best defensive team in the season's second half. Nevertheless, the Ravens were playing confident football.

The Panthers reentered the stadium determined to change that. With the ball at the Carolina 24, Collins hit Willie Green and Wesley Walls on consecutive 13-yard passes to get it to midfield. The drive nearly stalled on fourth-and-one at the Baltimore 41, but Capers, showing faith in the revamped offensive line, sent Collins up the middle on a quarterback sneak. He pushed for two yards, and the drive was kept alive.

Carrier did the rest. He caught a 26-yard pass to bring the ball down to the Baltimore eight, then snatched a six-yard TD throw from Collins on third-and-goal. The Panthers led again, 17–13, with seven minutes left in the third quarter.

Baltimore would not go away, though. The Ravens offense had been slowed down, but the Ravens still had enough left to exchange field goals with the Panthers, giving Carolina a 20–16 lead early in the fourth quarter. The game was still in doubt when Carolina got the ball back on a punt at its own 37 with 10:14 left in the game.

It was as good a time as any for an unlikely hero to emerge.

PANTHERS FULLBACK SCOTT GREENE LIVED WITH THE misfortune of a last name already claimed by two of Carolina's most well-known players, linebacker Kevin and wide receiver Willie. Scott Greene was a pleasant, unobtrusive rookie—a squatty fullback with a crewcut who felt lucky to be on the team at all.

Greene was purely a special-teamer. At 5' 10" and 225 pounds, he looked like a cannonball running downfield and was good at bowling into other team's blocking wedges. A sixth-round draft choice out of Michigan State, he had been a two-time MVP for the Spartans but was a nobody in the Panthers locker room. Carolina had actually cut him in July, then brought him back onto the practice squad to serve as a tackling dummy.

Finally, in midseason, the Panthers could no longer ignore Greene's tenacity on special teams and his good hands as a backup fullback, so they promoted him to the bottom of the active roster. Still, he often got boxed out of his own locker by members of the media who always gathered around his verbose locker-room neighbor Wesley Walls.

The Baltimore game wasn't supposed to be any different for Greene—until Howard Griffith suffered a pinched nerve in the fourth quarter. The player who would have been the second-string fullback, Bob Christian, a player known for his advocacy of sexual abstinence before marriage, was on the injured reserve list for the season.

That left Greene. He jogged into the huddle, hoping he would not flub anything up. He joined the Panthers offense at a crucial juncture, with Carolina still holding that 20–16 lead.

For the first seven plays of the drive, he blocked with fairly good results. Then, on first-and-ten from the Baltimore 13, the call came in from the sidelines: a pass to Greene.

With Griffith out, Baltimore wasn't paying much attention to the fullback position, and that allowed Greene to sneak out into the flat. Collins hit him, he caught it, and bulldogged straight ahead for six yards. That, Greene figured, would probably be his one catch of the season. But on third-and-goal from the one, he was told to run another pass pattern—one that Griffith usually ran in this situation.

Collins had two options on the play as he faded back—either tight end Walls or the rookie. It wasn't surprising whom he chose to look at first, but Walls was double-covered inside. On the outside, however, Greene was all alone. Collins lofted a soft pass toward him that looked as big as a basketball.

"Just don't let me drop it," Greene breathed. He didn't. Carolina scored on what Collins would call the "biggest drive of the season so far." With 3:38 left, and a 27–16 lead, the game was basically over. Greene's catch had made blackbird pie of the Ravens.

"You can't stop Scott Greene, you can only hope to contain him!" backup quarterback Steve Beuerlein screamed in a happy Panthers locker room after the game.

Ironically, Greene didn't play again the rest of the season on offense. He carefully clipped out the picture of his touchdown in the next day's *Charlotte Observer.* "I'll never forget that day," he said. "Or that play."

Carolina's win assured the team at least one more week atop the NFC West. A win over Pittsburgh in the season finale would assure a first-round playoff bye and an automatic berth as one of the NFL's final eight teams.

"There's no place like first place," Carlton Bailey said.

THE DECEMBER 22 GAME VS. PITTSBURGH WOULD BE a pride game for the Panthers in many ways. Capers had made his NFL mark there as a defensive coordinator under Bill Cowher, his friend and now his rival. Kevin Greene had parted from the Steelers on bad terms after the 1995 season. The Panthers ran basically the same defense as the Steelers did—a 3–4, blitz-from-everywhere alignment. And both offenses concentrated on running the ball and not getting themselves beaten.

But for the two sides the stakes were very different on the NFL's final Sunday.

The day before the game the Steelers had been locked into the No. 3 playoff spot in the AFC when New England won a regular-season game over the New York Giants. So no matter what happened vs. Carolina, Pittsburgh would play the first playoff weekend at home.

For Carolina, on the other hand, this game had huge implications. Capers greeted the team at the Monday-morning meeting after the Baltimore win with a proposal: three days off if they won, and working right through Christmas Day if they didn't.

"Scrooge!" the Panthers yelled. "Grinch!"

"I noticed cheering after one [scenario] and booing after the other," Capers later said. "When I told them we would have to work on Christmas if things didn't work out the way we wanted them to against the Steelers, they had a few choice comments."

But the players knew Capers's offer was fair. A win would mean Carolina would not play again until the weekend of January 4–5. A loss would mean Carolina would have to prepare very quickly to play again, in a home wild-card playoff game December 28 or 29. In its simplest terms, a win against Pittsburgh meant Carolina could skip a step, and the players could enjoy Christmas, too.

A couple of notable things occurred in practice the week before the Steelers game. The school bus drove by again, with the kids screaming out the window, "Cowboys! Cowboys!" This time, though, the words sounded more like a promise than a threat, because if Carolina won this game, there was a good possibility the Panthers would host Dallas at home in a second-round playoff game.

The other notable occurrence: Wide receiver Brian Wiggins learned yet another position. Wiggins was a practice-squadder for most of the season, a cheerful wide receiver who filled in wherever he was needed during workouts. He had yet to play a down.

Sometimes the Panthers put Wiggins at defensive back when they needed one more at practice, but this week, they made him stand in for Pittsburgh quarterback Kordell Stewart. Wiggins ran for a touchdown that week in a scrimmage while playing Stewart. His teammates were impressed enough with his versatility to start calling him "Leon," a play on Dallas's jack of all trades, Deion Sanders. They also drew a backward Nike "swoosh" on some of Wiggins's clothing.

Kevin Greene, in major media demand all week because of the obvious story angle of his playing against his former team, carefully avoided the cameras. He didn't want to give the Steelers any bulletin-board material. "I wasn't going to let the media build this up as some Kevin Greene revenge game against Pittsburgh," Greene said.

DECEMBER 22 STARTED OUT COLD AND CLOUDY AND stayed that way. It was a surprise for the fans used to the balmy temperatures the Panthers had enjoyed for almost all of their afternoon home games. The temperature was 43 degrees at kickoff, and the wind-chill factor hovered around freezing most of the game.

Of course, Cowher, Pittsburgh's coach, wanted to win the game, but because he couldn't alter his playoff seeding, he had already decided to take some of his pieces off the board. Four defensive starters would not play at all. Running back Jerome "The Bus" Bettis would be put in the shop after a couple of series. Same thing with quarterback Mike Tomczak. Cowher wanted to take a long look at the athletic but raw Kordell Stewart at quarterback that Sunday.

The Panthers liked all of those changes, except for Stewart's likely insertion. They were more scared of Stewart than of anyone else on Pittsburgh's team. His unique skills as a wide receiver/quarterback/runner had earned him the nickname Slash, because of the punctuation mark needed to describe his role with the Steelers. Brian Wiggins had done a good job of impersonating Stewart during the week, but no one could duplicate Stewart's speed out of the pocket.

At first, though, this game looked like it would be easy. Bates took the opening kickoff at the 15 and raced 27 yards, setting Carolina up only 58 yards from the Steelers goal. It took only ten plays to cross it.

On a methodical drive where no play covered more than 12 yards, Collins threw three times to Walls. The tight end caught all three of them, including the last one for a nine-yard touchdown.

Carolina would add a safety on the second play of the second quarter when Tomczak, trapped in the end zone by Greene and Lathon, heaved the ball to . . . no one. Intentional grounding in the end zone is illegal, so the Panthers got two points for the safety that would have been inevitable had Tomczak not thrown the ball away. Greene and Lathon celebrated by holding their arms above their heads and pressing their hands tightly together, the signal for a safety. Carolina led 9–0, with 14 minutes left in the first half, but Pittsburgh, with nothing to play for, still wouldn't fade away. The Steelers were admirable warriors, and later in that same quarter, they got a break.

Fullback Howard Griffith, normally a reliable ballcarrier, swung out in the flat at the Carolina five-yard line after a Pittsburgh punt had hemmed the Panthers back at their own two. Griffith got drilled at the seven by Pittsburgh free safety Darren Perry and lost the ball. Pittsburgh's Willie Williams recovered at the Carolina seven.

It took the Steelers three plays—and some jawing back and forth between Tomczak and Greene—to get into the end zone.

Greene pressured Tomczak into an incompletion on second down, and after Tomczak had already thrown, Greene didn't try too hard to hold up on his follow-through and knocked the quarterback down. The play was clean, according to the official, but Tomczak didn't think so. He gave Greene a shove. "He was just saying that he missed me and that he loved me," Greene would joke later.

On third down, Pittsburgh went to one of their favorite goal-line plays: five wide receivers, with their best receiver, Andre Hastings, in the inside slot position. This play, which would foreshadow the most momentous play of the game, was designed to get Hastings isolated against either a safety or a linebacker—a mismatch in either case.

Hastings got open, Tomczak threw it with Greene in his face, and Pittsburgh scored. The extra point made it 9–7, Carolina, with 10 minutes still left in the first half. And that was it for Tomczak. Cowher pulled the veteran in favor of Slash.

Pittsburgh's next play was unorthodox genius. The Steelers had noticed that Carolina's first row on the kickoff return team cheated a little when trying to rush back to block for Bates, often starting a step or two early. So far all year no NFL team had had the guts to take advantage of that with an onsides kick—it was too risky—but the Steelers did. Kicker Norm Johnson squibbed the ball 14 yards and fell on it himself. The only Panther who had any shot at getting to it was Anthony Johnson, who dove unsuccessfully and found himself buried under a pile of black-and-gold.

Johnson was slow getting up, and Capers worried during those few seconds about how wise he had been to have a 1,000-yard rusher still playing special teams. Despite his concern, he had vowed not to second-guess himself on this point.

"That's the essence of our football team," Capers would say later. "There's really nobody who's exempt from any team. What he [Johnson] does on the kickoff team is extremely important. We think he's as valuable in that role as he is carrying the football. To me, it [having Johnson play special teams] does something for the total attitude of your football team. The kicking game here is just as important to us as offense or defense. If you treat the kicking game like a second-class citizen, the players view it that way."

A.J. struggled to get up. And Pittsburgh gave up its chance for more quick points when Toi Cook intercepted Stewart's first pass at the Carolina 49. But the Panthers couldn't move the ball, either, so Rohn Stark came on to punt. His kick bounded into the end zone, setting up one of the most bizarre plays of the season.

TOMMY DONOVAN WAS TWENTY-FOUR YEARS OLD—A friendly, gregarious type of average build whom you wouldn't look at twice if you passed him on the street—unless he was playing his alter ego: Sir Purr.

Sir Purr, the Panthers mascot, was an athletic fur ball who could dance so well that many of the players in the first season hypothesized that the man inside the costume had to be black. "Got to be a brother," they would say after watching Sir Purr's signature routine, a herky-jerky dance at the two-minute warning after every home game. "Got to be!"

In fact, Donovan was a white guy who could dance. He was also a veteran mascot. While attending the University of South Carolina, Donovan had won the role of Cocky, the Gamecocks mascot, and had played him for three years. In 1994, as a junior there, he won the collegiate mascot national championship. As Sir Purr, Donovan always looked for something to do to get the Panther crowd into the game.

When Rohn Stark's punt bounced into the end zone where Sir Purr stood, Donovan never thought about the fact that the ball was still live until either it left the end zone or a player hopped on it.

He just dove.

"It never registered that I was interfering with the game," Donovan said. "But the crowd went nuts. I looked up and all these players were around me, laughing and hitting me and saying, 'Good job. Way to down that punt.'"

As stern-faced officials approached him, Donovan realized what he had done. The Panthers might receive a penalty for this. Sir Purr may have committed the cardinal mascot sin of actually helping the other team!

There was only one thing to do.

Hide.

"I hid behind the goalpost," Donovan said. "Then, to get even farther away, I hid behind one of the groundskeepers."

It isn't difficult to find a six-foot-tall furry Panther on a football field, however, and head official Dick Hantak easily tracked him down.

"Sir Purr," Hantak said gravely, "If you want to be out here, you can't come on the field like that."

To preserve his animal image, Sir Purr was supposed never to talk, but he thought in this situation he should make an exception. "I made a mistake," he said. "I'm so sorry. Please don't penalize us. It won't happen again."

By this time, Cowher had almost doubled over in laughter at a replay on the scoreboard of Sir Purr's dive onto the field. ESPN would later replay Sir Purr's leap and run a graphic under his name that read: SIR PURR. PUNT RETURNS: ONE. YARDS: ZERO.

Capers never cracked a smile about the incident until the next day, however. The field-position king was too concerned about whether Carolina would lose 15 yards. No one else can keep blinders on for an entire football game quite like Capers. If Jesus finally returned to Earth in the middle of a Panthers play, Capers's first question would be "Are we going to get penalized for having twelve men on the field?"

Hantak cut Sir Purr a break, since there was no way Pittsburgh was about to return the punt. No Steeler had been within 15 yards of the ball. But Donovan still felt bad, figuring he might have subtly altered the momentum of the game. When Pittsburgh's Stewart finally stopped running a few minutes later, he would feel even worse.

On first-and-ten from the 20 after Sir Purr's brush with infamy, Stewart faded back to pass. When nothing opened up, he decided to run. He shot through the line like a bullet. He split four Panthers defenders right up the middle with an astounding burst of speed. No one even laid a hand on him, including Panthers speedster Tyrone Poole, whom Stewart easily outran.

The result was an 80-yard scramble for a touchdown—the longest scoring run by a quarterback in NFL history. Sir Purr, fearing retribution from fans or players, walked back into the tunnel under the stadium and didn't reemerge until 10 minutes later.

The TD gave Pittsburgh a 14–9 lead at halftime.

"I turned on my 'Slash' speed," Stewart said of the run. "I'm in the record books, baby."

And Carolina was in trouble.

EVEN WITH PITTSBURGH PLAYING A DEFENSE MADE UP of several second-stringers, the Panthers offense couldn't get into the end zone. Carolina's first series of the second half looked promising, but on third-and-two from the Pittsburgh 17, Collins threw quickly under heavy pressure toward Griffith. The pass sailed away from Griffith, who had no shot at it, and Kasay had to come in to kick a field goal to cut the lead to 14–12 early in the third quarter.

Lathon—who had basically stopped criticizing Collins after the critical moments in the team meeting—couldn't help himself this time. He tracked down Collins as the quarterback pulled off his helmet and jogged toward the sideline. "Hey, Kerry," Lathon said. "I respect what you do. Those linemen have to block for you and give you some time. But you have to make those plays! You have to put some more touch on the ball!"

Collins was furious. "You have got to be kidding," he said, boiling. "I don't tell you how to play linebacker! Don't tell me how to play quarterback! You don't know what you're talking about!"

Collins hadn't forgotten that Lathon had intimated that he, Collins, had a drinking problem during the team meeting. He had told Lathon that he didn't know what he was talking about before, but that didn't make him any less angry this time.

Now, Lathon was angry too. He grabbed Collins by the jersey and they yelled at each other again before Lathon pushed Collins away.

Capers noticed the confrontation and asked Lathon what had happened. "I told him *exactly* what I just said," Lathon said. "Kerry got pissed off and I'm sure it had to do with what was said before [at the team meeting]."

Kasay kept bailing the offense out, however. Two more times in the second half, Kasay knocked in field goals after Panthers drives stalled. He set an NFL record with the last one, giving him 37 successful field goals in a single season.

"My job is just to kick the ball," Kasay said later, pooh-poohing the record. "Let's not get too philosophical about it."

Kasay's last field goal made it 18–14, Carolina, early in the fourth quarter, but the Panthers were finished scoring by then. They didn't make a single first down in the fourth quarter. It would be up to the defense to hold that lead in a fourth quarter that was "as dramatic as you could get," Capers would say later.

Cowher, coaching like someone who had nothing to lose (which he didn't), wasn't about to punt or kick a field goal for the entire quarter. He was going full speed ahead—touchdown or nothing.

"It was really a magical sort of situation," Panthers owner Jerry Richardson recalled. He would later call this game his favorite of the season.

Pittsburgh's first fourth-quarter drive ended at the Carolina 29 when Stewart couldn't find Andre Hastings on a fourth-and-three play. But it wouldn't be that easy. Carolina quickly punted, and Pittsburgh took over with 9:52 left in the game. This time the Steelers moved all the way to the Carolina six.

On fourth-and-three, Stewart faded back and saw Ernie Mills slanting over the middle with a step on Tyrone Poole. Stewart laid the ball in perfectly, right at the goal line. Mills dropped it.

"Oh, how I wish I had that one back," Mills would say months later, still haunted by the play. "I just took it for granted that I would catch it. I never squeezed it."

Still, Pittsburgh had plenty of time. The Panthers ran three plays and punted again, and the Steelers took over at the Carolina 40 with 3:29 left.

The 72,217 rowdy fans edged forward in their seats. This would be the drive that decided whether Carolina got the first-round playoff bye or not. And everyone knew it, including Panthers reserve safety Chad Cota.

COTA, A SEVENTH-ROUND DRAFT CHOICE OUT OF OREgon in 1995, had matinee-idol looks and a quiet demeanor. From a small Oregon town, he was more comfortable on skis or a snowboard than in the middle of the defensive backs' fast-paced repartee in the locker room. He looked like he could still be in college, or just out, serving drinks behind the bar at Bennigan's. But he could play the game.

Cota had gotten more and more time from Brett Maxie during the season, as the aging Maxie kept getting nagging injuries. Cota had fumbled his first interception away—against Minnesota—but had made three more since then and had come to be counted on as a key part of the Panthers' pass defense.

He was young and wide eyed enough to admit to having felt a bit of awe when he had guarded Jerry Rice against San Francisco earlier in the year. "Playing against him—it was just weird being out there," Cota said. "And then I ended up tackling him in the game. So if everything goes bad, at least I ended up tackling Jerry Rice."

Cota was an Oregon kid all the way. He had stayed in-state for school and had gone to the University of Oregon, where he played on the Ducks' "Gang Green" defense. Coached by Rich Brooks (who was the St. Louis Rams head coach in 1996), Cota helped lead his team to the 1995 Rose Bowl, where Oregon lost to a Kerry Collins–led Penn State squad.

Now Cota would be playing in the Panthers' biggest defensive series of the season. And like the rest of the Panthers, he seemed helpless to stop Pittsburgh's inexorable march downfield.

Stewart had finally gotten his passing rhythm going. A 15-yard pass to Hastings took the Steelers down to the Carolina nine with 1:53 left in the game.

"We've gotta have it," linebacker Sam Mills told his teammates in the huddle.

The next 90 seconds would all be spent inside the Carolina 10-yard line in a frenzied finale to the regular season. On first down Stewart threw for a six-yard gain. The ball was now at the three. On second down, Stewart got tripped up by Mike Fox on a scramble, but that loss was nullified as Kevin Greene got flagged for defensive holding: automatic first down for Pittsburgh at the one-yard line.

Capers, on the sideline, felt his face turn red. He would not feel more emotional during a game situation all year, he said later, "because of all that was at stake."

Then Pittsburgh blinked. Offensive guard Brendan Stai false-started, and the Steelers had to move back to the six.

On first down, Stewart looked for Ernie Mills but threw incomplete. On second, he scrambled, but Shawn King, in as a pass-rushing substitute, was there to stop him for a two-yard loss.

It was third-and-goal at the eight. The fans screamed for the Panthers to "hold 'em, hold 'em!"

But Carolina had the wrong defense on the field.

Sam Mills was supposed to be out of the ballgame, but in the heat of battle, something went awry. The Panthers didn't notice that the Steelers had their five-receiver setup—the same one that worked for a touchdown earlier in the game—on the field until it was too late.

Mills saw it by the time he got back in his defensive stance, but by then it was too late to leave and let Damon Pieri—a quicker, smaller player—run in to take his place. "I saw five wide receivers and I knew I was the slowest guy out there," Mills said. "I thought, 'This could be interesting.' "

Cota saw it, too. He knew this was the same play where the Steelers had isolated Hastings inside earlier in the game. So, on a gamble, he started sprinting toward Mills just as Stewart pulled the ball back and prepared to release it.

Panthers radio announcer Bill Rosinski called what happened next like this: "Stewart back to throw, fires in the end zone. What is it? What is it? INTERCEPTED! The Panthers have it! The Panthers have it!"

Cota and Hastings had reached for the ball almost simultaneously, but Cota had a better grip on it. "I had it," Cota said. "He was trying to get it from me. I knew I had it. I didn't even know they were debating it."

"He made a great play on it," Pittsburgh's Hastings admitted. "At the time we hit the ground, we both had the ball, but he had a little bit more leverage than I did."

"He anticipated the throw and made a great, great play," Panthers defensive coordinator Vic Fangio said of Cota. "It's one of the plays that will live here forever."

Fans saw two players, one from each team, wrestling in the end zone. By NFL rules, if each had an equal hold of the ball, the offensive player would be ruled the victor and the touchdown would count. But Cota demonstrated his grip by rolling away from Hastings and coming up with the ball.

It was the play that Fangio said changed the Panthers forever.

"I just think some kind of love affair—I mean a true love affair—started then," Fangio said. "The town was in love with the Panthers before that, but from that fourth quarter on it was much bigger. After that you'd read in the paper and the classified ads that guys were willing to give up Charlotte Hornets tickets or Masters tickets to get one ticket for the Cowboys game."

THE GAME WAS OVER, AND COTA WAS THE LATEST IN a long line of Panthers heroes. In celebration, Eric Davis flung his helmet straight down into the turf, and it skipped like a rock 25 yards to the Panthers sideline. Safety Pat Terrell jumped into the stands and got pounded on the back by delirious Panthers supporters.

"Who would have thought?!" Terrell yelled. "Who would have thought?!"

Queen's rock anthem "We Are the Champions" blared over the loudspeakers as the players ran off the field. Capers shook his cap at the fans as he ran into the tunnel—a major emotional gesture for the even-keeled coach.

Across the country in San Francisco, the 49ers were reduced to cursing at their television sets. If Carolina had lost, the 49ers could still have won the division with a Monday-night win over Detroit the next day. With this result, San Francisco was doomed to a wild-card bid.

Toi Cook exulted, "There were a lot of wineglasses hitting the wall in San Francisco when Chad made that interception!"

Cota ran off the field, ball held high toward the stands. Panthers linebacker Greene stopped him just inside the tunnel.

"You're going to have a long, wonderful career in this league and you're going to look back and realize how big of a play that really was," Greene breathlessly told Cota.

The Panthers would have Christmas off after all. And the defense—which led the NFL in sacks with 60 and again didn't allow a point in the second half—had won the West for the Panthers.

"You wouldn't want to be anywhere else," Greene said, remembering the goal-line stand. "You've got your backs to the goal line. It's a rotten situation. You dream of stuff like that. That's what makes football players football players—sucking it up and dealing with it and winning the game defensively."

Lathon wasn't even in the game late—he had been sidelined with a badly bruised hip. But in the locker room, before the reporters got there, he became overcome by emotion in the huddle.

With tears streaming down his face, Lathon bawled, "We did it together. Panther pride on three! One, two, three . . ."

". . . PANTHER PRIDE!"

Lathon didn't even mind that he had lost his $2,000 bet to Greene as to who would have the most sacks. Greene had finished with 14½; Lathon, 13½.

An hour after the game, Cota still had the football that he had intercepted tucked under his arm.

"You can let go of that ball now," Panthers cornerback Eric Davis teased Cota. "We won."

Said Cota: "Ain't nobody getting this ball, bro'."

THE ONLY PERSON WHO MAY HAVE BEEN HAPPIER about beating Pittsburgh than Cota was Kevin Greene. Defeating his old team put him in a jolly mood.

It's hard to say which would have been more unlikely back in training camp: the Panthers winning the NFC West or Greene and Lamar Lathon posing together in Santa Claus suits. But there they were, just a few days after the Pittsburgh game, all decked out in red and white, waiting for *Charlotte Observer* photographer Bob Leverone to snap the shot that would appear almost poster size on the front sports page of the newspaper's Christmas Day editions.

The picture was symbolic not only of the team's holiday playoff vacation due to a first-round bye, but also of the friendship Greene and Lathon had built through the course of the season—a friendship that had played a major role in helping the Panthers become a championship-caliber team. Salt & Pepper had come a long way from the season opener against Atlanta, when Lathon had despised Greene. Now, Lathon no longer viewed Greene as the enemy, but rather as a close ally and friend—so close that they could joke about *anything*.

"I've never heard of a black Santa Claus!" Greene had said when Lathon was putting on his Santa suit.

"What makes you think Santa has to have blond hair and blue eyes?" Lathon fired back. "And, while we're at it, where's my black wig? I can't wear this white hair. I can hear the kids now when they see this picture. 'What's wrong with him, Mama? He's an albino Santa Claus.'"

The line made both of them laugh loudly. It was said in fun, with no harm intended toward anyone. Then Greene noticed that Lathon's wig and beard weren't on straight, so he tried to adjust them.

"What are you doing?" Lathon asked.

"Trying to help you out," said Greene.

"I think we've gotten too comfortable with one another," Lathon said with a chuckle.

Despite that gesture of tenderness, the rivalry between them was still evident.

When Leverone was getting them set for the picture pose, he asked Lathon to stand on a step-up box he'd placed on the floor and asked Greene to stand next to Lathon.

"No, no, no!" Greene said. "Why does *he* get to be on a pedestal?"

Leverone explained that while Lathon would stand on the step, Greene would stand slightly ahead of Lathon, to Lathon's right.

"Oh, okay, I'm in front," Greene said, relieved. "Yeah, that's good."

SO WHAT HAD HAPPENED? WHAT HAD BROUGHT SALT & Pepper together after such a rocky start at the beginning of the season?

The bonding probably began on the night early in the season when Greene invited Lathon to his house for a country dinner. Greene's wife, Tara, prepared chicken à la king and homemade biscuits. A few weeks later, Lathon invited the Greenes to his home. His personal assistant, Ivery Black, served a feast that included Alaskan king crab legs, prime rib, and lasagna.

"After we ate, we looked at old pictures of me—with hair!" Lathon said. "We even talked about wrestling together someday. We figured we could set up a match and call ourselves 'The Spice Twins.'"

On the football field they had been great together all year. It was an amazing feat that two teammates could finish first and second in the NFL in sacks. That was even more than Capers had hoped for when he signed Greene back in May.

"Lathon and Greene are both tremendous football players," St. Louis Rams coach Rich Brooks had said during the regular season. "They can kill you. When you're trying to decide how to block them, it's kind of like choosing your poison. Lathon is really special, but one of the biggest differences in him this year is having Greene on the other side. Lathon was clearly the guy you had to worry about last year. Now you have to worry about two of them."

Though he was reluctant to admit it early in the season, Lathon eventually acknowledged how much better Greene's presence had made him.

"Lamar originally thought Kevin would take some of his thunder, but it turned out that Kevin was the best thing that ever happened to Lamar," said cornerback Eric Davis. "Darion Conner [the other starting outside linebacker in 1995] was not going to push Lamar. But Lamar wanted to be better than Kevin. He wanted everyone to see that he was better than Kevin."

As the competition between them carried on during the regular season, the chemistry improved as well. Lathon loved agitating Greene, to the point that Greene called him "the biggest instigator I've ever seen." Almost every day in practice, usually during stretching warmup exercises, Lathon would sling a couple of verbal darts at Greene. Sometimes, when Greene would feel exuberant and would yell something to try to fire everyone up for the workout, Lathon would respond, "There's no media out here, Kevin, so shut the hell up."

It happened so many times over the course of the season that their teammates lost count. Almost always, it drew laughs from the other players.

Lathon said that even though he was kidding, he was also making a statement. "Basically, I was letting everyone know that Kevin is a media whore," Lathon said. "And he is. He lives for it. The media obliges him because they love that stuff, too. I just wanted to humble him and let him know nobody really cared." Nobody, perhaps, except

Lathon. If Greene was a "media whore," you had to wonder what that made Lathon.

"Deep down, I still don't know how well they like each other," said defensive end Gerald Williams, who played with Greene in college at Auburn and on the Steelers. "You have to understand that in professional sports, everyone is vying for the same camera."

Mills said he always believed the Greene-Lathon tandem would work, that he knew the friction between them in training camp and the early season would subside. "Both of those guys were on a mission to show the other one they were capable," he said. "Kevin wants a certain amount of career sacks, so he is going to come out and get in the quarterback's face. Lamar felt like he was brought here to be the sack guy on this team."

Mills said it was only natural that players at the relatively flamboyant position of outside linebacker would crave attention as much as Lathon and Greene. Lawrence Taylor did when he was with the New York Giants, and so did two of Mills's former teammates in New Orleans, ex–Pro Bowlers Rickey Jackson and Pat Swilling. "I think Kevin requires a little more attention from the fans and Lamar requires a little more from his teammates," said Mills. "Kevin is more of an entertainer, as you see with his wrestling background. He feeds off the fans. I think it drives him. And when I say 'fans,' put the media in there, too.

"Lamar can play a game, and as long as his teammates realize he was great out there, he's just glowing. When he was selected to the Pro Bowl, that's the happiest I've ever seen Lamar. He knew the players were part of the voting process and he really appreciated the fact that his peers recognized him."

For Greene and Lathon, it was all about respect. And after the season they'd had, both of them were receiving plenty of that.

AS THEIR FIRST PLAYOFF GAME TOGETHER APPROACHED against Dallas, Greene and Lathon were like brothers. They had big plans for chasing down Cowboys quarterback Troy Aikman—but not before tossing their Santa's "sacks" over their shoulders and finishing the pose for the Christmas picture.

After Leverone got them set—Lathon on the step-up pedestal with Greene standing slightly to the right—Leverone asked them to show him some "crazy energy."

Greene smiled. Lathon growled, "I hate you, Kevin!"

After a few more snaps, Leverone turned and aimed the camera at Greene.

"Hey, hey, give me some air time over here," Lathon said.

"He's focusing on me right now, my man," Greene said with a wink.

Together, Salt & Pepper had finally arrived.

CHAPTER FOURTEEN

The Unforgettable Game

SOMETIMES, LIFE EMBARRASSES YOU WITH RICHES.

Sometimes, you win the lottery and kiss the prettiest girl at the dance and make your parents proud and cause a child to smile—all in the same day.

That's what it felt like for the Carolina Panthers in the latter part of 1996. Just when it seemed like it couldn't get any better after the dramatic win over Pittsburgh, it did. That's because in the first round of the playoffs—the one that Carolina got to watch because of Chad Cota's magnificent interception vs. the Steelers—Dallas pounded Minnesota 40–15.

That meant the Cowboys would visit Ericsson Stadium and Carolina for a second-round playoff game on January 5, 1997. You couldn't script it any better. Hollywood would have dismissed this as frivolous fiction: *The defending Super Bowl champs reduced to playing in an expansion team's stadium? Please!* But this was real.

"This is the type of game," Panthers linebacker Carlton Bailey said, "that you wait all your life to play."

And to watch.

Single-game ticket sales nearly caused a riot. During the '96 season, the Panthers held out about 7,300 tickets per game for fans who couldn't afford or didn't want to buy a permanent-seat license. Those 7,300 tickets to the Cowboys game sold out in four minutes.

"It was exciting—a very wild ride for those four minutes," said Phil Youtsey, the Panthers director of ticket sales. "We had two hundred forty points of sale—one hundred twenty phone lines and one hundred twenty ticket outlets. That's absolutely huge in the industry. That's a 'Rolling Stones'–type event."

About 3,100 people showed up at Ericsson Stadium to try to buy tickets that morning. Only 55, the ones who drew numbers 1 through 55 in the "line lottery," got tickets. Scalpers were asking for, and receiving, up to $1,000 per ticket for the game.

Yes, America's Team was definitely coming: Troy Aikman; Emmitt Smith; Michael Irvin; Deion Sanders—a Fab Four that had been part of the Cowboys' spectacular streak of three Super Bowl championships in the previous four years.

Panthers safety Pat Terrell worried about all of them.

But mostly, he worried about his dad. His father, Grady Terrell, had undergone a kidney transplant only a month before. Grady's younger brother Gerald, Pat Terrell's uncle, had donated his kidney. Both had been laid up in the hospital after the painful, delicate operation. It had gone well, but now Terrell was concerned.

Grady Terrell had hardly been out of the house since the surgery, yet he was determined to see his son play in what would be Terrell's first-ever playoff game. The elder Terrell brothers, along with several friends, were going to charter a small plane from St. Petersburg, Florida, to fly up for the game on Sunday.

"We don't really have that kind of money," Grady Terrell said. "But we know these sorts of games don't come along very often."

That was very true. Panthers linebacker Sam Mills had spent his entire career waiting to win one playoff game. Perhaps this would be his last chance. Cornerback Tyrone Poole was so excited all week he could barely breathe. The Cowboys were his high school heroes, especially Neon Deion, and now he would be facing them. He just hoped he wouldn't slip in his coverage, as he occasionally had the week before vs. Pittsburgh.

Lathon, always looking for a motivational edge of the "we-don't-get-any-respect" variety, found a nugget early. He saw a quote from Dallas coach Barry Switzer on ESPN that seemed to indicate that Switzer was a little unclear as to exactly where Charlotte was. Switzer noted that the Cowboys had never traveled this far south for a playoff game. Since Charlotte is northeast of Dallas, the players figured Switzer had no concern for the second-year franchise. If Carolina could beat the Cowboys, Lathon would cook up a little something special for Switzer after the game.

But Switzer had bigger problems than a questionable sense of direction. Early in the week, he was faced with yet another crisis in an expanding series that had headline writers around the country labeling the Cowboys AMERICA'S MOST WANTED.

This time the charges turned out to be completely false, but that was only proved a couple of weeks after the game, when a 23-year-old Dallas woman named Nina Shahravan recanted a number of lies she had told about being forced to have sex with Dallas offensive lineman Erik Williams while Cowboys wide receiver Michael Irvin was present. In fact, the woman later admitted that the sex with Williams had been consensual. Irvin wasn't even there.

No one knew Shahravan was making up her story the week of the Cowboys-Panthers game, however, so scandal rocked the Cowboys headquarters at Valley Ranch yet again.

Six of the last thirteen players suspended by the NFL for drug abuse had been Cowboys, and the media quickly took to calling the Cowboys "South America's Team" and their headquarters "Valley Raunch." Included in the drug-related suspensions was Irvin, who had been suspended for the first five games of the season after pleading no contest to a felony charge of cocaine possession.

These new charges led the national news media to recount the tale of the Cowboys' "tarnished star" image of late. Switzer was forced once again into what had become a traditional role for him in his coaching career both at Dallas and on the collegiate level at Oklahoma: defender of what appeared to be an outlaw program.

When confronted with questions about his team's image problem on Wednesday, four days before the game, Switzer replied testily, "I quit worrying about that damn stuff thirty years ago."

As the questioning went on, Switzer got even angrier. Anyone who thought the Cowboys' problems came from the top down was, he said, "full of shit. I've made a thousand 'do-good' talks over the years," Switzer said. "Some kids listen, some don't."

The Cowboys' "America's Team" image had been tainted earlier in the season when a place called "the white house" was exposed as a residence where some players used to take their girlfriends to be out of the sight of their prying wives. Former secretary of education William Bennett had even suggested earlier in the season that Dallas was "hurting this country's morale."

Longtime Cowboys safety Bill Bates told Dallas reporters four days before the game that what was happening to the Cowboys' image "makes me sick to my stomach."

But a wounded animal is a dangerous one. Aikman—unsullied and 11–1 in his postseason starts—declared, "I'm still proud to wear a helmet with the star on it." And he still had Emmitt Smith to hand off to.

Dallas had clobbered Minnesota on the ground for 255 rushing yards (116 by Smith), and many analysts figured that the rushing game would be where this game would be lost or won. The whole Cowboys offensive line was going to the Pro Bowl, and they were the size of 18-wheelers.

Smith thought the Panthers defense was sound. "Their two outside linebackers, Greene and Lathon, are the two most talked-about outside linebackers in the league," Emmitt said. "That defense may have old men's age, but they are playing like young men in the heart."

THE PANTHERS HAD THEIR OWN OFF-FIELD PROBLEM before the Dallas game. Dom Capers suspended reserve defensive lineman Shawn King for the postseason for chronic tardiness. He had grown increasingly fed up with King's inconsistent work habits. He had missed one mandatory running session and two mandatory weightlifting workouts, and Capers wasn't pleased.

"In Shawn's case, it was a matter of credibility," Capers said later, explaining his decision. "I felt in my heart that I'd been as fair to Shawn King as I could be, in terms of letting him know ahead of time what the problems were and what the consequences would be in terms of tardiness. I had told him the next time there'd be a fine and we'd double the fine. And the second time, no ifs, ands, or buts, there'd be a suspension involved. So when the second time came, Shawn knew."

King later admitted to *The Charlotte Observer* that he had flunked a drug test in late December, testing positive for marijuana several days before his suspension. He said he had smoked pot on and off since he was fourteen years old, and he checked into a drug rehab center shortly after getting suspended without pay.

Since the positive test was only King's first, he wasn't automatically suspended by the NFL, as Whitley had been after testing positive for crystal meth. But King was the second Carolina player who had tested positive for drugs during the 1996 season. Carolina contended even after King's admission of drug use that the team suspension had come because of excessive tardiness and was not related to his marijuana problem.

The suspension for tardiness actually made the Panthers look good nationwide, although Capers hadn't planned for that. Carolina looked like the strict team, the one so clean that they would squeak if you rubbed a hand across their helmets. Dallas—the three-point favorite—played the renegade.

Four days before the game, verbose Panthers cornerback Toi Cook said that the two teams' owners seemed "diametrically opposed from a morality standpoint. That's not saying Jerry doesn't have morals. I just think Jerry Richardson is striving to put together a team you could take home to Mom."

It could be argued that many of the Cowboys could be taken home to Mom, too—Aikman and Smith among them. Some of the other players, however, seemed more at home in a strip club, and that was another problem for Dallas.

There were other problems, however. Dallas's depth was depleted. Injuries and free agency had sapped a team that had won three of the last four Super Bowls.

"This was not the Dallas team that beat Buffalo twice in the Super Bowl," Bill Polian said. "Not close to it. The Cowboys, San Francisco, and Green Bay all had more talent than we did in 1996, but Dallas was relying a lot more on the 'triplets' [Aikman, Irvin, and Smith] than it used to have to."

And Smith had been banged up all year at tailback with a variety of injuries.

Worst of all for Dallas, the Panthers coaching staff had two weeks to prepare for the Cowboys.

Carolina was always good in this situation, mainly because of Capers's obsessiveness. Capers's team had drilled Atlanta in the opening game after having most of the preseason to get ready. Carolina had blasted San Francisco 23–7 coming off their bye week in September. Capers thought the week before the San Francisco game was the sharpest Carolina had ever looked. And after some preparation, he thought these two weeks before the Dallas game might be even sharper.

Switzer believed that Dallas's main advantage would be the way that cornerbacks Deion Sanders and Kevin Smith could blanket the Panthers outside receivers, Willie Green and Mark Carrier.

The Panthers quietly agreed with that assessment as far as Sanders was concerned, but they thought they could get to Smith. He would be the corner they would go to all afternoon. Furthermore, defensive lineman Leon Lett had been suspended for drugs, and so Carolina also figured they would run the ball constantly at his replacement.

And to ensure a little psychological edge, Carolina would make Dallas wear its blue jerseys. It was a well-known fact in the NFL that the Cowboys lost more often wearing blue than white, so the Panthers chose to wear their own white jerseys, a departure from the normal black jerseys the team had worn at all winter home games.

But on their side Dallas had tradition, having played in 51 playoff games in their team history. This was Carolina's first.

Eric Davis, who had been involved in some huge Dallas–San Francisco battles before, loved the idea of this one. "If you want a chance to be The Man, you have to *beat* The Man."

THE PANTHERS HAD A MIDWEEK SCARE WHEN KEVIN Greene missed practice Thursday due to a bruised right shoulder suffered in practice. But he was fine before game time, and probably would have played even if his shoulder had fallen off on Saturday.

The Panthers' Thursday practice without Greene was ragged, however. Several fights broke out. Wide receivers dropped balls. Linemen jumped offside. These were the sorts of errors that usually gnawed at Capers so much that he would huddle up the team and make them start again. Not this time, though. His players appreciated his leniency, which was prompted by Capers's sense that the team was tight enough already and needed some slack. Friday's practice was much sharper.

The offensive line—ripped in the team meeting two months ago and now as a result bonded tight—also had a nice moment. The day before the Dallas game Greg Skrepenak asked for some time from linebacker Sam Mills to make a presentation in front of the rest of the team.

Running back Anthony Johnson had been the one player to defend the O-line in that brutal team meeting. Then he had followed every hole—and carved out a few more of his own—for 1,120 yards. Skrepenak, whose average salary was approximately seven times that of Johnson's $275,000, had talked to the other linemen about buying Johnson a Rolex watch. They knew A.J. didn't make much money by NFL standards. And they thought he deserved it.

Skrepenak gave a touching speech in front of the team before handing Johnson his prize.

"I have one son," Skrepenak said, "and another one to be born in a month. As I am raising my sons, I can tell you that I would want them to grow up to be like A.J. That's because of his work ethic, his character, and his belief in God. He is everything I wish my sons could be.

"Honestly," Skrepenak said in a soft voice, "I wish I could be more like him."

• • •

BY SATURDAY MORNING, CAPERS WAS READY TO PUMP up his team. As usual, he got up at 5 A.M. and headed straight to the stadium. He pulled out three examples of great Panthers plays—offense, defense, and special teams—from the past.

At the team meeting that morning, Capers praised the team for being a "team" in every respect of the word. He talked again about his philosophy—about why the biggest, fastest, and strongest players don't always triumph, but that the best teams do. This was an obvious reference to Dallas, the only team to place more players in the Pro Bowl than Carolina.

Then Capers showed the highlights of some of his favorite Panthers plays. He closed with these words: "Men, we're playing a good team. But every man in here knows if each man in here goes out and does a good job and refuses to accept anything but his best, you know what the outcome will be. The best team will win tomorrow. And I feel the best team is sitting here in this room."

Things went much more smoothly in Carolina before the game than in Dallas, where minicams and reporters constantly followed every move of Irvin and Williams as the false scandal developed. "We were able to lay in the weeds and wait for them to come," Panthers fullback Howard Griffith said.

It was certain by Saturday that Williams and Irvin would play. No charges would be filed against them to prohibit that. And it was also certain whom the winner of this game would play in the NFC championship: Green Bay in Green Bay. The Packers had defeated San Francisco 35–14 on Saturday.

The night before home games the Panthers always stayed at the Westin in uptown Charlotte. They were used to 1 P.M. home games, but Sunday's Cowboys-Panthers game wouldn't start until 4 P.M. By noon the team was going stir-crazy, especially Collins.

"About twelve-thirty, I decided I was going to go out and drive around," Collins said. He whipped around Charlotte's upscale Dilworth and Myers Park areas in his 1996 black BMW, listening to Pearl Jam. After a while, he got bored and decided to call his best friend back home in Pennsylvania, Brian "Pookie" McCarty, from his car phone.

"Brian," Collins started.

"What the hell are you calling me for, K.C.?" McCarty said, totally nonplussed. "Don't you have a game to play? Aren't you nervous?"

"Not really. I'm bored, man," Collins said. "I'm driving around. So, how's your job-hunting going?"

"*Job-hunting!*" McCarty screamed. "Why are you asking me about job-hunting? What about the game?"

But Collins just wanted to talk. McCarty was more nervous than he was about what was going to happen in 3½ hours. McCarty already had his beer and popcorn out, ready to watch the first playoff game of the afternoon.

"Brian, I'm guaranteeing a victory today," Collins said. Then, by chance, Collins wheeled the BMW around a corner and saw Helen Carr, an attractive friend of Collins's who is a graduate student at Queens University in Charlotte. She was out jogging.

"Gotta go, Pook," Collins said quickly. "Hey, Helen!"

Carr turned and spotted her quarterback friend. She invited Collins up to her nearby apartment. They talked for about 30 minutes, mostly about her imminent return to work. Then she finally asked him: "How do you feel about the game?"

"Calm," Collins replied. "Look, I need to get going, I guess."

"Well, you go," Carr said, smiling. "I'm not going to wish you luck because you don't need it. But do me a favor. Kick some Cowboy butt."

AN HOUR BEFORE THE GAME, THE PANTHERS SHOWED the first real sign of how huge this game was to the franchise. It happened when Polian spotted a Dallas helmet lying right in the middle of the area where the Panthers were going to warm up. The helmet was Irvin's. He had taken it off and left it there for some reason.

Was it an intimidatory tactic? A simple oversight? No one was quite sure. But Polian knew he didn't like it. A Panther could conceivably trip on the helmet while backpedaling in warmup drills. Plus, it was a space infringement, since Dallas was warming up all the way across the field.

"The helmet was a hazard," Polian said. "It would have interfered with warmup. I didn't know whose helmet it was. I simply took it and tossed it back toward the Dallas bench."

Some Panthers players saw Polian take the helmet and throw it. They later described the action a little more vividly. "It looked like a shotput," laughed Panthers wide receiver Dwight Stone, who'd seen the throw.

Irvin's chinstrap wasn't attached to the helmet, however, so it still rested on the field as the Panthers warmed up. Chris Polian, Bill's son and a member of the Panthers pro scouting department, saw the chinstrap. He flung it in the direction of the helmet. Right about then, Irvin came back. He couldn't find his helmet at first, then saw what had been done with it. He was furious. He stormed over to 25-year-old Chris Polian, screamed at him, and then angrily walked away.

The Panthers players thought it was a great scene. If they needed any further motivation, that would do. As Collins said later, "I thought it was great. I mean, I'm Irish, too. I know kinda how Bill thinks. He doesn't take crap like that. He doesn't take it and his son didn't take it. So what if it was Michael Irvin? They don't give a crap about him. They're from New York City."

Lathon strutted around the field shortly afterward, yelling into a camera, "Time to earn a little respect! Time to earn a little respect!"

The Panthers went back into their locker room with about 20 minutes to go before kickoff. Capers gave a focused, calm pregame talk. Everyone saw the TRUST EACH OTHER! command on the blackboard. And then the players ran back out, ready for the biggest game the team had ever had.

FANS AROUND THE COUNTRY KNEW THIS ONE WAS going to be big about an hour later, when Pat Summerall and John Madden, Fox-TV's number 1 announcing team, began their live broadcast at 4 P.M. Sunday. The two hadn't seen the Panthers play live all season, for Fox had been slow to realize what a good developing story the Panthers were and kept assigning the pair elsewhere. One sign in Ericsson Stadium read: HI JOHN, PAT: 'BOUT TIME YOU GOT HERE.

But the pair was determined to make up for their absence. They were both very excited about the game and the newness of Carolina. Summerall thought privately that Dallas had far better talent than Carolina, but wondered if the Panthers might not pull off an upset because they weren't a divided team.

The telecast opened with highlights of several Panthers players. Summerall intoned over a shot of the stadium, "Today, for the first time, Dallas journeys through Carolina, as the championship drive continues." Next, viewers saw a shot of Charlotte's skyline. Summerall continued, "And downtown Charlotte, which is close by Ericsson Stadium, is rocking today. Ericsson Stadium, a magnificent edifice, the home of the Carolina Panthers. The divisional playoff match between the Dallas Cowboys and Carolina is about to begin."

Madden looked and sounded normal. His hair was askew. His eyebrows were so bushy that they seemed to stick three inches out from his face. His enthusiasm was boundless. "I think this is the greatest," he bubbled. "Carolina gets its glory today . . . and it's something. You get the Carolina Panthers. Who would have thought? Here's a team that wasn't even a team three years ago and they are just two games away from the Super Bowl."

Finally, it was time. Tara Greene, Kevin's wife, belted out the national anthem again. Kevin's teams had a 4–1 record, he noted, when she sang at his games. Carolina hadn't played a game in two weeks, and the season-ticket holders who formed the bulk of the crowd hadn't cheered in two weeks, either. So they were in full voice on this gorgeous, 67-degree day with a 15 mile-per-hour wind.

The Panthers had 72,808 fans inside the stadium—it was easily the loudest and the biggest crowd ever at a Panthers game—and the noise was deafening. The roar would continue throughout the game. The Panthers had provided blue towels to each fan, which would be swung in the air in unison for every big play, forming a big blue sea in the middle of Charlotte. Red, white, and blue bunting draped over the retaining wall added to the festive atmosphere.

Carolina won the coin toss and elected to receive. They immediately pounded the ball inside to Johnson for eight yards. The Panthers wanted to remain committed to the run all afternoon. They felt their vastly improved offensive line could beat down average Dallas players like Tony Casillas.

The Panthers also used Mark Carrier heavily early in the game. The first three passes Collins threw were directed at Carrier. "I knew I'd be an integral part of the offense," Carrier said. "But things didn't work out so well at first."

Collins's first pass to Carrier was incomplete. His second—on first-and-ten from the Carolina 42—was intercepted by diving Dallas safety Darren Woodson. And *boom,* just like that, the Cowboys had the ball at their own 47 with the game only two minutes old. Collins, even after the pregame drive that was supposed to relax him, looked very shaky. He walked off to the sideline shaking his head. Backup quarterback Steve Beuerlein tried to comfort him. "Hey, the guy made a great play," Beuerlein said. "What are you going to do?"

TV watchers around the nation nodded their heads knowingly. Here was where the blowout was supposed to begin.

But almost as quickly as that huge play came another one rolling on top of it—perhaps the most important play of the game. On second-and-10, Aikman faded back and found Irvin streaking across the middle. Poole had slipped on the play, leaving Irvin wide open. Irvin caught the ball and headed downfield.

But Lathon charged after him and grabbed him from behind. He slammed Irvin straight down like a hammer driving a nail. The wide receiver's right shoulder jammed into the turf with a sickening *cra-a-a-ck!*

The tackle was hard, clean, and perfectly legal.

"My intensity level was probably higher than his intensity level," Lathon said. "Hey, I met a two-hundred-pound guy. I'm two-sixty-five. I put a good lick on him."

Just like that, Irvin was out of the game. The controversial receiver had caught one pass for 22 yards. Lathon had fractured Irvin's right shoulder. And the landscape of the game had suddenly changed.

Lathon would apologize later. "I never mean to hurt anybody while playing," he said. And the Panthers linebacker admitted that the game would have been "very different" had Irvin been able to play.

There was no doubt that Irvin's absence was a major advantage for Carolina. "You have to take away the weapons," Kevin Greene said. "I'm not saying you go out to hurt anybody, but you take away the weapons."

Irvin was gone. He would reappear on the sideline in an exquisitely tailored, six-buttoned gold suit, complete with vest and sunglasses. If they had been shooting a *GQ* cover for fallen superstars, he would have been on it. But he wouldn't bother the Panthers secondary the rest of the day.

Soon, Aikman was in worse shape than he would let on. The Cowboys were so reliant on Irvin that no one else was really familiar with his passing routes. The Cowboys switched around for the rest of the game, using Sanders, Kelvin Martin, and Kevin Williams, but Aikman would have to play this game without his go-to receiver.

The Cowboys still had Emmitt Smith in their arsenal, however, and he ran the ball on four of the next five plays, as Dallas quickly drove the ball down to the Carolina one. But this was where Dallas had had trouble all year. The Cowboys were twenty-fourth of 30 teams in scoring touchdowns once they got the ball inside the opponent's 20-yard line.

On second-and-goal, under pressure from reserve linebacker Andre Royal, Aikman threw incomplete. On third-and-goal, a pitch to Smith to the left side was stuffed by Sam Mills and Chad Cota. The Cowboys would have to take a field goal. Chris Boniol's 22-yarder with 8:27 left in the first quarter made it 3–0, Dallas.

CAROLINA WANTED TO GO AFTER DALLAS CORNER-back Kevin Smith, so Collins started throwing at him on the next possession. On third-and-eight, Collins threw an incompletion to Willie Green. But Smith—whose five pass-interference penalties were the second-highest number in the NFL in 1996—got tagged for a daily double. He was guilty of both defensive holding and pass interference on the same play.

The 22-yard penalty was immediately followed by another 22-yard gain. It was Collins to Green—a Joe Pendry specialty. The offensive coordinator was well known among his players for going to the same play two or three times in a row if it was working.

Quickly, Carolina drove to the Dallas one on a run by Johnson and a seven-yard pass to Carrier. And on first-and-goal from the one, Pendry called a play Carolina hadn't used all year, a risky play that the offensive coordinator had put in just for this game. Carolina had copied the play from Washington. Wesley Walls would line up on the right side in a goal-line situation and chop the legs out from the opposing defensive end. Then, when Cowboys defenders were satisfied that Walls was going to be blocking and not receiving on the play, he would scramble to his feet and fade to the sideline. If Dallas bit, Walls would be wide open.

The first part worked sensationally as Walls blocked Dallas's Tony Tolbert. Down on all fours, Walls then managed to scramble up. But he felt a little dizzy. "I had to kind of back out from under him," Walls said. "I was almost running backwards trying to get out of there, and my equilibrium was kind of messed up."

Collins's play-action fake drew the defenders in, and Walls finally managed to get open only 10 yards away. Collins, trying too hard to be careful, only threw it about eight. "Oh, no, you skipped it!" Collins thought to himself. "Just please, please, please have enough to get there!"

Madden exclaimed, "Kerry Collins got so excited because Wesley Walls was so wide open he darn near took too much mustard off it!"

But Walls's great hands saved the Panthers again. Dizzy and all, he dove forward for the ball, got his hands under it, and scooped it up for a touchdown. With five minutes left in the first quarter, Carolina had assumed a 7–3 lead.

Dallas's next series went horribly, thanks to what may have been the best play Panthers reserve lineman Les Miller ever made in his life.

Miller had been home hunting pheasant in Kansas during the 1995 season. He had been cut by New Orleans and had decided he was sick of football. You could only get bird dogs Pete and Max to hunt so many times, though, Miller found. By '96, he was tired of shooting and ready to play. Luckily, Carolina called him to be a defensive line backup.

Miller's defensive philosophy was simple. "The way I play is, I just try to find who's got the ball and then just get 'em," Miller said. "I get the other people out of the way and get 'em."

That was exactly what he did to Dallas, on third-and-seven from their own 21 late in the first quarter. Miller got a great jump and came blasting straight up the middle. Cowboys offensive linemen Ray Donaldson, Nate Newton, and Emmitt Smith—840 pounds' worth of Cowboys—tried to stop him. Miller, who weighs 285, whipped them all. Then he smashed into Aikman for a 13-yard loss to the Dallas eight.

Because of that play, Carolina got the ball on the Dallas 42 late in the first quarter. Quickly, Carolina was driving again, as Collins threw to Walls for 13 yards.

A miniature crisis was about to erupt, however. Three Panthers plays took the ball to the Dallas 20. Fourth-and-one. Would Capers go for it? He would. Collins ran a quarterback sneak for the yard the Panthers needed.

Six plays later, Carolina faced another delicate situation—third-and-goal from the Dallas 10.

Collins faded back. Walls was covered in the middle and Green, running an outside route called a Q to the front corner of the end zone, was blanketed by Smith. Collins didn't even think about throwing to Deion Sanders's side.

He hurriedly considered his options. Smith had gotten burned a couple of times before: How about there? There was only a hole about the size of a football that could possibly work, but Collins decided to try it. The ball looked way too far for Green. But the Panthers receiver dove, got both hands on it, and yanked it into his body just before crashing down into the end zone.

"It was a perfect throw," Collins would say later. "I'm not one to pump myself or anything like that, but it was right where it had to be. It was one of the best throws I've ever made."

Dallas's Smith walked away in disgust. Green jumped up, smiled, and pointed a gloved hand toward the crowd. Touchdown! Carolina led 14–3, and the game was only 17 minutes old.

"Kerry Collins threw a perfect pass!" Madden yelled. "Whew! This guy's something!"

But the Cowboys weren't going to fade quietly into the good night, especially not in the second quarter. As the sun set on Ericsson, Dallas began a grinder of a 14-play drive. No play was longer than 15 yards, but Dallas moved the ball steadily down the field with Aikman's short, precise passes. Once again, in the red zone, the Cowboys almost faltered. Emmitt Smith had a crack from the two and a crack from the one, and couldn't score either time. On third down, Dallas sent fullback Daryl Johnston into the left flat. The Panthers' Carlton Bailey was beaten badly, but Aikman's pass was thrown well behind Johnston. The Cowboys player nicknamed Moose surprised everyone and made an amazing catch, twisting his body sideways and roping in the ball with one hand. Dallas had cut the lead to 14–9 with 4:19 left in the half, and Switzer wanted more. He decided to go for two points. A successful conversion would leave the Cowboys down by only a field goal. But the Panthers messed up the two-point play: Kevin Greene knocked away an errant Aikman pass. The Panthers would stay up 14–9.

Not for long, though. Carolina couldn't make a first down and was quickly forced to punt. In came long snapper Mark Rodenhauser—who got paid $275,000 solely to snap the ball for punts and field goals.

RODENHAUSER HAD A LOT OF FREE TIME ON HIS hands since his job was so limited. The Panthers kept him around because one bad snap can turn a game on its ear. In fact, most teams in the NFL save a roster spot for a player who is exclusively a long snapper.

Unlike many NFL players, Rodenhauser used his free time to develop the skills he figured he would need after his first career was over. He was the closest thing to a Net-head the Panthers had. He wore glasses and was an amateur desktop publisher, having formed his own Internet access and consulting company during the 1996 off-season. He was great with words, graphics, and computers. Rodenhauser and Bill Polian probably had the best vocabularies in Ericsson Stadium.

But Rodenhauser most impressed his teammates with his talents for computerizing inside jokes for the Panthers.

In his first year with the team, 1995, Rodenhauser read a story in *The Charlotte Observer* in which then Panthers running back Derrick Moore proclaimed his love for the Julie Andrews character in *The Sound of Music*. The next day, Rodenhauser had taken a shot from the film of Andrews spinning around on the mountain and had morphed Moore's head onto it. Moore, one of the true characters of the Panthers' first year, said, "I never thought I would have looked that good in a dress."

Rodenhauser also once made a mockup of a cereal box that featured rotund Panthers security director Ed Stillwell. The fake cereal was called "Ed Stillwell's Cholesterol Crunch—1,000 percent of the minimum daily allowance of fat, sugar, and cholesterol." And he made a fake weekly tabloid that featured Dom Capers as the missing "Fifth Beatle," complete with a mop-top haircut that would have made John, Paul, George, and Ringo proud.

Rodenhauser's football claim to fame was that in nine seasons in the NFL he had never made an uncatchable snap. He fired the ball backward 15 yards into a punter's hands perfectly, every single game.

That's why all of Ericsson Stadium shrieked in shock late in the second quarter when Rodenhauser's snap sailed three yards over punter Rohn Stark's leap and 37 yards into the end zone. He had inexplicably held on to the ball a fraction of a second too long, sending it high and out of the reach of the desperately leaping Stark.

"I felt like crawling under a rock," Rodenhauser said. "There's no place to go out there. You're laid bare."

Stark ran into the end zone and smartly batted the ball away from rushing Dallas players. It counted as a safety. Dallas had gotten the two points it wanted after all.

Now Carolina's lead was down to three, and the first half still had three minutes to go. Rodenhauser moped on the sideline. A few teammates came over to him to pat him on the shoulder pads, but most let him grieve alone.

By NFL rules, Carolina then had to punt to Dallas from their own 20. The Cowboys sent Deion Sanders back to take it, and he skittered 28 yards to the Dallas 48. If Carolina didn't watch it, the Cowboys would at least gain a tie by halftime.

One first down later, Dallas faced a third-and-nine at the Carolina 39. Aikman faded back to throw, looking for Kelvin Martin, a smart but slow receiver, at the Carolina 24. But the previous game's hero, Cota, stepped in front of the ball, caught it, and raced 49 yards down the sideline to the Dallas 27.

With 1:49 left to go, Carolina moved the ball to the Dallas six. But the Panthers ran out of time and sent John Kasay on to attempt a field goal with six seconds left in the first half. Rodenhauser came in to snap the ball.

This time, the snap was perfect. Kasay knocked it in, and Carolina extended their lead to 17–11 at halftime.

IT WAS A TENUOUS LEAD AGAINST THE DEFENDING world champions, and it looked even more so when the first big play of the third quarter went Dallas's way. Dallas had to punt after its first series, and John Jett unleashed a mammoth 59-yarder.

The Panthers' Winslow Oliver ran backward, caught the ball, dropped it, and picked it up. When he got tackled he dropped it again and Dallas's Daryl Johnston rolled on it at the Carolina 16.

The Cowboys only needed a touchdown to take the lead, and they moved to the Panthers five with little problem. But again, the Panthers defense stiffened. Two runs by Smith to the left were steamrolled by Greg Kragen and Sam Mills. "Evidently, they wanted to rely on their offensive line," Greene would gloat later. "They wanted to run over us. We stood up and took the challenge and stuffed their ass."

On third-and-goal from the three, Aikman threw incomplete under pressure from Lathon and Mike Fox, and Dallas had to take another field goal. Carolina clung to a 17–14 lead with 10 minutes left in the third quarter.

The thing was, though, that Anthony Johnson had this *feeling*. He had run the ball nine times for only 28 yards in the first half, but the offensive line seemed to be taking care of business inside. He thought he could get more. "From the first play, I felt we could beat them up-front," Johnson said.

It was time to try. Three times on Carolina's first series in the second half, Collins handed to Johnson. Three times the crowd roared as Johnson ripped off gains of 12, nine, and 12 yards. Johnson ended up gaining 44 of the Panthers' 50 yards on the five-minute drive, which ended in a 40-yard Kasay field goal.

With that, Carolina was up 20–14, with only five minutes left in the third quarter and 20 minutes left in the whole game. After a quick defensive stop, Pendry went right back to calling Anthony Johnson's number. The third quarter ended before Carolina's drive did, and Fox-TV's cameras caught a pumped-up Greene holding up four fingers of each hand and yelling with the crowd. "Four! Four!" he screamed, knowing that the Panthers defense had only given up three fourth-quarter points all year at home.

Johnson was almost always good in the fourth quarter, too. He sandwiched a pass-interference penalty on Kevin Smith with six consecutive runs of 10, four, one, three, zero, and two yards. It wasn't spectacular, but it was enough to get Carolina in position for another Kasay field goal. This one made it 23–14, Panthers, early in the fourth quarter.

BY THIS TIME, TEAM EQUIPMENT MANAGER JACKIE Miles had had enough. Dallas had kept trying to throw at cornerback Tyrone Poole the whole game, ever since he slipped on that first play while trying to guard Irvin. Poole had been almost frantic.

"I was so nervous," Poole said. "I can honestly say I was more nervous than I'd ever been. I had grown up watching Dallas, ever since I'd known anything about football."

But even after Poole settled down, he kept slipping. Miles thought he knew why. Poole wanted to be just like Eric Davis on the field—confident, aggressive, and smart. And Davis was wearing shoes with half-inch spikes, so Poole had decided he had to do that, too.

The problem was that Davis had a remarkable sense of balance. He would have been great in one of those lumberjack contests where two guys are out on a log, each one trying to spin the other off.

"Eric could play a game wearing ice skates and never fall down," Miles said.

"Or maybe even cowboy boots," Davis laughed.

Poole, however, was more fallible. Miles had tried to get him to switch to a longer spike in the Pittsburgh game, but he wouldn't. Finally, in this game, he forced Poole to switch shoes on the sideline, to ones with ⅝-inch spikes. It wouldn't stop Dallas from going after him, but at least it would give "Total Package" Poole a better wrapping.

The Cowboys, down nine, weren't quite desperate at this point, but they were close. They had Sanders playing some offense now, and normally he didn't do that much anymore. With Irvin gone, they needed a big play. So on the Cowboys' next series, on second-and-12 from the Dallas 30 early in the fourth quarter, the play call was for a reverse to Sanders.

Sanders circled left, picked up a good block from Aikman on Lathon, and saw some daylight. He had gained 16 yards before the Panthers converged like a swollen river upon him. Poole—in his new ⅝-inch spikes—was there. So were Mills, Kragen, and Carlton Bailey. Four players piled into Sanders, and the Dallas star landed awkwardly, facedown.

The Panthers got up, but Sanders stayed down. He hurt terribly. Doctors weren't sure what was wrong at the time, but it turned out that the impact of the four-way tackle had broken a small bone just below Sanders's eye. Months later, he would still suffer from blurred vision. And for this game, he was out. Now two of Dallas's four stars were gone. Noted Madden: "That's what they always said. When Deion plays offense, wait until those defenders get a chance to hit him."

Bill Polian, up in his private booth, felt it was over when he saw Sanders getting helped off the field. "At that point, they had no one that Aikman could hit for a quick strike," he said. "There was no longer any chance of a miraculous play, of Aikman hitting someone long. When Deion went out, they lost that capability."

Aikman wasn't buying that, though. Neither was Emmitt Smith, who unleashed his best run of the afternoon five plays later. He trucked the ball 25 yards to Carolina's nine-yard line.

First-and-goal again. Twice Carolina had stopped Dallas in these situations. Once, the Cowboys had scored. This time, the Cowboys gave up on trying to run. Aikman threw three passes—one for a seven-yard gain and two incompletions. On the second one, Dallas tight end Eric Bjornson, guarded closely by Poole, dropped a catchable ball.

So it was Boniol time again. The kicker's 21-yard field goal made it 23–17, Carolina, with 5:33 left in the game.

Dallas was still within a touchdown of winning. And soon, they would get the ball back, even after two wonderful field-position plays by the Panthers. The first came when Michael Bates sped 51 yards with the kickoff return. Then, after Carolina couldn't make a first down, Johnson showed again why he had been so valuable on special teams all season. On fourth-and-two from the Dallas 41, Carolina punted. Rodenhauser made a nice snap, Stark laid the ball up high, and Johnson zoomed downfield. Just as the ball was about to hit inside the Dallas five, Johnson stuck his right hand out. The ball bounced and—with Johnson's helping hand—almost stopped. "Right place, right time," Johnson would say later. "I barely even saw that ball."

The Panthers' Dwight Stone downed it at the Dallas two. The 72,808 people in the stands screamed with delight and swung their blue towels.

It would be up to the Panthers defense once more. Dallas was 98 yards away from a go-ahead touchdown but, with 3:44 to play, still had plenty of time to score. Terrell and his mates trotted out once more with the game on their shoulder pads.

In the stands, the Terrell family had been on its feet most of the game. Terrell's uncle and father, Gerald and Grady Terrell—the kidney donor and recipient—had been yelling for Pat all game. Terrell's first playoff game had been a thriller, but Grady's son hadn't done anything too special yet.

As Terrell ran out onto the field, he knew it wasn't over. "I knew they had ninety-eight yards to go, but it seemed like about thirty yards with Troy Aikman standing over center," Terrell said.

It took Aikman little time to chip away 35 of those yards—on one completion and two penalties on Poole. Poole's cleats were sticking fine now; in fact, he was getting too close. He had had three penalties called on him in the fourth quarter, and Aikman was picking on him on nearly every play.

"I knew they were going toward Tyrone," said Terrell, whose position as free safety allowed him to roam the field during many pass coverages. "So I started shading that way. I wanted to play the game, but I also wanted to play Aikman's mind." His cousin, Calvin Terrell, had a premonition right about then: "Watch Pat on this play," said Terrell, who had worn a number 40 jersey to the game in honor of his cousin. "He's going to do something."

On first-and-10 from the Dallas 37, with 2:30 left in the game, Aikman dropped deeper than usual. The protection was good.

"Must be either a screen pass or a deep ball," Terrell thought. So he started sprinting toward Poole on the left sideline—he wouldn't have been able to do anything about a screen pass anyway. In the stands, 20 Terrell family members—most from either Florida or Tennessee—rose as one as Aikman planted his back foot. He heaved the ball 50 yards toward Poole and Kevin Williams, who were jockeying for position at the Carolina 32.

Aikman had miscalculated a little, though, and Terrell got a good jump on it as he watched the ball sail down from the sky. "Goodyear blimp," Terrell thought to himself. "Looks just like the blimp."

And he imagined a message flashing on the football: "The ball was saying to me, 'If you catch this, you're going to Green Bay,'" Terrell said.

"If he catches that," tight end Wesley Walls thought to himself, "I'd probably even give him my last Bud Light."

Three players jumped for the ball. Terrell came down with it.

The Terrell family went nuts, but they were drowned out by a stadium doing the same thing on a much grander scale.

Poole and Williams both fell away from Terrell as he caught the ball, so he chugged 49 yards down the sideline—Aikman had to knock him out of bounds—to the Dallas 19.

Terrell tried to jump into the stands after the interception, figuring that in a larger sense he would be embracing his father and uncle. "I really wanted that interception for them," he said.

Deeper in the stands, the Terrells hugged anyone they could find. The $2,700 they had paid for the chartered plane was some of the best money they had ever spent.

TERRELL'S INTERCEPTION FINISHED IT. CAROLINA RAN three plays into the middle of the line to set up Kasay's fourth field goal, which put the game out of reach for the Cowboys with 1:48 left. The 26–17 margin meant Dallas would have to score twice with no timeouts.

Instead, Aikman got sacked by Lathon. Smith got tackled for a three-yard loss. And then Aikman drilled a pass right to Mills, who caught it at the Dallas 25. Mills thought about falling down, but saw no one near him and almost reluctantly ran the ball to the Dallas one.

"I was going to take a knee, but I realized there was nobody around me," Mills said. "So I figured I'd run a little while. I ran the whole time with two hands on the ball. So I wasn't really going that fast—not that I have that many gears to work with anyway."

Eric Davis celebrated that interception by lying flat on his back on the field, kicking his legs and pumping his arms in the air in sheer joy. Many Panthers fans felt the same way.

A woman would call into *The Charlotte Observer*'s game hotline a few minutes later to proclaim: "Sam Mills. Sam Mills. Sam Mills. I'm a forty-six-year-old mother of four. But I tell you what—if I saw him right now, I would give him a big ole hug and kiss."

The game ended there, inside the Dallas five, with Collins taking a knee twice. The fans screamed in jubilation as they swung their blue towels. As the final seconds ticked away, Panthers radio announcer Bill Rosinski shouted out to his listeners, "The Panthers have done it! The king is dead! The king is dead!"

GREENE WAS INTENT ON GIVING CAPERS ANOTHER water bath. "Help me over here, Andre," he called to backup linebacker Andre Royal.

"All right, we get to dump the coach!" Royal yelled. "I've never done that before."

They splashed Capers. Royal held the empty water cooler up like a trophy, swinging it around his head.

On television, Madden gushed, "Who would have thought that Dallas would lose in this round and that the winner would be the Carolina Panthers?"

Switzer and Capers met at midfield and shook hands. Summerall noted on-air that the controversial Dallas coach looked "relieved" to have lost.

Lathon had saved up a good quote about Switzer's not knowing where Charlotte was. He just needed to find someone to say it to. That wasn't a problem, since reporters were swarming the field. When a handful gathered around Lathon, he whooped, "So now I propose a question for you, Barry Switzer! While you're sitting at home next week, do you know where Charlotte, North Carolina, is now, BABY?!"

It was one of the quotes of the year, spewed out with such emotion that Lathon seemed on the verge of either fainting, fighting, or crying. It got replayed again and again on TV the next few days.

The funny thing was that Switzer did know where Charlotte was. He had simply misspoken earlier in the week. He had actually been to Charlotte several times before. "I don't know what he [Lathon] was making reference to because I lectured in Charlotte before he was ever born," Switzer said several weeks later. "When I was coaching in college, we used to have clinics there and I would speak at them."

Nevertheless, Lathon's quote perfectly captured the moment. The Panthers had found the end of the rainbow, and everything was just as golden as they imagined. They streamed into the locker room high-fiving one another and yelling.

Jerry Richardson and Capers embraced and in a ragged, happy voice, Capers squeezed his boss and said, "Oh, baby, that was a great one today!"

THE PANTHERS' TWO VETERAN RECEIVERS KNEW HOW special the moment was, and they knew whom they needed to share it with. Willie Green and Mark Carrier spent a moment in the locker room by themselves. They heard the roar still coming from above them—many of the fans were still inside the stadium, screaming. "We've gotta go back out there!" they said almost at once to each other.

Green proposed the idea in the team huddle right after a brief prayer. "We need to go back outside and thank our fans because if it wasn't for them, we wouldn't be here!" Green shouted.

The idea caught everyone's attention. Fullback Howard Griffith led the Panthers back out of the locker room, past a surprised group of reporters waiting to interview the team. The fans shrieked when they saw the players come back out. They had seen Carolina win all nine games at home in Ericsson. They had seen the Panthers defense give up only 19 second-half points all season. And now they were getting to say good-bye. And thanks.

"The fans loved it," Green said. "And they deserved it. They believed."

The Panthers started circling the stadium in an orderly way, slapping hands with fan after fan. The players were in various states of undress. Some still had helmets and shoulder pads on. Eric Davis wore only a T-shirt. Lathon was shirtless—if he had been a fan, he would have been thrown out for that.

After a while the spontaneous conga line fell apart. Some of the big linemen were so exhausted they couldn't trudge a lap around the stadium. Other players' right hands got so tired that they started jogging backward, using their left hands to touch the fans.

"Mike Fox was ahead of me, and when we got halfway, he just couldn't go anymore," Carrier remembered. "When we got to the end, I was exhausted, too. But it was worth it."

"It was a great time," Collins said. "You felt so alive. It's so great to experience those kinds of things."

SUMMERALL AND MADDEN STILL SAT IN THE BOOTH, watching the impromptu parade. Later Summerall would say privately, "If there's ever been an example of a team beating a divided group, I think that was it. The Panthers played as a team. The Cowboys played like, 'I don't know these guys I'm playing with. And the ones that I do know are in trouble and I don't know if they're going to be back and I'm tired of listening to these shenanigans.'"

The Panthers players eventually filed back into the locker room. Most sat on their stools, overwhelmed by what they had done and in no hurry to end it. Terrell had obtained locker-room passes for his dad and his uncle, and he gave them both fierce hugs.

Leigh Steinberg, the agent to many of the game's superstars and the man on whose life the film *Jerry Maguire* was loosely based, waited outside the locker room for his clients. Steinberg represented both of the quarterbacks in this game, Aikman and Collins. Like many, he was surprised at which one of them had emerged the winner. "That squeaking noise you hear," Steinberg said, "is the sound of the shift of power in the NFL."

Capers would later call his mother and tell her softly, "That one was for Dad." He still thought often of Eugene Capers, and of how much he wished he had gotten to share moments like these with the man who had meant the most in the world to him.

As for the school bus with the kids who had yelled "Cowboys, Cowboys!" for so long, the Panthers never noticed them again.

CHAPTER FIFTEEN

Ice Bowl II

COLD.

Bitter, freezing, miserable cold.

That was the weather forecast for Sunday, January 12, in Green Bay—a temperature of around zero to five degrees and a wind-chill factor of 20 below. Those shivery conditions would be the setting in which the Panthers would try and pull off what could be their most amazing upset yet: a victory in the NFC Championship Game.

The Packers-Panthers game was immediately labeled "Ice Bowl II." It was a natural nickname. The last time the Packers had been in a game of this magnitude, Bart Starr had sneaked one yard for the winning touchdown against Dallas with 13 seconds remaining for the 1967 NFL championship in the first Ice Bowl.

While the Panthers studied the film of the 1996 Packers, a team that featured the highest-scoring offense and stingiest defense in the NFL, team equipment manager Jackie Miles scurried around collecting every cold-weather tip he could find.

He came up with some beauties: He had some of the Panthers wear baby powder in their cleats to help keep their feet dry. He told others to smear antiperspirant in their socks for the same purpose. Miles handed out hot bouillon soup on the sideline to keep players warm. He pressed the team chaplain into duty to hand out cold-weather capes. He provided miniature "heat factories"—tiny packets that when squeezed provided a burst of warmth—for players like Kerry

Collins to tuck inside their jerseys. And he brought along Canadian "broomball" shoes—broomball is an obscure sport played on ice—just in case the field was layered with ice.

Most of the offensive linemen vowed among themselves not to wear anything on their arms. They liked the macho look that gave them. But it served a practical purpose, too: Defenders wouldn't have anything to grab on to.

Almost everyone else, though, planned to layer their clothing as if they were going on a ski trip to Colorado. Much of the clothing was made from thermal polypropylene, the sleek stuff that many Olympic skiing outfits are made from.

"I'll use everything they've got," Willie Green said. "If I could wear a fur coat out there, I would. Then I wouldn't have to worry about the cold—just the animal-rights activists."

Bitter cold weather was a new thing to this southern team. Carolina had never played a game where the actual temperature was below freezing. They came the closest during the Panthers-49ers game in Clemson on December 19, 1995, when the actual temperature was 34 degrees and the wind-chill factor was 15.

The Panthers had gotten blasted in that one, 31–10, but they talked bravely about the upcoming game. "Hey it's going to be cold," Eric Davis said. "So what? You think it's going to be warm for them? You go out and play football. It's like playing in the rain. You can't make it stop, so you just go play."

"Hey, we'd go to Iceland to play this one, it doesn't matter," said Pat Terrell with a smile.

With the cold-weather issues taken care of, thanks to Miles's dogged preparation, the Panthers turned to what would be Sunday's real problem: stopping Green Bay quarterback Brett Favre.

Favre was undoubtedly the best, most colorful player in the NFL. For two consecutive seasons he had been the league's Most Valuable Player. He scrambled around in the pocket until he saw a receiver he liked, and then he threw the ball with bullet force. No one in the NFL except possibly Denver's John Elway could throw it harder.

Favre hated the cold weather, too, even though he had a record of 18–0 as a starting quarterback when the temperature was 35 degrees or lower. He was a southern boy through and through, with an affection for flip-flops, ripped T-shirts, hunting dogs, fishing and double-wide trailers. "He's a character," teammate Reggie White said. "He does things that'll make you shake your head sometimes."

But mostly, Favre made the lives of opponents unbearable. And what was most remarkable about Favre—the finest player Carolina would face all season—was how he had spent his 1996 off-season.

Favre, 27, had gotten addicted to the painkiller Vicodin during the 1995 season. He had once popped 13 of them in a single day. They helped him cope with the pain of five surgeries in six years. After a while he couldn't live without them.

But Favre got scared straight in February when he suffered a seizure while already in the hospital for surgery to his left ankle. He thrashed around on a hospital bed like a landed fish, banging his head backward uncontrollably. Doctors' intervention prevented him from swallowing his tongue. His seven-year-old daughter screamed out in fear before being ushered out of the room. "Is he going to die, Mom?" she asked.

In May 1996, Favre checked into a Kansas rehabilitation clinic after admitting his Vicodin addiction. He stayed in rehab 45 days.

Soon the jokes began. What did MVP stand for on Favre's 1995 trophy? Answer: "My Vicodin Problem."

When he returned to the NFL, it was huge news. At the press conference for his return, Favre made a bold pronouncement: "You know I'm going to beat this thing. I'm going to win a Super Bowl. There's a lot of things I'm going to do. And all I can tell people if they don't believe me is 'Just bet against me.'"

Just bet against me.

Those four words echoed throughout the NFL in 1996. While Carolina's extraordinary season was the best team story in the NFL, Favre's was the best individual one. Everyone who had bet against Favre during the 1996 season had lost. The Green Bay QB played the game the way most players dreamed of playing: with imagination and verve and explosive talent.

He was the closest thing in the NFL to a saxophone player on a wild jazz riff: You never knew where he was going to end up, but you were pretty sure he was going to be damn good getting there. He threw 38 touchdown passes in 1995 while on Vicodin; he threw 39 in 1996 off it.

"One thing we know for sure about Favre," cornerback Davis deadpanned. "It wasn't the drugs."

And still, for all that success, Favre's coach occasionally wanted to kill him. "Oh, yeah, many times I do," Green Bay coach Mike Holmgren said with a laugh on the Wednesday before the game. "That would be a great headline, huh? Coach strangles MVP."

But Favre had won over his teammates with his grit and sheer talent. No one questioned who was in control of this team. It was the guy from Kiln, Mississippi, with a chaw in his mouth.

"He's like Billy the Kid," Packers wide receiver Andre Rison said. "He's cool. He's James Dean. He has an air about himself that's different than any quarterback in the NFL. He's not a wannabe. He's the MVP."

That was the man the Panthers had to deal with: a driven, determined, destructive offensive force.

On Wednesday, four days before the game, Favre told reporters that he believed the Packers were a "team of destiny." In Green Bay people believed that wholeheartedly. The players and fans of Green Bay felt as though they had hopped on some magical mystery tour of the NFL that wasn't about to stop until it reached the Super Bowl in New Orleans.

MAGIC AND MYSTERY, THOUGH, WEREN'T GOING TO GET it done on the field.

Players were.

So the Panthers and Packers started tinkering with their game plans, trying to outguess each other in the most crucial aspects of the game.

In Green Bay, Packers offensive coordinator Sherman Lewis watched film of the Carolina defense, and he worried—mainly about Lamar Lathon. "The guy is playing like Lawrence Taylor," Lewis told other Green Bay assistants. "Like L.T., I'm telling you! He's playing at a level of intensity I've never seen. The guy is all over the field."

Lewis watched Lathon again and again. He chased plays down from behind. He shed blockers in front of them and made tackles. Although

Kevin Greene had edged Lathon by one sack for the NFL title, Lathon had finished second (to Sam Mills) for the team lead in tackles.

The Packers worried about Lathon so much—especially since he was matched up against unspectacular left tackle Bruce Wilkerson—that they finally decided that they would double-team him most of the game. And when they ran the ball, it would usually be up the middle or away from Lathon, and straight at Kevin Greene.

"This is the most academic week we've ever had," right guard Adam Timmerman told his teammates. After hours and hours of preparation, the Packers' hard work paid off. While studying game film, the coaches noticed that the Panthers players would cheat toward the line of scrimmage—especially on the tight end's side—when they were coming with a blitz. That would be one thing Green Bay would try to exploit.

Carolina, meanwhile, wanted to stick to a simple game plan: Stay basic on offense and dangerous on defense. Capers noted to his staff that the Packers looked more like Carolina than any other team they had faced all year; they were a bunch of team-oriented role players surrounding a few stars.

In the defensive meeting room that week, Capers asked his staff who the Packers' best offensive lineman was. There was a long pause. Finally someone hedged an answer, saying that one Packers lineman had played well the week before. But there was no obvious choice. As with Carolina's line, each player contributed to the success.

The Panthers' main concern was getting down early—say, 14–0 or 21–0—and having to play catchup. If Carolina could just hang with Green Bay until halftime, Capers told his staff, the Panthers would have a great chance to make it to the Super Bowl.

That's what had happened all season. Carolina had allowed fewer second-half points in a 16-game schedule than any team ever, and that's what the coach felt confident would happen now.

"This is the most complete team we've ever played, though," Capers fretted. "When you're Number One in total points scored and Number One in total points allowed and pretty good on special teams, it's hard to be much better than that."

And this was the hardest place Carolina would ever have to play.

The Packers' home-field advantage was the strongest in the NFL. Most NFL games have at least a couple of thousand no-shows. For Green Bay's 35–14 playoff rout of San Francisco the previous week, there had been exactly three no-shows.

"And those three people probably would be shot if people knew who they were," Favre joked.

THE PANTHERS LOCKER ROOM, USUALLY POPULATED by about 20 media people during the midweek open locker-room sessions, suddenly became the place to be. There were 100 reporters clawing for quotes and soundbites at the Wednesday locker-room session.

Panthers linebacker Carlton Bailey gazed at the scene and laughed. "All the doubters are coming in now," he said.

As the week went on, both teams' strategies coalesced.

Anthony Johnson again would be the early key for Carolina. The Panthers had run the ball very well against Dallas, and they would try to go to that well one more time vs. the Packers. If the offensive line could just push the Packers defense back a little bit, everything else would open up.

On defense, Green Bay felt confident enough that it would just try to beat the Panthers one-on-one without any trickery. The Packers defensive line was nicknamed "Three Trees and a Stump." The trees were Reggie White, Sean Jones, and Santana Dotson; the stump was Gilbert Brown.

Panthers center Frank Garcia, the man who would try to remove that stump, figured that Brown's listed weight of 325 was 25 to 35 pounds off—on the low side. He may have been right. Brown wasn't telling. He was content to let his legend (and his stomach) grow larger than life.

Brown already had a hamburger, the Gilbert Burger, named for him at a local Green Bay Burger King. He said it was roughly the size of two Whoppers.

Coach Holmgren loved having Brown inside, saying he was "the size of a guy and a half" in the middle. In fact, Brown was so big that he had two nicknames. Besides the Stump moniker, teammates also used the label "the Gravedigger," since the middle of the defense was where the other teams' running games usually went to die.

On offense, the Packers decided to do what every other opponent of Carolina had chosen to do: throw at Tyrone Poole. "We wanted to work Poole," wide receiver Antonio Freeman said. "We had seen some previous film where he seemed to lose his feet a lot. He seemed to fall down a great deal, and we wanted to use that to our advantage."

On Thursday, when the Packers started working on their red-zone plays, they inserted one for Freeman. Expecting one-on-one coverage from Poole, they told him to fake inside and then run a fade route to the corner of the end zone. The play worked well in practice.

The Panthers worried about Green Bay's running backs. Oddly enough, they wanted Favre, the best quarterback in the game, to throw 50 times.

"We've got to make them one-dimensional," Kevin Greene said. "We absolutely must stop the run. If they run on us, they'll pass at will, too, because we'll never know what to expect. We'll be back on our heels the whole game."

That turned out to be a telling comment.

ONLY ONE THING IRRITATED CAPERS ABOUT THE WEEK. The Panthers would have to travel to Green Bay on Friday—one day earlier than usual—to do a press conference. Capers hated his schedule getting messed up, but there was nothing he could do about it.

Favre, on the other hand, had things irritating him all the time. He threw up several times during the week. He had never felt pressure this intense. This was the game the Packers had lost the previous year to Dallas. Defensive end Reggie White called him nearly every night on the phone, reminding him of the game's importance.

"This is for the Super Bowl, Brett," White would say.

Favre didn't need to hear that.

As usual, Carolina was a major underdog. The Panthers were supposed to lose by 12 points. The Panthers didn't care. Sunday seemed like the promise at the end of a dream.

By Friday, nearly everyone who mattered had converged on tiny Green Bay, Wisconsin (population 100,000), the smallest town to host an NFL team.

Pat Summerall and John Madden would telecast the game again for Fox-TV. They had a vested interest in the result of both that game and the Jacksonville–New England AFC Championship Game, to be played later the same day. For the first time in five years, TV's most famous pairing would get to announce the Super Bowl too.

Summerall had quietly developed his own rooting interest. "I was in many ways hoping it would be Jacksonville and Carolina," Summerall would later admit. "It would be refreshing. I don't think my bosses were hoping that, but that's what I wished."

On game day, it was clear but very cold. Packers fans cooked bratwurst in the parking lots and tried to stay warm. They were veterans at this sort of thing, outfitted with hand warmers and hats and heavy Packers jackets.

"This is like us vs. the whole state of Wisconsin," Panthers cornerback Toi Cook breathed, surveying the mass of green and gold.

The game was scheduled to kick off at 11:30 A.M. local time, so both teams arrived early.

The Panthers players, after hearing so much about the cold, were relieved when they walked outside. It was freezing, but nothing they couldn't handle. The turf was another source of good news. Having been totally replaced only four days before, it seemed solid.

But the stadium . . . none of the Panthers had ever seen anything quite like it. While a Panthers game at Ericsson Stadium might draw a dozen banners from fans, this one had more than a hundred. Most of them had something to do with Fox-TV or Vince Lombardi, whose stone-faced image is still etched over the entire city. Some of the best banners even made the Panthers laugh. Among them:

I TAWT I TAW
A PUDDY TAT

VINCE WANTS HIS TROPHY BACK

IT'S NEVER TOO COLD
FOR THE GREEN AND GOLD.

FROZEN
OUTER
XTREMITIES

FAVRE 3:16

VINCE IS PROUD

NOTHIN' WOULD BE FINA
THAN TO KICK OL' CAROLINA
SUNDAY MOOOORNIN'

NFL Films caught Kevin Greene cutting a wrestling pose before the game and getting himself jacked up.

"Kids grow up knee-high to a grasshopper dreaming about playing in a game like today," Greene yelled to the camera. "It's the freezing, frozen tundra of LA-A-A-A-A-MBEAU FIELD! I'm glad I'm here!"

Panthers owner Jerry Richardson was sure his team would win. He was so sure, in fact, that he took out the envelope that his tickets had been in and scribbled a few things he wanted to stress in his victory speech: "Humble. An honor. Power of collective effort. Credit goes to the players, coaches, and fans." He folded the small envelope back in his wallet, figuring he'd have a use for it in about three hours.

THE GAME BEGAN WITH A TEMPERATURE OF THREE degrees and a wind-chill factor of minus 17 degrees. And like children coming in from the cold after playing in the snow, both teams looked like they were just trying to thaw out.

Green Bay's coach Holmgren always "scripts" his team's first 15 plays, but they didn't work particularly well against Carolina. Favre was off; he would complete only two of his first eight passes. He was as nervous as a cat, firing the early-game throws that Holmgren sometimes called "rocket balls."

But Carolina wasn't making anything happen either. One disturbing trend had already developed on the Panthers' first two series: Brown was eating up Garcia inside. The Stump was firmly rooted in this game.

After the first three possessions ended in punts, the game's first big break came.

On second-and-10 from the Green Bay six, Favre faded back and looked for Don Beebe, a former Panther who had found a second life in Green Bay. But Mills, reading the play beautifully, stepped right in front of Beebe and hugged the ball tight to his chest. The Panthers sideline exploded in celebration. Mills ran the ball back to the Packers two, and suddenly it looked like it could be a game.

Lathon, hyped as always, wandered by Favre shortly after the play. "I respect you," he said. "You're a good player. But it's going to be a long day."

Favre didn't say much of anything to that. He just listened. And fumed.

Lathon still had not learned *not* to talk to quarterbacks. It hadn't worked out in Philadelphia with Ty Detmer, with Collins in the Pittsburgh game, and now with Favre.

Two plays later, the Panthers nicely executed a play-action pass. As Green Bay rushed to double-cover tight end Wesley Walls in the end zone, fullback Howard Griffith sneaked out to the right side. He was alone.

Collins lobbed him the ball, he caught it on his knees, and just like that, it was 7–0, Carolina, with 10 minutes gone in the game.

Green Bay missed a long field goal on their next possession and Carolina punted again on theirs. But then, on third-and-one from the Green Bay 36-yard line, on the last play of the first quarter, a bad omen surfaced for Carolina.

His name was Dorsey Levens. He had gone to school at Georgia Tech, in ACC country, but few Carolina fans had ever heard of him. He didn't even start—that was Edgar Bennett's job. But he subbed in a lot and was a very effective role player.

And on this Sunday, he was about to have the game of his life.

The first indication of that came on the last play of the first quarter.

Levens took a handoff from Favre, cut right through a gaping hole, and sped through the Panthers linebackers. He had only Eric Davis left to beat for a touchdown, but Davis had an angle on him and forced him out of bounds at the Carolina 29-yard line. Still, it was a 35-yard gain, and it got the Packers fans swinging their towels again as the teams changed end zones with the Panthers clinging to their 7–0 lead.

On the next play, it was Levens again.

The Packers had never used this play before, even though it had been in the game plan for about a month. Tight end Keith Jackson stayed in the slot and Levens split out wide.

What Green Bay wanted was for Eric Davis to follow Jackson inside and for Levens to go deep against one of the Panthers linebackers.

"It was basic," Levens would later say. "Line up, go deep, and try to beat the guy. It was designed to get one-on-one on the linebacker, but the linebacker passed me off to the cornerback, to Davis."

Davis made one smart move on the play—sticking with Levens. "It was like, 'Choose your poison,'" Davis said.

He appeared to have chosen correctly. By staying outside, Davis gave Carolina exactly the matchup it wanted in the end zone: a Pro Bowl cornerback vs. a reserve running back.

Favre lofted it up there anyway. He wanted to gamble. Ronnie Lott, a former teammate of Davis's at San Francisco and now a Fox announcer, watched it from a few yards away in the end zone.

Like two basketball players going for a rebound, Levens and Davis positioned themselves. Levens managed to get in front of Davis and get both hands on the ball. Davis got his left hand in the middle of Levens's body and tried to rip the ball free. It didn't work.

Levens came down with the ball—with one of his cleats a half-inch inside the end zone. Touchdown, Green Bay.

"When I saw the ball in the air, I didn't even see Eric Davis," Levens said. "I didn't even know anybody was near me. He did get a hand on it but I had leverage."

Summerall griped on the air that Davis had looked "lackadaisical" on the play. Lott said later that he screamed at Davis, "Get to the darn ball!"

"The mistake he made was, he should have turned and found the receiver and looked back for the football," Lott said. "He lost where the receiver was and then he didn't have any time to find out how far he was away from the receiver to make the play."

Madden sensed that the Panthers' pride had been badly shaken.

"That broke their backs," he thought to himself. He didn't say it on the air, though.

THE PANTHERS' SPINE ACTUALLY STAYED INTACT FOR a while. Favre, under heavy pressure, fumbled the ball away on Green Bay's next series early in the second quarter. Lathon sprinted toward the ball and hopped on it.

Carolina quickly moved 37 yards in four plays to a first-and-goal at the Green Bay eight. But there the Panthers stalled. Collins threw two straight incompletions and Kasay came in for a 22-yard field goal to make it 10–7, Carolina, with 8:40 left in the first half.

Green Bay got the ball again. And now that Favre had calmed down, the Packers were very hard to stop.

The home-field advantage started to kick in, too. Packers fans, sensing that maybe Carolina wasn't going to be the easy opponent they had hoped, were in full throttle.

"When they made a couple of big plays, it showed me quickly how big home-field advantage would be," the Panthers' Terrell said. "Plays that would get a couple of claps in most places were getting a five-minute, continuous roar."

The giant scoreboard showed a video of Packers defensive end Reggie White singing "Amazing Grace" interspersed with clips of his crushing sacks, and it nearly brought down the house.

For all that, though, Green Bay's next drive almost petered out before it began. But the Packers offensive line had noticed that Mills and sometimes Greene called out "Pass" or "Run" on almost every play, trying to guess what the Packers were about to do.

Timmerman, Green Bay's right guard, figured the Panthers were simply watching to see how much weight the offensive linemen placed on their "down" hands in the three-point stance. Linemen often unconsciously anticipate a running play by mashing down harder on their hand and a passing play by having less weight on it (because they are getting ready to sit up and pass-block).

So the linemen decided to make a real effort to fool the Panthers. On third-and-three, they all mashed down hard on their hands.

"Run!" Mills yelled out.

Favre faked the run and threw instead to Bennett for five yards and a first down.

"That's about right when we were figuring out what they were doing," Timmerman said. "I felt from then on like we were almost anticipating what they'd do before they did it."

Green Bay moved steadily down the field, mainly on Levens's runs. Finally, they faced a third-and-three from the Carolina six-yard line with a minute left in the first half and Carolina still leading 10–7.

It was time for Freeman's play.

Favre looked at Freeman briefly on the left side and made eye contact with him. Green Bay had the coverage it wanted, Poole on Freeman, one-on-one. Favre nodded at Freeman and took the snap. Freeman started hard inside like he was running a slant. Poole bit on the move. Then Freeman cut outside. Poole slipped.

Freeman would later describe it this way: "I gave a little fake and gained some separately," Freeman said. "By the time I turned around, Brett had put the ball in the corner of the end zone. I faded into it, scored the touchdown, and five days later . . . cover of *Sports Illustrated!*"

It was true. *SI*'s cover the following week showed Freeman just about to catch the ball and Poole desperately trying to catch up.

Poole got a consolation prize for that cover, however. Because you could tell in the picture that the cleats he wore were Reeboks, Poole eventually received a $3,000 bonus from the shoe company. His shoe contract stated that anytime his Reeboks were visible on the cover of a national magazine, that was what he would be paid—even if he was getting beaten by five yards in the most important game of the year.

Shortly after the pass play, Freeman recounted this conversation between the two: "You got lucky," Poole said. "You know I slipped on that one." Poole blamed the field for his slip, saying that it was icy in that corner of the stadium because of the shade.

Freeman nodded his head then. Later, though, he laughed about it. "That's the way the play was designed," he cackled. "He's supposed to slip. I give him one move. He bites. I go the other way. He slips."

In one of the Lambeau Field suites, Packers general manager Ron Wolf saw Freeman haul in the ball and knew—just knew—his team was going to the Super Bowl. He would say later that the game ended right then.

Still down only 14–10, the Panthers got the ball back with 42 seconds left in the half on their own 27-yard line. Capers thought about it. The Panthers were 40 yards from a field goal. Should they concede a four-point margin and the momentum? Or should they be aggressive? Capers adjusted his headphones. He puzzled on it a second, and he decided to go for it.

"If we take a knee with forty-something seconds left, we're conceding the momentum," he thought to himself. "We're just letting them go in there with all of it. . . . You're in a championship game. Be aggressive."

So they were. On the first play, Willie Green went deep down the left sideline. Collins heaved up an overthrown ball—one that looked well beyond everyone's reach—but Green Bay's Tyrone Williams made an extraordinary one-handed interception. That put the ball right back into Favre's hands at the Green Bay 38 with 35 seconds left.

"Oh, my goodness!" Green Bay safety Eugene Robinson exclaimed. "I have never seen an interception like that!"

Quickly the Packers moved into position for a field goal. By halftime it was 17–10, Green Bay.

Still, Capers felt decent about the game at the half, even though Green Bay had scored 10 points in the final 48 seconds. "What really did us in was, we didn't play very well the last three minutes or so of the last half," he would say later. But at the time he felt that the Panthers were in a decent position. Carolina had come from behind in the second half of six of its 13 wins. He reminded the team of that again at halftime, referring to his nicely printed first-half notes, and sent them out again into the cold.

Favre, however, was still red-hot. Green Bay ran off an 11-play drive to start the quarter, including Favre's most astonishing play of the day.

ON THIRD-AND-SEVEN FROM THE CAROLINA 24, GREENE finally had a chance to grab hold of Favre. The intense linebacker came in on Favre's right side, wrapping him up high to assure Favre couldn't make a normal last-ditch throw. So Favre, seeing Levens scooting over the middle a few yards away, grabbed the ball with both hands, and threw a two-hander from his stomach. Levens caught it, ran eight yards, fumbled, and recovered. First down, Packers.

Greene looked at Favre disbelievingly. "Wow," the Carolina linebacker said.

Capers thought about writing something down, but he didn't. What could you say about a play like that? "From now on watch the two-handed shovel-pass-catch-fumble-recovery"? For the first time all season, in fact, Capers didn't take a single note during the second half.

Carolina finally stopped that Packers drive at its own 15, but Chris Jacke's field goal made it 20–10, Green Bay, with seven minutes gone in the third quarter. Now the Packers had scored on three consecutive possessions, and Carolina players were getting frustrated about the ineffectiveness of their blitz. Green Bay faced 11 third-down situations of third-and-three or less in the game and converted nine of them.

"The huddle was getting very quiet," Terrell said. "It hadn't been like that all year."

And they were getting cold. Lathon, who hadn't even worn a T-shirt under his jersey, felt colder than he had ever been in his life. "It was some frigid-ass tundra," he said.

Another trend had developed, too. Green Bay was running to the right side on many of its plays—directly at Kevin Greene.

"They came right over that right side," Madden would say later, remembering the game. "I was surprised they went at Kevin Greene. They hit that thing in there. They were just able to do it, over and over."

Carolina hung in gamely, however. The Panthers launched their own long drive of the game on the following third-quarter series—helped by a gorgeous play from Carrier. On third-and-six from the Carolina 47, Collins rifled a pass to Carrier. Carrier spun, put one hand down, somehow kept his feet, and sprinted 27 yards to the Green Bay 26. The Panthers worked their way to third-and-three at the Green Bay five, when Collins tried for Carrier again but missed him.

Capers, burned by his first-half gamble, this time took the conservative route. He ordered a field goal. Walls would say later that Capers's decision "jolted" the Panthers. In hindsight, Carolina should have gone for it: The opportunities were dwindling fast. The field goal pushed Carolina back within a touchdown at 20–13 with 3:23 left in the third quarter. But here came the Packers again, feeling more and more confident on each possession.

"By this time, there really wasn't any pressure," Green Bay's Timmerman said. "They were starting to sit back in the second half, and that's not what they are designed to do. But you could tell they were getting kind of frustrated with the blitz, so they went away from it."

Well, not quite. Greene came flying in from the right side on second-and-six from the Green Bay 30. Favre waited, then calmly lofted a screen pass over Greene's head to Levens. With a mass of blockers on the right side, Levens started running again. The Panthers had gotten caught badly, and no one was even in position to make a tackle. Sixty-six backbreaking yards later, Poole came all the way across the field to knock Levens out of bounds at the Carolina four.

"That was huge," Davis said later. "If we had any hope of getting back into the game, that pretty much killed it."

An obviously stunned Panthers defense saw Bennett waltz into the end zone on the next play. It was 27–13, Packers, with a minute left in the third quarter.

THE FINAL NAIL IN THE COFFIN WAS DRIVEN IN ON Carolina's next series by the Gravedigger. He knocked the ball out of Johnson's hands, causing a fumble that Green Bay recovered at the Carolina 47. "My worst offensive play of the year," Johnson would say a month later. "It still sticks with me. And I didn't even get another offensive play. We had to throw from then on, so Winslow Oliver was in there for me."

The Packers scored another field goal—the fifth straight time they had scored on offense. That made it 30–13 with 10 minutes left in the fourth quarter.

Although Madden had blamed Greene for the Panthers' staggering inability to stop the run, in fact the whole defense played poorly. Lathon noted that he and Greene had whipped other teams' tight ends all year on blocks, but on this day Green Bay tight end Mark Chmura had handled both him and Greene many times.

"Late in the game, they started bringing Chmura to my side, and I started getting some of the same stuff they were doing to Kevin," Lathon recounted. "They whipped his ass. Then they came over to my side and got me."

For the rest of the game after Green Bay went up 30–13, there was no more scoring. Carolina just couldn't get up the field anymore on the Packers' strict defense. "I think sometimes Kerry didn't know what we were playing," Green Bay safety Robinson said. "He was so focused on what they were doing, he wasn't paying that much attention to our alignments."

By the end, Favre was out of the game, celebrating on the sideline, and aging quarterback Jim McMahon was doing cleanup duty for Green Bay. The Packers, who rushed for a stunning 201 yards, had soundly beaten the Panthers 30–13.

"I would have never dreamed in a thousand years they would have hammered our butts for over two hundred yards rushing," Greene said. "We had people filling the wrong gaps, not filling the right angles. It was totally uncharacteristic for our defense. I never thought we would play like that."

A month after the game, Lathon would let his frustrations boil over. "Man, I've been wanting to say this for a long time," he said. "We did not do the things we had been doing to get there. We were conservative, in my mind. Granted, they outmanned us sometimes. But still, the zone blitz wasn't in effect that day. I rushed maybe four or five times. Every time I rushed, they double-teamed me. We didn't do the things we had done in the past games to get us there."

"Carolina had a chance early and took advantage of it," Madden said a couple of weeks later when asked to review the game. "They got that first score. But then Green Bay went out and whipped them after that. They played more physical than them."

THE PACKERS STAYED OUT ON THE FIELD LONG AFTER the game ended, accepting the NFC championship trophy and exulting with their fans.

"That scene at Lambeau Field afterwards was just great," said Madden, touched by the fans' unconditional love of the Packers. "That's a memory I'll have with me forever. You can't create something like that."

When they eventually went inside, Holmgren would tear up and try to duck away from the cameras as he congratulated his team.

There were tears of a different sort on the Carolina side, however. The Panthers trudged into the visitors' locker room cold, tired, and beaten.

"That locker room was unlike any I'd ever been in," Davis said later. "For the most part, guys got along. That's why it hurt so much. I'd never been on a team like that where everyone pretty much cared for one another. San Francisco was never like that. . . . But it was Green Bay's time to win. We wanted to win. Green Bay *had* to. If they lose that game, they're destroyed."

Capers felt awful.

He had never been to a Super Bowl before as a coach, and he had missed by one game again. But he vowed internally to use this game-tape as inspiration for next year. And he collected himself to talk to his players, trying to lift their spirits in the midst of the gloom. "I don't want anyone leaving this locker room feeling bad," he ordered. "At the beginning of the year, I don't think anyone would have given the Carolina Panthers the chance to be playing for the right to go to the Super Bowl. I don't believe we have anything to be ashamed of."

But the team took the loss extremely hard. The cramped visitors' locker room at Lambeau Field was as silent as a mortuary. After eight consecutive wins, the Panthers had honestly forgotten how badly it hurt to lose. They had expected to shock the world once more in this game, to take over Bourbon Street in New Orleans in two weeks.

Normally mild-mannered Matt Elliott shouldered his way through a group of TV cameramen. Some players cut the tape off their wrists and ankles, wadded it up, and furiously slammed it into wastebaskets. Other players cried quietly by their lockers.

"Hearing two weeks of hype about Green Bay in the Super Bowl—that's going to be like a knife stabbing you," Willie Green said. "I won't watch the Super Bowl. I won't torture myself. Guys like me and Sam Mills: What are our chances of getting back to this game again?"

"A loss is a loss, and it stinks any way you look at it," Collins said somberly. The quarterback looked around the locker room, wondering who would be around for the 1997 season. "It was weird," Collins said. "It's like it automatically shifts, like, BOOM! You could tell everybody was going a thousand different directions."

Someone asked Mills about next year and what sort of chance the Panthers would have. He started to answer, then stopped. "I hate those words, 'Next year,'" he said softly.

Davis, a relentless optimist throughout the season, knew the season was over. He shrugged a sports jacket over his shoulders. He looked terrible. "To understand, you'd have to go out there and take those licks in the cold," Davis said. "You'd have to run around in training camp when it's 100 degrees. You'd have to see the guys crying in the huddle and deal with the frustration in the locker room. So much goes on during a season. You put everything you have into it, in front of the whole world. And you fail. It hurts."

Poole, once again burned badly in a high-profile game, was crushed. With his eyes wet, he said, "I tried to play my best. In the NFL, a little bit—a little slip—can mean a lot."

Walls, for once downcast, called the end of the season "sudden" and "shocking."

Richardson still had the folded-up victory speech in his wallet. He decided to keep the envelope there, rather than throw it away, as a reminder and a motivation for next season.

"If we had played Green Bay in Charlotte, I think we would have won," he said. "And I think if we had won, we would have had two weeks to prepare for the Super Bowl and we would have won that. . . . We've talked so much about the value of home-field advantage. I thought I understood it, but I really did not understand it."

LAMAR LATHON WAS ONE OF THE LAST PLAYERS OUT of the shower. He had tried to be classy at the end, when he knew it was over, congratulating the Green Bay fans and some of the players. He shouted, "You deserve it!" over and over again to the Packers supporters as he left the field.

But now he felt the finality of it all, and he vowed to remember this feeling when the Panthers were playing for home-field advantage in the playoffs in future years—remember what it felt like to be a vanquished, visiting team. "Hearing 'We Are the Champions,' seeing them celebrate—that was very hard," Lathon said. "That's going to haunt us."

That was apparent when you watched Lathon put away his helmet for the last time. He saved it for last, leaving it out the way a child would leave out his favorite toy until the last box needed to be packed on moving day. Finally, he grabbed the helmet off the top of his locker and looked at it. He turned it over in his hands. He traced a finger over one of its dents. Then, in one swift motion, he stuffed the helmet in a large bag and zipped it shut.

On the flight home, the Panthers talked about next year. They tried to remember what a fine year it had been. And then, when they finally got bused back to Ericsson Stadium to pick up their cars, it got easier to place the entire season in perspective: There were 3,000 Panthers fans waiting in the dark in the stadium parking lot to greet their heroes. Jerry Richardson's dream stood like a monolith behind them.

It was cold in Charlotte. The fans shivered. No one had organized this ahead of time. TV stations had merely announced when the team would return. Still, they had come. These fans wanted to say "Thank you" once more for an extraordinary season.

Mills looked at the crowd as he stepped off the bus and was touched. "Parents were holding up their little kids, who probably barely knew what football was all about," he said. "In my mind, I knew a lot of those fans were probably the same people who were there at that pep rally [before the first game of the season]. That's the way it started, that's the way it ended. A lot was accomplished in between those times."

The players shook hands with the fans. They signed autographs. A few of them spoke at a hastily set up podium.

And it was Collins—the second-year quarterback who had become a true leader this season—who put the year in perspective. "What you've witnessed," Collins told the fans on that cold, dark night, "is the beginning of a dynasty."

EPILOGUE

THE FAX ARRIVED IN JERRY RICHARDSON'S OFFICE AT 3:17 P.M. on January 13, 1997, the afternoon following the Panthers' loss to Green Bay in the NFC Championship Game. It was a seven-paragraph letter from Rev. Billy Graham, sent from the evangelist's home in Montreat, North Carolina.

"Having spent a great deal of my years in Illinois and Minnesota, and visited Green Bay, Wisconsin, when the temperature was thirty below zero, I prayed extra hard Sunday that the Lord would give the whole management and team extra strength," Graham wrote in the letter. "I believe He did."

Despite the loss to the Packers, Graham saw victory in the Panthers' 1996 season. "What you all have done this past year is a miracle from God," Graham wrote. "You have put Charlotte on the map and shown the world the strength that Christianity gives to a city, state, and team."

One week later, on January 20, Richardson was already planning for the '97 season. He held a meeting with his sons Mark and Jon, president Mike McCormack, general manager Bill Polian, and coach Dom Capers.

"The organization has to know what we expect," Richardson said. "You have to tell it over and over again. You can't tell it one time. You have to keep reinforcing it."

The meeting was the first step in the team's effort to get to the NFC Championship Game again—and win it. Richardson prepared an extensive memo and handed it out. "The main purpose of this meeting today is to discuss what we need to do to create a winning and enjoyable work environment," Richardson's memo began. "The success of our second season, which was our ninth year in business, was not an accident. We have the potential to have another successful year in 1997."

His written introduction also included an ominous warning: "Our collective success will bring new challenges to us that could erode our organization."

Richardson had seen the Baltimore Colts disintegrate in 1960 and he didn't want it to happen to the Panthers. After the Colts won the '59 NFL title with a 9–3 record in Richardson's rookie season, they slipped to 6–6 the next year, losing their last four games after starting out 6–2.

"We had players who started seeing things differently," Richardson said. "All of a sudden [quarterback] John Unitas was getting more attention than [receiver] Lenny Moore and Big Daddy [Lipscomb, a defensive tackle] wasn't getting as much attention as Gino [Marchetti, a defensive end].

"So I've seen it happen and it's huge for us. When you do as well as we have, you can get full of yourself and think you're real special and lose sight of what got you there. People in the organization can start getting an elevated view of themselves because of the collective success of the team."

Richardson wanted to move fast to try to prevent anyone in the Panthers organization from getting an inflated ego.

As for Richardson's expectations for '97, they are higher than ever. He made that clear when he was discussing the future of defensive coordinator Vic Fangio, who interviewed for the San Diego head coaching job in early 1997.

"Vic's value is only going to continue to go up," Richardson said. "The only way it will go down is if we fail. And we're not failing. We've never failed at anything we've done with the Panthers—not one single thing.

"We're not going to fail now either, because we know what to do and our people clearly understand what to do. We've created as good an environment as I know there is in this league to have winning football. I don't know of anyone who's got one better—not one single NFL team. So why aren't we going to win?"

ONE OF RICHARDSON'S MAIN REGRETS ABOUT THE '96 season was the way the uncertainty about general manager Bill Polian's future with the team mushroomed into a major national story. There were broadcast and print reports throughout the year that the New Orleans Saints and New York Jets wanted to hire Polian and that he might be receptive to their offers, even though he had two years remaining on his contract with Carolina.

Neither Polian nor anyone from the Panthers refuted the speculation. They rarely acknowledged it at all, and Polian consistently said he didn't want to dignify the reports with a response. It didn't end until Richardson denied the Saints or any other team permission to speak to Polian following the playoff loss to Green Bay. In retrospect, Richardson wished he had handled the situation more directly.

"It bothered me that we didn't put it all to rest and I blame myself for that," Richardson said. "I don't blame Bill. I blame me. I should have called Charlie Dayton [the team's vice president for communications, who oversees the media relations department] and I should have said, 'This is over.' I didn't do that and it was a mistake."

Richardson felt the situation added excess baggage to the season. "We had put so much energy into the 1996 season," he said. "One of the things we didn't want to deal with was something that was unnecessary, and that was an unnecessary distraction. If it didn't pertain to making the Panthers better, it was a distraction. And I can tell you that that did not help us."

Once it was settled that Polian was staying with the Panthers, Mike McCormack announced his retirement. Richardson wanted him to stay another year, but he and his wife, Ann, longed to move back to Seattle to be closer to their children and grandchildren.

"I was hired to put the pieces in place and we've done that," McCormack said. "We had a good year and things are running smoothly. It just seems like the right time. I've always said, 'I think you can go too long.'"

WHO COULD PASS UP A FREE TICKET TO THE SUPER Bowl? Dom Capers, that's who. For the second time in three years, Capers had fallen one win short of making it to the biggest game of the year.

Two years earlier, the San Diego Chargers had upset the Pittsburgh

Steelers for the AFC title in Capers's final game as the Steelers defensive coordinator. He would have preferred to stay far away from Super Bowl XXIX in Miami in 1995, but the Panthers had just hired him and wanted to show their new coach around. So he went.

But this time was different. There was no reason for Capers to travel to New Orleans to see the Green Bay Packers play the New England Patriots in Super Bowl XXXI. The trip would have been agonizing because of how close the Panthers had come to being there themselves.

The game went exactly as Capers expected. He believed the Packers were the best team in the NFL in 1996 and they looked like it in a 35–21 win over the Patriots. Return specialist Desmond Howard had a dazzling game for the Packers with 244 yards on 10 punt and kick-off returns and was named Super Bowl MVP. Quarterback Brett Favre was another worthy candidate for the award, as was defensive lineman Reggie White, who had three sacks.

One week later, Favre and White teamed with eight Panthers on the NFC Pro Bowl team in Honolulu, Hawaii. The Green Bay and Carolina representatives shared the same locker room and the same resort hotel.

White kidded with Greene that they should get together and become a wrestling tag-team combination. Greene loved the idea and spent much of the week trying to convince White it was something they really should do. In fact, the two would wrestle on the same card in Charlotte in early May. Lathon, much to his disappointment, was not part of the "Slamboree."

Panthers quarterback Kerry Collins was a late addition to the NFC team, after San Francisco's Steve Young had to pull out of the game early in the week because of a rib injury.

Collins joined the seven teammates who had already been selected: Michael Bates, Eric Davis, Kevin Greene, John Kasay, Lamar Lathon, Sam Mills, and Wesley Walls.

Giving the week even more of a Carolina flavor was the fact that Capers and the Panthers coaching staff were the coaches of the NFC team by virtue of the loss in the conference championship game to the Packers. The NFL figures the best consolation prize it can give the coaches of the teams that missed the Super Bowl by one game is a free trip to Hawaii.

For those Panthers who made the trip, Pro Bowl week was exactly what they needed to help forget their disappointing loss three weeks ago. It was especially rewarding for Capers, whose first full-time coaching job had been at the University of Hawaii in 1975 and '76.

"There's a feeling of nostalgia coming back here," Capers said. "It brings back a lot of fond memories for me. It was such a unique experience getting a chance to start my career in a place like Hawaii.

"I was a young guy from the little town of Buffalo, Ohio, and Hawaii was a long way from there. But I was fortunate that a lot of local people took me under their wings and looked after me. You always remember those things."

Capers was reunited with some of his old friends at the Pro Bowl, including the man who hired him back then, Larry Price, the former Hawaii coach who had retired and become a popular radio personality in Hawaii.

If you were a friend of Capers's, you were a friend of Price's. He loved to reminisce about his hiring of Capers 22 years earlier. "Back then, it was our second year of Division One football," Price said. "We were in an unusual situation. We only had five coaches. I was looking for somebody who had been a grad assistant with a good program who wasn't married and was a disciplinarian."

Capers fit all those criteria, but Price said there was one problem. "I talked to Dom on the phone and I liked him, but as soon as I met him, I got this sinking feeling," Price said. "I thought, Oh, no.' He looked like a movie actor to me. He was a good-looking rascal—built like a Greek god with this big smile on his face. I don't know what I was expecting, but he looked like he was chiseled out of granite. He looked like Apollo. I was worried about him having a fan club and women chasing him all over the island."

Capers burst into laughter when he heard what Price had said. "That's Larry," Capers said. "He loves to bust your butt."

If Capers wasn't the Panther having the best time at the Pro Bowl, perhaps it was Lamar Lathon or Kerry Collins—both were playing the game for the first time.

Lathon said he wanted to be "the star of stars" and get selected as the game's outstanding player, but Capers knew that was highly unlikely because Pro Bowl rules didn't allow linebackers to blitz, which meant Lathon probably wouldn't have a chance at any sacks.

Collins felt like he was in football paradise.

"This is the daddy as far as I'm concerned," Collins said. "This is about as good as it gets. It really got to me when I was under center for the first time and I turned around and pitched the ball to [Detroit running back] Barry Sanders. It was a real 'Wow!' thing for me."

Collins, one of three quarterbacks on the NFC team, played the third quarter of the game and a few plays at the start of the fourth. Even though one of his passes was intercepted and returned for a touchdown, he said playing in the game was a good experience and a confidence builder for the future.

The February 2 game was about as exciting as the Pro Bowl could get, ending in a 26–23 AFC win in overtime, thanks to a 37-yard field goal by Indianapolis Colts kicker Cary Blanchard.

ONCE THE GAME WAS OVER, THE PANTHERS TURNED their attention to the '97 season. They used the early stages of the NFL's free-agency signing period to improve their defense and replace an offensive starter who left for another team.

Their top target was Steelers outside linebacker Chad Brown, but he quickly signed with the Seattle Seahawks. Carolina then turned to Houston Oilers inside linebacker Micheal Barrow. After three days of negotiations and discussions, Barrow signed a five-year, $18.75 million contract and provided one of the best moments of the off-season at his introductory news conference.

After getting presented his new number 56 Panthers jersey by Polian—a Carolina tradition—Barrow stepped to the podium. "Bill," Barrow said to Polian as cameras rolled, "I talked to the owner, Mr. Richardson, and he said if he was here, he would give me a hug. So I'll take a line from the movie *Jerry Maguire*, when the man said,

'Show me the money.' I want you to show me a little love and give me a hug."

Polian laughed, stood up, and hugged Barrow.

Barrow, a fast and brash linebacker who was an emerging star with Houston, was brought in to replace Carlton Bailey at inside linebacker and to spend his first year learning how to call the Panthers' defensive signals from Mills. Capers said he wanted Barrow to be able to take over that very important responsibility when Mills retires.

Carolina signed two unrestricted free agents from the Steelers, defensive end Ray Seals and wide receiver Ernie Mills, both of whom Capers liked from his days as defensive coordinator in Pittsburgh. Ernie Mills was signed after it became apparent that wide receiver Willie Green, one of twenty-one Carolina free agents, was going to sign with the Denver Broncos. But the first of the Panthers free agents to leave the team was fullback Howard Griffith, who also signed with the Broncos.

Griffith and Green both departed because the Broncos offered them better contracts than Carolina. This luring away of players was one of the surest signs yet that the Panthers had matured into a full-fledged NFL franchise: Now they were faced with the frustration of other teams trying to raid their cupboard in the era of free agency. But the Panthers did a good job of that despite the loss of Griffith and Green, and the key free agents who re-signed with the Panthers included Sam Mills, Anthony Johnson, and Greg Kragen.

THE PANTHERS WEREN'T SUPPOSED TO GET A PREmier player in the NFL draft, because of their successful season. They were picking late in the first round—twenty-seventh overall out of 30 teams—and it's often difficult to grab an impact player that late in the draft.

But Carolina got lucky. Colorado wide receiver Rae Carruth, predicted by most analysts to be one of the top 15 players available in the draft, was overlooked early in the first round and was still available when the Panthers' turn to select arrived.

The Panthers had intended to use their first-round pick on a defensive player—either a lineman or a pass-rushing outside linebacker—but with Carruth on the board, team officials decided they couldn't pass him up. "We never thought he would be there," said Capers. "Our main criterion with our first-round pick was to get an impact player, and we think Rae can be that."

Carruth was college football's top big-play receiver in 1996, ranking as the only player in the nation to average more than 20 yards per pass reception. With their next four picks, the Panthers returned to their defense-oriented draft plan. They selected Nebraska safety Mike Minter in the second round, Notre Dame inside linebacker Kinnon Tatum in the third, and then picked two outside linebackers, Wisconsin's Tarek Saleh in the fourth round and Ohio State's Matt Finkes in the sixth.

Carolina didn't have a fifth round pick because they had traded it the previous year to the Oakland Raiders in exchange for receiver Rocket Ismail. But with their final pick, in the seventh round, they chose Mississippi tight end Kris Mangum, a player who resembled Panthers Pro Bowler Wesley Walls.

All in all, the draft was a success.

PANTHERS OFFICIALS BELIEVED THAT THEIR MOVES in the off-season combined with the anticipated return of running back Tshimanga Biakabutuka and wide receiver Muhsin Muhammad from 1996 injuries would make them a much better team. But they wondered if it would show on their '97 record.

One of the direct results of their successful second season was a much tougher schedule for Year 3. The NFL uses a weighted scheduling system in an attempt to bring about parity. The best teams play the toughest schedules.

Carolina's opponents in '97 include Dallas, Green Bay, Denver, Kansas City, and Oakland, and in addition they will play San Francisco and the other three members of the NFC West twice.

Just how far the Panthers had climbed up the NFL ladder of respectability and popularity became evident when the league released the dates, times, and television schedule for its 1997 games. Carolina was delighted to learn it would appear on national TV five times, including Monday-night football games against the 49ers (in Charlotte on September 29) and the Cowboys (at Dallas on December 8).

Polian said the schedule was proof that the Panthers had grown into a "national team," a select distinction reserved for the teams whose appeal reaches far beyond their geographic boundaries.

Sam Mills, who signed a Panthers contract for two more years in March 1997, said Carolina's sudden success had turned the team into an organization other clubs in the NFL would love to emulate. "If you look around the league, we're becoming the model, more than just about any other team in the NFL," Mills said. "When you talk about defense, you see teams trying to run our zone blitz more and more. When you talk about stadiums, everybody would love to have a stadium like what we have in Charlotte. There's also the type of players we have on our team. I think you're going to see teams getting more and more away from problem players. I think you'll see owners, general managers, and coaches saying, 'Hey, we need more harmony on this team.' It's pretty obvious we're doing a lot of things right in Carolina."

Indeed, it was an opinion shared by many across the country. Fox-TV's NFL commentator, Ronnie Lott, who played on Super Bowl championship teams during his career as a 49ers safety, oozes with praise for the Panthers. "Great teams are built on organizations," Lott said. "Yes, you've got to have talent, but everything is built off organizations who understand how to win close games, understand how to draft the right people and get the appropriate people to fill the holes that develop. That's how dynasties are built.

"I like what I see in Carolina. They have certain principles and ethics in place that I think will allow them to continue winning football games. You look at them and you can see they've got a great young quarterback [Collins] who's only going to mature. I think Wesley Walls is going to be a rock of granite for that organization."

Meanwhile, the Panthers grew more valuable off the field, too. In its June 1997 issue, *Financial World* magazine ranked the Panthers sixth in value out of 113 professional sports teams, with an estimated value of $240 million.

One of the reasons the Panthers look poised to be a premier team for the remainder of the 1990s was the way they finished the '96 season. If they hadn't followed their loss to a winless Atlanta team with eight consecutive victories, they wouldn't be talked about in such glowing terms.

To pinpoint the key to their arrival even more specifically, you have to return to the players-only team meeting following the loss to the Falcons. Many Carolina players believe the true turning point was the precise moment when Lamar Lathon stood up and talked bluntly to Kerry Collins in front of all his teammates.

Running back Anthony Johnson, one of the most respected players on the team, didn't offer his opinion during the meeting about whether he agreed with Lathon that Collins needed to cut down on his public drinking and partying, but Johnson said after the season that he was glad Lathon had the nerve to make a statement on the issue at a time when the Panthers needed a dramatic change.

"I thought it was good for the team to get cleansed and to heal some wounds due to the feelings some players had toward others," Johnson said. "I think, for the most part, it purified some things in the minds of those individuals.

"I personally thought it was something Kerry needed to address because at some point it could affect the team or him. I told him later that guys on the team looked up to him, but that we expected his leadership to be in accordance with the way we approached the game."

Collins was standup about it from the second Lathon confronted him. Even though some of the things said were embarrassing to him—and infuriating, too—he never dodged the questions. Through it all, it was obvious that his self-confidence as a player, person, and leader stayed intact.

"Everybody maybe should look at the bigger picture of this whole thing," Collins said. "Regardless of how somebody might think about me, was I the quarterback in the NFC Championship Game? Did I make it to the Pro Bowl? For a second-year quarterback, I think they should be happy with what they have and *who* they have as their quarterback, regardless of what I do off the field. I'll stand by my credentials any day."

And Dom Capers never stopped standing behind Collins. Asked if he was ever concerned about Collins's social life during the '96 season, Capers said he was happy with the way the quarterback had developed. "I think Kerry has gone through a normal maturing process and he'll continue to mature," Capers said. "I think he'll benefit tremendously from the experiences he's had, both good and bad. Having been in the playoffs, he now has a much better understanding of what it takes to be one of the best players in the business."

The Panthers didn't feel as strongly about center Curtis Whitley, who had missed four games during the 1996 season after testing positive for crystal meth. On July 14, 1997—four days before training camp opened—Whitley was cut even though he remained eligible to play in the league. The NFL suspended defensive end Shawn King for six games for marijuana use, but the team kept him on the roster and allowed him to participate in training camp. King went to camp knowing he'd be watched closely not only by his coaches but also by his teammates, who had big plans for the months ahead.

THE PANTHERS SHOULD ENTER THE 1997 SEASON favored to repeat as champions in the NFC West. The rest of the division seems to be in turmoil. Every other team in the division has a new head coach.

Three veteran coaches who have taken other teams to the Super Bowl have arrived to challenge Carolina: Mike Ditka in New Orleans, Dan Reeves in Atlanta, and Dick Vermeil in St. Louis.

Reeves moved south after coaching the previous four years with the New York Giants. Ditka and Vermeil came out of "retirement" to head the Saints and Rams. It had been four years since Ditka coached with the Chicago Bears and fourteen years since Vermeil quit guiding the Philadelphia Eagles and brought the word "burnout" into everyday vocabulary.

But the real shocker during the off-season was the sudden resignation of 49ers coach George Seifert and the hiring of University of California coach Steve Mariucci to replace him.

San Francisco was desperate to regain control of the division from Carolina. The 49ers believed Mariucci, who used to tutor Brett Favre in Green Bay, was a rising star in coaching who was sure to get hired by an NFL team soon. The 49ers likened him to a football version of Boston Celtics coach Rick Pitino—a slick, charismatic talent. Their plan was to make him their offensive coordinator temporarily and to promise that he would take over the team after Seifert was gone. Seifert, who had one year remaining on his contract, didn't like the arrangement and quit.

That left Mariucci as the head coach and the man who could become Dom Capers's greatest coaching rival. The new season will tell.

FROM JERRY RICHARDSON TO BILL POLIAN TO DOM Capers to the players, the Panthers' goal in 1997 is to win the Super Bowl. There will be no satisfactory consolation. It will be an all-or-nothing mentality.

"It all starts with having a hunger," Capers said. "And I believe we have that."

Now the Panthers are a team others will try to knock off their pedestal. It's a position Eric Davis knew well when he was with the 49ers, and he believes it's a position the Panthers will enjoy.

"Now football is fun," he said. "We're expected to win. Now is the 'Do not panic' time."

Lamar Lathon believes it will be prime time for himself and the Panthers.

"We've basically had a peek at the promised land; it just wasn't our time," Lathon said. "But we've seen it. Now we know what to do to be able to combat our loss to Green Bay: win our games, get the home-field advantage throughout the playoffs, and then we'll be where we want to be."

Lathon had his breakout season in '96, finishing second to Kevin Greene in the NFL in sacks with 13½. Now he wants to dominate and become the NFL's top defensive player.

"I'm not satisfied," Lathon said. "I was second-team All-Pro and I was mad as hell about it. Chad Brown [of the Pittsburgh Steelers] is not better than me and Kevin Greene is not better than me, but they made the first team. My goal is to be the best outside linebacker in the NFL."

As for the Panthers, Lathon said, "In years to come we're going to have something to brag about around here. It can't happen soon enough for me."

Collins was thinking the same thing when he stepped to the podium at Ericsson Stadium that night in January and told the fans who had gathered there that they had witnessed the beginning of a dynasty in 1996.

"It was a spontaneous thing for me to say," Collins said. "I was thinking about it while I was waiting my turn to be up there and talk. It's exactly the way I feel. I won't settle for anything less.

"That's how good I think this organization is and that's how good I think I can be. I believe all the pieces are in place."

ACKNOWLEDGMENTS

THIS BOOK WOULD NOT HAVE BEEN POSSIBLE WITHOUT the cooperation of our superb employer, *The Charlotte Observer*. The fact that the *Observer*'s top management people allowed us to pursue this project independently will always mean a great deal to us. We would particularly like to thank publisher Rolfe Neill, editor Jennie Buckner, and managing editor Frank Barrows for giving us the go-ahead.

As for Gary Schwab, the executive sports editor of the *Observer* and the best boss either of us has ever had, we cannot thank him enough for his creativity, his patience, and his suggestions for the manuscript. We also appreciate his decision to team us up on the Panthers beat in the first place. Without that, we never would have developed the strong friendship and work relationship we now share.

We owe a huge thanks to the Panthers players, coaches, and front-office men who let us into their lives during and after the 1996 season. So many were exceedingly generous with their time. Head coach Dom Capers is consistently wonderful with the media, and we appreciate that every day of the year. The time he spent with us for this book—and for the newspaper during the 1996 season—went above and beyond the call of duty. Thanks, Dom.

Three players in particular deserve special recognition: quarterback Kerry Collins, linebacker Lamar Lathon, and center Curtis Whitley. Each of them spent hours helping us fine-tune our information and were unceasingly helpful as we tried to raise *Year of the Cat* from a kitten. Through multiple interviews and the numerous demands we made on their time, they never complained and answered every question we posed—including the most difficult ones—with honesty, insight, and humor.

Another group of Panthers players and management leaders was also wonderful to us in lengthy postseason interviews, and we would like to thank them mightily. They include Toi Cook, Eric Davis, Willie

Green, Kevin Greene, Anthony Johnson, Mike McCormack, Sam Mills, Bill Polian, Dwight Stone, Pat Terrell, Wesley Walls, and Gerald Williams.

This book would never have been written without Panthers owner Jerry Richardson, who brought the club to Charlotte in the first place and gave us something to write about. We applaud the way he treats everyone he meets with dignity, and we greatly appreciate the support and assistance he gave us throughout this project. Special thanks also to his delightful wife, Rosalind, who is always a lady in the truest southern sense of the word, and to his assistant, Diane Hoch, whose patience, efficiency, and courtesy are unfailing.

We owe a special debt of gratitude to Charlie Dayton, who heads the Panthers media relations department and is a man we trust and admire. He and his assistants, Lex Sant, Bruce Speight, Deedee Mills, and Avis Roper, are helpful to us year-round.

Other Panthers players, coaches, officials, and employees we'd like to thank include Carlton Bailey, Michael Bates, Steve Beuerlein, Tshimanga Biakabutuka, Blake Brockermeyer, Mark Carrier, Chad Cota, Mark Dennis, Tommy Donovan, Matt Elliott, Vic Fangio, Roman Gabriel, Howard Griffith, Rocket Ismail, John Kasay, Greg Kragen, Brett Maxie, Jackie Miles, Joe Pendry, Debbie Pulasky, Chris Polian, Tyrone Poole, Toni Price, Linda Raulerson, Mark Rodenhauser, Bill Rosinski, Andre Royal, Brad Seely, Greg Skrepenak, and Brian Wiggins.

Others who deserve special thanks include Terry Bradshaw, Helen Carr, the Reverend Billy Graham, Graeme Keith, Ronnie Lott, John Madden, Brian McCarty, Joe Menzer, Max Muhleman, Larry Ross, Leigh Steinberg, and Pat Summerall.

We also owe thanks to all of our other colleagues at *The Charlotte Observer* who helped us through the past season and with this book: deputy sports editor Mike Persinger, who coordinates our daily coverage of the team in the paper with expertise and flair, as well as Rick Bonnell, Susan Gilbert, Scott Goldman, Ron Green, Ron Green, Jr., Bob Leverone, Laura Mueller, Harry Pickett, Chris Record, Tom Sorensen, Dick Van Halsema, and Tom Tozer.

We never would have finished this book but for the adept leadership of our editors at Simon & Schuster, Jeff Neuman and Frank Scatoni, and our literary agent, Stuart Gottesman, who believed in us from the beginning.

Thanks to all of them—and to our families for their love and unwavering support.

INDEX